Gay Men's Relationships Across the Life Course

D1714389

Gay Men's Relationships Across the Life Course

Peter Robinson
Swinburne University of Technology, Australia

Foreword by
The Hon. Michael Kirby AC CMG

© Peter Robinson 2013
Foreword © Michael Kirby 2013

All rights reserved. No reproduction, copy or transmission of this publication may be made without written permission.

No portion of this publication may be reproduced, copied or transmitted save with written permission or in accordance with the provisions of the Copyright, Designs and Patents Act 1988, or under the terms of any licence permitting limited copying issued by the Copyright Licensing Agency, Saffron House, 6–10 Kirby Street, London EC1N 8TS.

Any person who does any unauthorized act in relation to this publication may be liable to criminal prosecution and civil claims for damages.

The author has asserted his right to be identified as the author of this work in accordance with the Copyright, Designs and Patents Act 1988.

First published 2013 by
PALGRAVE MACMILLAN

Palgrave Macmillan in the UK is an imprint of Macmillan Publishers Limited, registered in England, company number 785998, of Houndmills, Basingstoke, Hampshire RG21 6XS.

Palgrave Macmillan in the US is a division of St Martin's Press LLC, 175 Fifth Avenue, New York, NY 10010.

Palgrave Macmillan is the global academic imprint of the above companies and has companies and representatives throughout the world.

Palgrave® and Macmillan® are registered trademarks in the United States, the United Kingdom, Europe and other countries.

ISBN 978–0–230–24412–2

This book is printed on paper suitable for recycling and made from fully managed and sustained forest sources. Logging, pulping and manufacturing processes are expected to conform to the environmental regulations of the country of origin.

A catalogue record for this book is available from the British Library.

A catalog record for this book is available from the Library of Congress.

Typeset by MPS Limited, Chennai, India.

To the 97 men who gave their time to be interviewed

Contents

List of Tables

Foreword

In the social sciences, and in the quest for law reform, empiricism reigns. Having theories and bright ideas is good. But having detailed facts and collecting detailed data and opinions usually affords a much sounder basis for judgement and the design of new public policy and law.

A good illustration of these propositions can be found in the life and work of Dr Alfred Kinsey. Before Kinsey there were many theoreticians who offered postulates about homosexuality and homosexuals. Of course, some of them had a small sample of specimens upon whom they based their theories and conclusions. Thus, Sigmund Freud was a practising psychiatrist. He based his enlightened opinions about sexual minorities on the small cohort of patients he had treated or observed. It was on that footing, in 1935, that he wrote his famous 'Letter to an American mother'. In that letter he declared: 'Homosexuality is assuredly no advantage, but it is nothing to be ashamed of, no vice, no degradation, it cannot be classified as an illness; we consider it to be a variation of the sexual function. Many highly respectable individuals of ancient and modern times have been homosexuals, several of the greatest men amongst them (Plato, Michelangelo, Leonardo da Vinci).' Yet although this had an impact in the circle of practising psychiatrists, it cut no ice with the general public, or with the politicians who represented them as lawmakers.

This is where Alfred Kinsey made his mark. A more unlikely marksman is hard to imagine. He was a professor of zoology at Indiana University, in a conservative state of the United States, working in the rural setting of Bloomington. He was the world's leading expert on gall wasps, a variety of bee. Yet, in his mature age, he turned to the taxonomies of human beings. He embarked upon an empirical study of the sexual lives of his fellow Americans. He conducted a huge number of interviews. He followed a set interviewing pattern. And he came up with most remarkable data, including about the incidence of homosexuality:

- 37 per cent of the male population had at least one overt homosexual experience to orgasm between the ages of 16 and 45.
- 13 per cent of the male population had had more homosexual than heterosexual experience over at least a three-year period.

- 10 per cent of the male population had been more or less exclusively homosexual for at least a three-year period, with 8 per cent being completely homosexual for at least that period.
- 4 per cent of the white male population was exclusively homosexual (rated on his scale 0–6) for their entire lives.

Kinsey's 1948 report on *Sexual Behaviour in the Human Male* landed like a bombshell in the United States, dispelling all kinds of ignorant, medieval opinions concerning sexual conduct, and specifically homosexual conduct. Its impact was enhanced and enlarged by Kinsey's report on *Sexual Behaviour in the Human Female*, published in 1953. Armed with these reports, Kinsey's flair as a public speaker and protected by the First Amendment to the United States Constitution, it became impossible to put the genie back in the bottle. The news travelled far and wide through the modern media. Specifically, it spread to all the English-speaking countries, which had been in the forefront of criminalising adult private homosexual conduct. What had been thought to be the weird behaviour of a tiny and wilful minority, contrary to scriptural instruction, was revealed as widespread, natural conduct amongst a sizeable minority that was stable and persistent. It was so even in the face of cruel criminalisation and vicious religious and social stigma.

It is no coincidence that, a decade after the second Kinsey report was published, the British Parliament moved, in 1967, to amend the laws in England. Australia followed in 1974 with reforms adopted first in South Australia under Don Dunstan. Gradually parliaments and courts on every continent were getting rid of the fiendish laws that punished sexual minorities. And once the criminal laws disappeared, pressure built up to provide affirmative rights: to pensions and social security; to protection against discrimination; and to legal recognition of stable relationships. This is what can happen when social science reveals the realities about human life in all of its variety.

This book by Peter Robinson is another step on the path that Alfred Kinsey charted. It does not boast of the huge numbers of interviews conducted by Kinsey and his colleagues. To that extent the sample (being data collected from 97 gay men living in Auckland, Hong Kong, Los Angeles, Melbourne, London, Manchester, Mumbai, New York, and Sydney) is tiny, given the world of 7 billion human beings. Nevertheless, the author has added a dimension of detail that Kinsey's methodology did not permit. He has conducted elaborate interviews that reveal a rich source of primary data and permit the subjects to offer information about their experiences and opinions that the statistical approach of

Kinsey did not allow. Of course, it would have been preferable to have offered a larger sample for analysis. However, the author explains the difficulties, interruptions, and obstacles that he encountered even limiting his enquiry to fewer than 100 interviewees.

Another difference from Kinsey is that the author has gone outside the semi-comfortable circumstances of his own country to foreign lands, including some of them (India and Hong Kong) that have significantly different cultures and social values. This has permitted disclosure of features of the lives lived by gay men that are common and some that are different, according to cultural and social norms. It may be said that the lives of gay men in Mumbai and Hong Kong are significantly different from those lived by other gay men in different towns and villages of India and China. But the same can probably be said of the lives of gay men in Sydney and Melbourne when compared to Deniliquin and Goondiwindi. Kinsey is still bitterly criticised by his critics for the imperfections of his data that are denounced as unrepresentative, selective, and misleading. The same critics would probably attack Peter Robinson's sample on the same grounds. However, as with Kinsey, there is sufficient authenticity to make the study and its disclosures worthwhile. In Kinsey's case, the authenticity was achieved by the sheer volume and number of the interviews. In the present author's case it is achieved by the detail that he has gathered. This demonstrates at once the similarities and differences that exist amongst gay men both in the lives they live and in the opinions they hold about those lives and the current issues that affect them. Amongst the important messages that emerge from the book and its analysis are:

- Almost half the men interviewed lived full and active single lives, with a strong capacity to build friendships and to enjoy support of a community.
- A significant number of the men formed long-term relationships resembling marriage that (except in the early blush of romance) were not overly sexualised.
- 22 of the men had stories to tell as fathers.
- Although more than 40 per cent of the sample were recorded as favouring marriage equality, a significant number (20 per cent) were opposed to the institution of marriage, regarding it as patriarchal in character and imposing a regime of hetero-normativity that they wished to escape.
- Most of the men interviewed had lived through crises of various kinds connected with the HIV/AIDS epidemic. But amongst younger men

in the cohort, there was some evidence of willingness to take 'strategic risks' in sexual conduct, alien to the safe sex messages to which older interviewees had been exposed at the height of the crisis.

As with Kinsey and his statistical taxonomies, this book challenges a lot of assumptions about the sex lives of the interviewees. They do not emerge as particularly sex obsessed; nor as incapable of sustaining long-lasting relationships; nor as doomed to lonely lives, bereft of friends. On the other hand, questions are presented as to whether different conclusions would be drawn from a larger cohort; from one that included an equal number of women interviewees; from one that included transgender and sex-worker participants; and one which was able somehow to reach out to sexual minorities living their lives in non-metropolitan areas, in the loneliness of regional and rural communities still very hostile to homosexuals, bisexuals, transsexual, and other queer minorities.

One of the questions which was raised in the recently failed attempt to secure marriage equality from the Australian Federal Parliament was whether extending legal equality to those gays who wanted to get married would inevitably lead on to other forms of marriage: the marriage of three or four people to one another; polygamous marriage for heterosexuals; marriage to children; incestuous marriage; and even (as one Australian Senator offensively put it) marriage to an animal. Whilst these questions were presented politely enough, they revealed the underlying hostility amongst opponents to contemplating the truth of Kinsey's basic discoveries and the consequential need to open marriage to at least those gay citizens prepared to accept its obligations and assumptions. One value of Peter Robinson's text is that it reveals, amongst the sample investigated, the boring similarity between most homosexual and heterosexual lives. If there are differences they would appear to be differences that predominate between male attitudes to sexuality and female, rather than between homosexual and heterosexual attitudes to stable relationships.

The book is easy to read. It makes the reader a kind of voyeur to the sexual lives of the subjects. But the glimpse that is afforded is dependent upon the truthfulness and completeness of the revelations of the interviewees. And upon this, Peter Robinson (like Alfred Kinsey) had no sanction to impose either upon those who exaggerated the sexual features of their lives or (more likely) those who discreetly revealed only as much as they thought was desirable for the interviewer to hear.

Because this book is anchored in the empirical principle, it is a useful addition to human knowledge. It will not have the mighty impact that the Kinsey reports did. And yet it was those reports that, ultimately, led to many others. And that made it possible for an Australian researcher such as Peter Robinson to embark upon the enquiry recorded in these pages. By securing and analysing more data about the lives of sexual minorities and by making that data available in book and digital form, Peter Robinson and his generation contribute to the unstoppable global move to end the hostility, to reform the laws and to terminate the stigma that has caused so much pain and misery to so many innocent and blameless people.

Sydney
21 February 2013
Michael Kirby

Acknowledgements

I would like to acknowledge here the help and assistance I received from friends and colleagues over the three and a half years that I spent researching and writing this book. A stalwart was Dr Helen Marshall, who not only read the book twice in draft form, first as I wrote each chapter and then again when I brought them together in the shape that you see now, but also offered sensible and calming advice when I sought to make sense of my primary data and to plan the architecture of the book. As well and in particular, I would like to thank Professor Russell Crawford, Dean of the Faculty of Life and Social Sciences, Swinburne University of Technology, for his encouragement when I arrived at the University and the practical support that he provided in the shape of a start-up, research account, which allowed me in 2011 to finalise transcription of ten outstanding interviews and in 2012 to employ sessional and casual colleagues to help with research assistance, proofreading, and editing. Other colleagues at Swinburne who gave me support or a friendly smile and encouraged me on my way were Associate Professor Karen Farquharson, Dr Paula Geldens, Dr Julie Kimber, Dr Peter Love, and Dr Dean Lusher, and I thank them here for their kindnesses. Special thanks go to Dr Aisling Bailey, who often asked me how things were going with 'the book' and if I needed a hand and then helped out with proofreading at short notice and the checking of chapters when one important deadline was nigh. At Monash University, Dr John Pardy was ceaseless in his interest and generous in the theoretical insights he offered as I sought to make meaning of my data. Universities are nothing without students, and I found in my students at Swinburne a genuine interest in the progress of this book, especially those who were enrolled in Qualitative Research Methods in 2012 and Sociology of Health in 2011 and 2012. And here I am thinking of Daniel Ashbury, Andrés Carberry, Filip Djordjevic, Ameera Katar, Stephanie Mathews, and Ashlie Rich, among others.

Together with colleagues, my friends have been a great help. They know who they are, and I would like to thank them for bearing with me as I moaned and groaned about this, my second labour of love. The first labour of love, as they know only too well, was *The Changing World of Gay Men*, which was also published by Palgrave Macmillan (2008). Among my friends, I would like to thank Humphrey McQueen for a great practical kindness in passing on to me Beatrice Webb's note-taking method.[1]

It is a reliable system for storing the small and large ideas we jot down when taking notes from other people's work, which never failed me when I wrote my PhD, my first book, and now this my second book. To my physiotherapist, Jon Park, I probably owe the greatest thanks. Using his hands and practical knowledge as he did over a two-year period, he looked after my shoulders and back when they were strained, keeping them pliable and relatively pain-free as I wrote, edited, and revised the words that now make up this book.

Other people who helped me along the way, whose help was equally as important as that which my colleagues and friends offered, were the acquaintances and strangers and acquaintances and strangers who have since become friends who helped me recruit the very interesting sample of 97 gay men whose interviews comprise the data on which this book rests. Here, I am thinking of people like Rehan Kularatne in London and Trevor McLean in Melbourne, who helped me get in touch with men to interview in Melbourne, London, and Hong Kong. I was helped in Melbourne also by Jack Loder, who put me in touch with a group of men who were in their 20s. In Mumbai, I was fortunate to meet online Shivanandra Khan OBE and in person Prince Manvendra Singh Gohil. Both men kindly helped me recruit interviewees when I visited Mumbai in December 2009. In New York, Professor Dan Pinello alerted people to my research project when I was there in June 2009, and this enabled me to interview more diverse men in New York and Los Angeles than would have been the case. A Manhattan resident Scott Davis helped me also to recruit interviewees in New York, in particular gay African-American men, and for his assistance and that of Dan Pinello I am very grateful.

I made two attempts to interview men in Hong Kong, and these are discussed in more detail in Chapter 1. On my first trip in December 2009, I interviewed three men with the help of Eric Herrera, organiser of a gay business and social organisation called Fruits in Suits.[2] After more planning and equipped with introductions from friends and acquaintances who knew people in Hong Kong, my second research trip to Hong Kong (June 2011) was a success and I recruited the remaining eleven Hong Kong interviewees. The success of the second research trip was due also to the help and support I received from Nigel Collett and members of the Pink Alliance, whom I thank here.

There were two phases to the interviews I held with Londoners. The first took place when I was visiting England in July 2010 and held face-to-face interviews with two men. The second phase was when with the help of a friend who once lived in Melbourne I got in touch with six men aged 33–47, some of whom I interviewed on Skype and some of whom sent me 'written interviews', the meaning of which I explain in Chapter 1. I recruited interviewees from Manchester when I was in England in July 2010. My decision to include gay men from Manchester arose from the city's gay reputation and as the setting of the British television series, *Queer As Folk*.[3] I spent three days in the field when I was in Manchester and had one day to enjoy its Indian restaurants and new light rail system. When there, I was very grateful for the help and advice I received from Dr John Goldring, Manchester Metropolitan University and Dr Richard Ward, Manchester University.

My visits to Sydney and Auckland occurred towards the end of my fieldwork, in October 2010. Peter Trebilco OAM helped me recruit gay Sydneysiders by passing on to the Pride history group, Sydney, my call for interviewees. Six men associated with Pride got in touch with me, and I interviewed them in Sydney in mid-October 2010 en route to Auckland. The final leg of my fieldwork took place in Auckland. I began preparations for Auckland early in 2010, when through a mutual friend I got in touch with Michael Stevens who was then doing research for his PhD on HIV infection among men who have sex with men. Michael gave me the names of two people who advertised my field trip and helped me recruit men for interview. They were Jacqui Stanford, a writer and subeditor at GayNZ.com and Vaughan Meneses, the manager of OutlineNZ. I would like to thank Peter Trebilco OAM, Michael Stevens, Jacqui Standford, and Vaughan Meneses for their kind help in Sydney and Auckland. Finally, I would like to thank all the men I interviewed whose first language was not English and who agreed to speak to me in a language that was not their mother tongue.

At Palgrave Macmillan, Philippa Grand kept a careful eye on my first book and offered me a contract for this second book. I have found in Philippa a fair-minded, considerate, and knowledgeable publisher and would like to acknowledge her help and guidance here. As well, I would like to acknowledge the work of Andrew James and Naomi Robinson, who assisted me in the writing and pre-production stages of the book, and then finally the production team at Palgrave Macmillan for the great work they did on the book's cover and in copy editing my original manuscript. Any faults that remain are my responsibility alone.

Notes

1. B. Webb *My Apprenticeship* (London: C. Longmans Green), pp. 364–70.
2. See Chapter 2.
3. British television series about a group of gay people living in Manchester. A North American series by the same name screened also in the early 2000s.

Introduction

What identified me as a gay person when I was younger was the edginess of what was going on in the community. And we are not edgy anymore. We are truly mainstream and that just kills me. ... I don't know if that is a feature of getting older or the gay community has assimilated in such a way that we have become boring.

(Marvin, aged 59, Los Angeles)

Younger gay men in Mumbai have a different kind of mentality. Their notion of fun or of party are different from mine and that means I do not involve myself with [them]. ... I would rather go to a house party and sit around and have conversations and drinks than go to a nightclub and dance the night away with all that [naked] skin and smoke and everything.

(William, aged 27, Mumbai)

My interest in the life course is twofold. First, I am interested in how resilient are gay friendship networks and gay relationships, and whether they will sustain gay men as they age. Second, I am interested in how the gay 'community' addresses the issue of gay ageing. I lived through the HIV-AIDS epidemic and, like many others, was impressed by the way in which as a group gay men responded to the external threat posed by the disease. I wonder now if gay men can/will respond similarly to the issue of ageing, which is of concern because of evidence suggesting that gay men are forced back into the closet the moment they take up residence in aged-care accommodation facilities.[1]

One of the more important findings reported in this book is that gay men 60 and older are on the whole fairly content with their lives (most were in long-lasting relationships) and optimistic about the future. Gay activists I interviewed were concerned, however, about the prospect of life in a nursing home – for themselves or for any gay person – and chiefly for the reason outlined above, that is, that they would be forced back into the closet. This is an important issue that needs more public and political discussion, especially when one considers that in a country like Australia, and I suspect the same is true in most western countries, the majority of nursing homes and aged-care facilities are operated by churches or church-based organisations – and not all of these are gay-friendly. Along with the fact that the gay world, its social institutions and practices are surprisingly similar the world over, I observed that in cities where gay, lesbian, bisexual, and transgender (GLBT) community organisations existed and were actively involved in social matters, awareness of gay life course and ageing issues seemed relatively high.[2] This is similar to an observation Dennis Altman made about the correlation between levels of gay community activism in the 1980s and HIV-AIDS awareness.[3] In Manchester, Melbourne, and New York, for example, there are gay organisations that work to raise funds and awareness of gay life course issues and lobby government. In Mumbai, I found also a high level of interest in ageing issues largely because of the social and political activism of three charitable trusts – the Lakshya Trust, which is based in Gujarat, the Humsafar Trust in Mumbai, and the Saarthi Trust, which is in Nagpur.

This book differs from the first I wrote in two important aspects.[4] First, its sample is international, comprising as it does material collected from 97 gay men I interviewed in nine major cities in six countries. Second, it is mainly concerned with how gay men understand and experience relationships across the life course. It is through the twin lenses of age and ageing that their life stories were examined – life stories that included accounts of relationships of 20 years' duration and more, arguments for and against gay marriage, the joys of the single life, and men's experience of fatherhood.

The sample

The non-representative sample on which this book is based comprises 97 men recruited from nine major cities in Australia, China (Hong Kong), England, India, New Zealand, and the United States. Interviews were conducted between July 2009 and December 2011. The sample is somewhat predictable because as an Australian male of my class and age, it made sense when designing the project to look to England and the USA if I wanted to recruit an international sample of gay men.[5] Because I lived in Melbourne, it made practical, and logistical, sense to interview men close to home – from Sydney, Melbourne, and Auckland. I would argue, however, that the sample is also eclectic because along with interviewees from Australia, England, New Zealand, and the USA it includes men from Mumbai and Hong Kong.

The first city I visited for the purpose of interviewing men for the book was New York in July 2009, followed by Los Angeles in August 2009, then Mumbai in December 2009, and Hong Kong in January 2010. In the first half of 2010, I interviewed men in Melbourne, Manchester, and London, finishing with rounds of interviews in Sydney and Auckland in October 2010. Additional interviews were held in Melbourne in late 2010, and then with men in London to whom I spoke between December 2010 and February 2011 by the Internet program Skype.

My first book was commended for including gay men from all classes and in so doing helped challenge a pervasive myth – that gay men are mostly if not all middle class.[6] The fact that this book includes data not only from men of all classes but also from interviews I had with 30 non-white gay men will help challenge another popular myth, which is that the gay identity is largely white and western. The non-white men that I interviewed for the book comprised an Aboriginal Australian man, African-American, African-Caribbean and Mexican-American men, Chinese men, Maori, and men from South Asia. There is more about the nature of the sample and my reasons for interviewing men from Hong Kong and Mumbai in Chapter 1.

Rationale

For a study that includes the life stories of a large number of non-Anglo gay men, it was important from the outset to test whether the interviewees ascribed the same meaning to their social, sexual, and affective lives. For more than a decade in India, for example, terms to describe non-heterosexuals have been the subject of fierce debate: 'a vociferous constituency ... protests the use of terms like *gay* for India's male homosexual population instead preferring the more functional *men who have sex with men* (MSM)'.[7] Despite the controversy in India about terminology – largely relating to the work of NGOs and local organisations involved in the HIV-AIDS crisis to use a terminology that enables them to contact men who do not identify as gay but who have sex with men[8] – all the men I interviewed from India as well as the South Asian men who lived in the West declared that they and their same-sex-attracted friends were 'gays'. As well, all the Chinese men I interviewed from Hong Kong understood the term gay and, with the exception of one man in his mid-20s who called himself 'queer', identified as gay. I would argue that the general acceptance of and identification with the term gay that I found among this non-representative sample was partly a result of the plain-language statement that I sent potential interviewees, which stated that I was seeking 'gay' men to take part in research on gay age and ageing.[9] It was partly a result also of what Dennis Altman argues is the effect of globalisation on non-heterosexual identities:

> The gay world – less obviously the lesbian, largely due to marked differences in women's social and economic status – is a key example of emerging global 'subcultures', where members of particular groups have more in common across national and continental boundaries than they do with others in their own geographically defined societies.[10]

The research that underpins this book rests on four assumptions, which are examined below. First, a connection exists between sexual preference and sexual identity so that a 'gay world' exists in the West, comprising bars, sex clubs, community organisations, which many gay men use in order to socialise or find sexual or relationship partners – and that similar versions of the same exist outside the West. Second, the idea of generation exists that often provides individuals with a sense of personal and collective identity. Third, the self is narratively constituted. Fourth, that age and ageing can be understood as socially constructed.

Sexual identity and gay world(s)

It is now fairly well accepted in scholarly circles that in the West sexual preference or sexual desire shapes identity, and that this in turn has given rise to sexual categories such as gay, bisexual, and transsexual, that is, that sexual desire and the associated sexual identity are socially constructed. The connection between sexual desire and sexual identity is explained by Steven Seidman as follows:

> Unless we are prepared to exclude all those sexual constructions that differ from 'our own', or to deny difference by interpreting them as minor variations of an identical phenomenon, we must concede that groups evolve their own sexual culture around which they elaborate coherent lives.[11]

This understanding that separate sexual categories exist has taken hold also in non-western countries where the influence of the West has been strong or prolonged, such as in the case of India and Hong Kong.

Of all the debates about the connection between same-sex desire and practice and sexual identity, the one I find most persuasive is James Boswell's argument in *Christianity, Social Tolerance, and Homosexuality*. Boswell argued that gay people have always existed in human societies, and that evidence of their existence in the past has come to us only from times that were sufficiently propitious for them to make themselves and their relationships public.[12] That the views and attitudes towards gay men that non-homosexuals hold are not constant and vary according to the social context of the day relates to an argument Norbert Elias made in *Civilizing Process* – that people born at different times in the modern period demonstrate different levels of sensitivity to shame and embarrassment.[13] Following Elias's argument, I have assumed that different age cohorts of gay men experience homosexuality differently, influenced as they are by prevailing, dominant narratives on sexuality and homosexuality.[14] In a similar vein, Dennis Altman argues that homophobia shadows every move gay men make.[15] By this he means that whenever and wherever they speak up, their opponents also do so and by the same means. Once anonymous homophobic abuse was scribbled on walls, in railway carriages, and public toilets. Nowadays, anti-gay slogans are scrawled in public places on the Internet when homophobes post abusive messages in response to views they wish to denigrate or belittle.

The world that many gay men inhabit comprises the scene – bars, sex clubs, saunas – and then what is generally known as the gay community, consisting of community organisations such as those established to care for people living with HIV-AIDS (PLWHA) and help gay men come out or improve their relationships.[16] In relying on the idea of a gay world, that is, a sub-culture that is separate from 'mainstream' society, I am consciously building on earlier work where I explained the formation of the gay world in countries like Australia and England as a response to gay men's need to socialise and as a safe harbour from the straight world where they were shunned or worse. For many gay men, the clubs and bars that it comprised formed a ghetto-like space where they could socialise in relative safety. During most of the twentieth century in large western cities like London, New York, and Sydney, the gay world was important for the formation of gay identity, particularly during the 1960s and 1970s when the gay liberation movement coalesced. At that time, men exchanged and disseminated new ideas about themselves and how they understood their identity as based on their sexual preference; they did so in the same bars and clubs where they went to drink, dance, meet friends, and look for sexual partners. Since then, however, the importance of the gay world as a safe haven has declined as the achievements of gay liberation have been more widely shared and social tolerance increased. Its *raison d'être* has declined also with the growth of the Internet, the dating and quick-sex hook-ups that it spawned, and the emergence of young gay men whose social lives are defined not by their immersion in the gay world but by assimilationist practices.[17] Young men with assimilationist values have so reshaped the gay identity in parts of the USA that Marvin (aged 59) from Los Angeles, whose views are quoted at the head of the Introduction, said that he no longer felt any connection to contemporary gay culture. It is possible that the cultural change taking place in western gay world(s) is as portentous as the change that took place in the late 1960s. Then, the baby boomers invaded and took over the camp world of their predecessors, publicly proclaimed the gay man as the new, modern homosexual and began establishing gay institutions to meet their economic, political, and social/sexual needs.

How was the gay world in Mumbai similar to or different from that in a western city such as Manchester? Even though I visited Mumbai and Manchester to interview men for this book, I did not make or find time to explore the gay bars and clubs in the cities, and so here use fleeting impressions, secondary material, and, in the case of Mumbai, draw on the views of interviewees to describe them. One Sunday lunchtime on Canal Street is too brief a time to form any but the most superficial impression of the gay scene (bars and clubs) in Manchester. What I remember seeing, however, were bars open to the street serving food and drink, small groups of mostly men, representing most body shapes, and loud, fairly anonymous dance music. The people in the bars and those eating from sidewalk cafés appeared polite, relatively affluent, well behaved, and friendly. Only the absence of children, conventional family groups, and a greater number of women suggested it was a gay neighbourhood. Paul Simpson has written at length about the gay world in Manchester and described the gay precinct as follows:

> The gay district itself consists largely of one main thoroughfare (Canal Street), which ... hosts the main bars overlooking the canal. The village also extends to two streets running in parallel and three smaller streets running perpendicular to the main thoroughfare. ... The gay district housed: 35 bars (mainly gay-identified with late licenses,

though six were advertised as 'mixed,' one is mainly 'lesbian' and one is mainly 'trans'); three nightclubs ... seven restaurants ... several fast-food restaurants; three hotels, two of which are attached to bars ... various businesses mostly targeted at gay men ... [and] The Lesbian and Gay Foundation ... situated just behind Canal Street.[18]

From Paul's description and my observations of Canal Street, the gay world in Manchester is similar in nature and composition to gay districts in other large, western cities. Because of the preponderance of bars and clubs with late-night licences as well as cafés, restaurants, and shops selling dance-party paraphernalia and leather costumes, Canal Street resembled Soho in London, Le Marais in Paris, Oxford Street in Sydney, and Greenwich Village in New York.

I did not visit any of the gay districts in Mumbai. Parmesh Shanahi's description of Mumbai's gay world suggests that middle-class, gay men meet and socialise in bars and clubs, dance until dawn, and use the Internet for social/sexual contacts in much the same way as do their counterparts in cities like Hong Kong, London, and New York.[19] And as William from Mumbai reveals, whose quote is one of two that head this chapter, not all gay men are drawn to the commercial scene of bars and clubs and, as Shivananda Khan and Jeremy Seabrook have pointed out, among others, there is a vast network of men from all classes in India who have sex with men.[20] From casual conversations with interviewees while in Mumbai and observations I made when in their homes, I left the city with three distinct impressions of the gay world in Mumbai. My first impression was that the men I interviewed tended to socialise in each other's homes or in cafés and restaurants, which might be explained by the fact that, with the exception of one man from a poor village family, all belonged to either the middle or upper classes. My second impression was that, as William's quote suggests, the dance clubs in Mumbai were crowded and noisy and attracted large numbers of young men. My third impression was that a lively sex trade existed and that large numbers of sex workers used the sea wall near the Gate of India as the central place to meet clients. These impressions reminded me of the picture that Andrew Holleran painted of the New York gay world in the late 1970s, that is, a vast, hedonistic, fairly chaotic, and mobile world populated by young or youthful men.[21]

I have used the terms 'gay', 'non-heterosexual', 'same-sex-attracted', and 'homosexual' interchangeably in this book to describe men who love men or have intimate and/or sexual relations with them.[22] The term 'men who have sex with men' is also used but mainly in the context of same-sex sexual practices in India where sex between men who do not identify as homosexual or gay is more widespread.[23]

Generation identity

The work of Karl Mannheim is generally the agreed starting point for anyone interested in generations and their meaning.[24] Mannheim believed that an understanding of generations would help social scientists explain social change, and looked for a means of defining the meaning of 'generation' and enabling us to scientifically separate one generation from another. The problem as Mannheim saw it was that a general law did not exist to 'express the rhythm of historical development, based on the biological law of the limited life-span of man [sic] and the overlap of new and old generations'. The problem for anyone wanting to use the concept of generations to distinguish between historical periods was, according to Mannheim, in proposing a method to overcome the difficulty that overlapping births and deaths caused in drawing a dividing line between two generations.[25] The difficulty was in knowing when the social environment had changed dramatically enough to identify two birth cohorts as coming from different historical cohorts. Since Mannheim first identified this problem, scholars have not stopped using the term to designate periods of lived experience, as shown by the continued use of the terms 'First World War' generation, 'Depression' generation, and 'Vietnam' generation, for example. In the context of gay worlds, twin defining experiences for western gay men since the 1950s have been (1) the gay liberation movement and (2) the HIV-AIDS epidemic.

The gay liberationists' programme called on gay people to come out, to proclaim their sexual difference and, until the HIV-AIDS epidemic, was the most significant, generation-defining event in the history of modern homosexuality. The act of coming out was not always a straightforward or painless experience for gays and lesbians from the 'baby boomer generation'.[26] The HIV-AIDS epidemic was a seriously traumatic event in the lives of more than one generation of gay men. It marked the generation of men born in the late 1940s and 1950s who had come of age when the epidemic broke in the West and who had been sexually active before its means of transmission were known. As well, as I argue in Chapter 7, the epidemic shaped the identity of later generations of gay men because by its existence it forced and continues to force gay men to consider who they are and how they conduct themselves, sexually and in other ways.

British gerontologists and sociologists have argued that the term 'age cohort' is both better than and preferable to 'generation', for four reasons. First, as others since Mannheim have noted, it is an inexact term that cannot and does not define a separate and unique group of people.[27] Second, it is not a helpful tool for understanding or explaining social inequalities.[28] Third, it does not reflect the lived experience of many people, for whom family and family relations are stronger identity markers.[29] Fourth, its identity is created after the event.[30] As a consequence of these arguments, I have mostly used 'age cohort' in the book. The only exception is in the case of Chapter 7 where I discuss HIV-AIDS and its effect on the identity of two birth cohorts of gay men. My reason for preferring 'generation' over 'cohort' in this single context is that the date of the arrival of the HIV-AIDS epidemic marked a clear and virtually unambiguous watershed between a time when it was unknown (and great numbers of gay men contracted it unknowingly) and a time when its presence became known and was made public. Once its means of transmission were known, a public health campaign began in Australia (as it did in other western countries like New Zealand and the UK) to inform gay men about HIV-AIDS and, using the then novel idea of 'safe-sex', to educate them about how to avoid contracting the disease. The most notable consequence of this public health campaign has been to change the sexual practices of a generation of same-sex-attracted men.

Narrative identity

To analyse the stories the men told me who were interviewed for this book, I used a form of narrative analysis known as the life-story method, which British sociologist Ken Plummer recommended for researchers working in the field of sexuality. According to Plummer, one of the advantages of the life-story method was that it provides a scholarly audience for new stories that were previously not heard – such as those of sexual-abuse survivors, people coming out late in life, transgender people, and the relatively familiar coming-out stories of gay and lesbian people.[31] In analysing the data I collected for this study, I was influenced by the work of historian David Carr, who argues that narrative is 'constitutive', that is, that the stories we tell about ourselves bring into being not only actions and experience, but also, and crucially, the self: 'Narrative ... is constitutive not only of action but also of the self which acts and experiences.'

In regard to the constitutive role of narrative and how it operates, Carr argues that the self occupies four positions in its own narrative, which it must occupy simultaneously. The third assumption on which the research for this book rests is that a person's life is shaped by the stories s/he tells about her/himself. Each of us, Carr says, is the author, storyteller, actor, and audience of the story that together and at once constitutes the self.[32] I would argue that such an understanding of how the self is constituted is especially useful when analysing life stories of non-heterosexual people because, for many of us, large stretches of our lives were and in some cases still are given over to establishing ourselves as the principal author of our own story, if not also its principal storyteller, actor, and audience.[33] Understanding narrative as constitutive enables a twofold research process. First, it assumes that the interviewee will explain by narrative the signal events in his/her life – in the case of the men interviewed for this book, how they lived their lives as single men or as fathers, for example. Second, it allows the researcher then to analyse his/her interviewees' narrative accounts and shape a larger narrative that tells the story of how, in the case of this book, small groups of men made sense of their lives as non-heterosexuals.

Social construction of age and ageing

It is generally accepted in sociology and similar disciplines that life stages such as 'youth' and 'old age' are socially constructed. The fourth assumption underlying this book is that a person's attitude to and experience of age and ageing are shaped by social factors and not solely by biology.[34]. Because class affects gender, for example, working-class women can experience a harsher old age than women from the middle or upper classes: 'the rich simply purchase good and expensive care for themselves on the "senior services market", while the less well off receive no help because they cannot pay for it'.[35] At this point I should explain that when I refer to interviewees' class position in the book, I do so in order to give a fuller picture of their lives and that I am not presenting this as a class analysis of gay men's life stories or relationships.

The low life expectancy of Aboriginal and Torres Strait Islanders in Australia illustrates the continuing negative effect ethnicity can have on a person's old age, as do accounts from India showing how a combination of class, gender, and caste operate to reduce a person's life circumstances.[36]

> The bulk of the poor not only are landless poor peasants and unorganized workers, but are also from the scheduled castes, backward classes and scheduled tribes. Among the poor households women suffer more, and also in general, women suffer more from poverty. Thus, understanding poverty is incomplete without seeing the interface of caste, class and gender.[37]

Sexuality as well can affect how an individual experiences old age. Media reports in Britain and Australia suggest that ageing gays and lesbians are concerned that they will experience discrimination if they have to move into nursing homes in old age.[38] This will not be the universal experience of gay men, however, for, as Edmund White has written, class is a stronger bond than sexual identity: 'Rich and middle-class gays are not likely to identify with the poor; they retain a loyalty to members of their own class, whether straight or gay.'[39]

The chapters

This book examines the lives of gay men as lived in response to two powerful social impulses, namely, the incentive to conform to heterosexual norms of relations and behaviour or to create new patterns of relations and behaviour that match their relationship needs. In the following chapters, I consider how different facets of gay men's identity are shaped by the relationships they maintain and in varying social contexts.

After the account of interviewing men for the book in the first chapter, I look at the life stories of men who lived single lives (Chapter 2), providing evidence that contradicts a myth about single people and gay men, which is that single people are invariably lonely and that gay men are invariably single. After this, the focus moves to the accounts of men with experience of long-lasting relationships. Among more interesting findings here (Chapter 3) are that not only were a substantial minority of the men in long-lasting relationships (10 years or more) but that the relationships closely resembled the companionate marriage, which I argue is evidence of gay men's willingness to mirror heterosexual relational models based on sustained commitment and longevity. Fatherhood is the next relationship type to be considered.

My analysis of the stories told by a small group of men who were fathers (Chapter 4) shows that the majority of these men became fathers as a result of their earlier heterosexual relationships. Included in this chapter were five stories of non-heterosexual fatherhood, that is, how the men became fathers as a result of relations with lesbian couples, surrogacy, or other means. This chapter provides evidence therefore of gay men's involvement in one of the relationships most strongly associated with heterosexuality and of their doing so by both conventional and experimental means. As well, it shows how social context determined the means by which two generations of men came to be fathers.

The next two chapters (Chapters 5 and 6) are devoted to the gay marriage debate. Chapter 5 focuses on the principal reasons that more than 40 men gave for supporting gay marriage – legal/property equality, relational equality, and recognition of relationship success through marriage. The arguments of the men who did not favour gay marriage are considered separately in Chapter 6. Differences of opinion about gay marriage were mainly along generation lines. The younger men (aged 31 and under) almost uniformly favoured adopting what many of the older men from the sample regarded as a failed, heteronormative institution. The younger men argued for doing so without any of them indicating any apparent awareness of the impact gay marriage would have on gay identity or relationships and because it suited their personal needs. By contrast, most of the older men (aged 51 and over) opposed gay marriage for personal reasons – because they considered cohabitation a satisfactory arrangement that suited them and for political reasons – marriage, they said, is a patriarchal institution and if introduced would lead to a return to heteronormativity for gay men.

Generation differences were apparent also in Chapter 7, the final chapter, where the focus was on how two age cohorts of all-Australian men understood the threat HIV-AIDS posed to them and what effect living in its midst had on their sense of self and sexual/social lives. My analysis of the stories from the two generations of men – a pre-HIV generation of men who were adults and sexually active before the disease was diagnosed, and a post-HIV generation of men who were adults and sexually active in the early 2000s – found only minor differences of nuance between how they were affected by the virus.

The five tables in Appendixes contain a small amount of quantitative material relating to the lives of the men interviewed for the book. Tables A.1 and A.2 comprise lists of the pseudonyms of the interviewees from the international sample and the all-Australian sample (for more information on these, see Chapter 1), together with the men's ages when interviewed, the cities where they lived, and their occupations by broad fields. Table A.3 shows a breakdown of the 97 men from the international sample according to their relationship status, that is, whether they were single or in a relationship when interviewed. These data are discussed in Chapters 2 and 3. Table A.4 provides a list of the pseudonyms of the single men from the international sample (*n* = 42), their ages, and where they lived. These data are the subject of Chapter 2. Table A.5 contains information about the lives of 14 men from the all-Australian sample and eight from the international sample who had experience of fatherhood. Together with the men's pseudonyms and ages are details of their marriages or relationships, their children, and in at least one case their grandchildren.

Connecting the chapters that comprise this book is a narrative about how age and age cohort or generation affiliation affect gay men's relationships. In each chapter I have organised my analysis of the men's stories around age groups so as to make my findings clearer and underline the importance of what I believe is crucial to understanding the lives of gay men – that their identity and the relationship choices open to them are historically contingent. It is no coincidence, for example, that the majority of men with fatherhood stories to tell were baby boomers and became fathers as a result of heterosexual relationships with women. These men decided in the 1960s or 1970s to have relationships with women because either they were unsure about their sexuality or the times were not propitious for them to come out or be gay. It is not a coincidence also that the older men from the sample mostly opposed the push for gay marriage and on the grounds that cohabitation arrangements had suited them. These men came to maturity in the 1960s and 1970s when the women's liberation rhetoric was being disseminated loudly and widely. They grew up in the midst of pronounced public debates on television, in university cafeterias, pubs, and union meetings about the value or otherwise of marriage. And they made long-lasting relationships work for them before homosexuality was decriminalised and without the need for state recognition or sanction. The younger men were not prepared, however, to accept anything less than what their heterosexual friends or siblings could expect to enjoy, and in my analysis of their stories about gay marriage made it very clear that in their eyes marriage was a matter of gay rights and they would not stop calling for marriage equality.

Location and class were less important in the end than I thought they might have been. I mention them in the book if and when the occasion arises, and do so to provide fuller background for my discussion of the men's stories but, as I explained earlier, I do not present this work as a class analysis or cultural comparison of gay men's lives or relationships stories. It is a study of the influence of age and generation on gay men's relationship experiences and stories, a study of similarity and difference.

1
Collecting 97 Gay Men's Life Stories

> Heterosexual people are persecuted on Valentine's Day for showing their emotions in public, let alone homosexuality. ... I am not saying homosexual people are second fiddle to them ... but if you imagine this is the condition of the heterosexual community [in India] what can you expect for homosexual people?
>
> (Kim, aged 23, Mumbai)

Introduction

By its very nature, a qualitative sample can never represent the population it purports to study. Qualitative samples can be 'quite large', as was the overall sample I used for this book, or they can be 'relatively small', as are a number of the city samples I used. Typically, qualitative samples can 'represent' or provide a sense of the possible range of views, experiences, processes found in the wider population but cannot represent their numerical distribution. For example, in Auckland, I interviewed 12 men who were drawn from a variety of classes and ethnic backgrounds, including two retired men who had had working-class jobs in the transport sector and three Maori. In New York, I interviewed 11 gay men, whose ages were from 33 to 72 and included five African- and Caribbean-American men and two men who were HIV positive. In Mumbai, I interviewed seven men, four of whom were in their 20s and five of whom were in relationships.

Gay identity and belonging are strongly shaped by the stories gay men tell each other about themselves and their life experiences, and will continue to be until the distinction between gay and straight disappears. For this reason, while a qualitative sample of gay men cannot represent the 'infinite variety' that Alfred Kinsey argued he found in gall wasps (and by extension Nature more generally) and sought to discover in his studies of human sexuality, small samples such as I gathered in New York and Mumbai do represent a reliable range of the views that gay men in those cities held on the matters I discussed with them, which form the basis of this book. They do not represent the views of bisexual men, men who have not yet come out, or men who have sex with men. Also, they cannot represent the views of other sexual minorities, even though there will be similarities. Finally, they cannot cover every variety of views held by gay men. They are a reliable representation, though, of the range of views that gay men held about their lives, their understanding of what age means to them, and what it means to age as a gay man.

Two non-representative samples

Drawing on data from two separate sets of interviews can be hazardous. There is a temptation to 'mix and match' incongruous sets of data, that is, material collected for different purposes. For example, if the researcher has a sample of former railway workers that he interviewed for a relatively contained, small project, is it appropriate to use these data in conjunction with data that a local government agency collected from retired people that included a subset of interviews with former railway workers? The efficacy and ethics of blending two data sets such as these depend on the following. First, how similar were (a) the questions the interviewees were asked, (b) the manner in which the interviewees were recruited, (c) the protocols that guided the researcher's practice in each instance. Second, how familiar with the data, which they did not collect themselves, were the researchers able to get once they gained access to them and proposed blending them with their own data. There is nothing mischievous or illegitimate about blending material from multiple projects as long as researchers devote time to acquaint themselves with the full biographical details of the participants from both sets and can explain to their readers how the sets differ and how they used them. They must make very clear that they are using two different data sets, are aware of the hazards, outline what efforts they have taken to reduce or eliminate them, and where or how the sets are different and/or similar.

I have tried to avoid hazards such as these when drawing on material from the two sets of data I collected myself. The first set of data, which is discussed in more depth below, was a non-representative sample of

80 gay men that I interviewed in Australia in the period 2001–3 for my PhD. The second set of data, discussed also below, comprised interviews with 97 men that I recruited in 2009–11 from nine major cities in Australia, Britain, Hong Kong, India, New Zealand, and the United States.[1] How did I avoid the pitfalls that I argue can arise from blending data sets? First, on each occasion, I was interviewing gay men on closely related topics. Second, in the one chapter in this book where I combine data from both sets of interviews, I used the men's answers to the same questions, to provide material for analysis about their parenting past.[2] Because I was responsible for recruiting and interviewing the 177 men from the combined samples of gay men I recruited in Australia and five other countries, following the same ethical practice throughout, I would argue the material the men provided in answer to similar if not identical questions can be used without fear of misrepresentation.

One nagging doubt remains, however, which is whether it is legitimate to blend material collected where there is a significant time difference, in this case, as much as ten years, notwithstanding similar if not identical questions. One approach to dealing with this was to use the interviewees' dates of birth as a means of sorting them by age and to look for differences. At first, this seemed a commonsensical approach, but doing so would mean having to choose a single year from which to reckon the men's age, for example 2006, which was midway between 2003 when I completed the interviews for the first data set and 2009 when I began interviewing for the second data set. There was one serious problem with this approach. It would mean forcing consistency on the two separate data sets in such a way that would affect the one unchangeable fact of the interviews I held with the men – the fact of who they were at the time of interview. A 51-year-old man interviewed in 2003 remains forever 51 in the data set to which he belongs. His age at the time of interview means that his views and opinions remain forever the views and opinions of a man who was 51 at the time of interview, in his case, in 2003. It would be wrong to adjust these facts for the sake of neatness or consistency, that is, to use his date of birth, in this case 1952, and present and analyse material from his interview as representing those of a man who was 54 or 58 or 62 in 2006. This relates to the question of age cohorts that I discussed in the Introduction. If, for example, I had been interviewing during the 1990s – when HIV-AIDS was still a life-and-death health risk to gay men in the West but included also the year when an antidote was discovered (1996) – I could have been dealing with two groups of men separated by ten years who effectively belonged to two different social cohorts. One social cohort comprised men who lived with HIV-AIDS before the antidote, the other social cohort comprising men who lived with HIV-AIDS in the era when the antidote existed. When using two different data sets the methodological solution is to retain the integrity of each set and to be clear about where and when one's interviews were held and to check for differences by date of interview.

One of my data sets (the 'all-Australian' set) is from my home country and was collected between 2001 and 2003; the other is international, collected after 2009. The Australians, recruited from capital cities, country towns and districts in south-eastern Australia, were aged between 20 and 79. With the exception of three Aboriginal men and a man who was Thai by birth, the men were of Anglo-Saxon or Anglo-Celtic descent and, with the exception of 13 working-class men, who were employed in the transport and hospitality sectors, all were tertiary-educated and had jobs in middle-class occupations such as law, the care professions, education, or the public service.[3] The international data set consisted of interviews that I collected from 97 men recruited in nine international cities, namely, Auckland, Hong Kong, London, Los Angeles, Manchester, Melbourne, Mumbai, New York, and Sydney. The interviews took place between 2009 and 2011, and the men were from all social classes and a variety of ethnic backgrounds. Their ages ranged from 19 to 87. Ethnically, while the bulk of men from this sample had Anglo-Saxon or Anglo-Celtic backgrounds, interviewees included five distinct ethnic minorities, consisting of one Aboriginal Australian man, five African- or Caribbean-American men, 10 Chinese men, three Maori, and 11 men with a South Asian background – or a total of 30 men.[4] In Chapters 2, 3, 5, and 6, I used the international sample exclusively. In Chapter 7, I used the all-Australian data set exclusively. And in Chapter 4, I used interview transcripts of 22 men drawn from the two data sets: 14 from the all-Australian sample and eight from the international sample.

The choice of English-speaking cities is predictable because as a white, Anglo Australian who was born in the 1950s, it made sense to me when designing the research project to recruit interviewees from England and the USA if I wanted an international sample of gay men. And because I live in Melbourne, I looked for interviewees from cities I knew and could get to without too much difficulty, namely, Sydney, Melbourne, and Auckland. Two factors shaped my decision to seek potential interviewees in India and Hong Kong. The first was a promise I made my editor to address a failing her reviewer observed in the original publication proposal – that it was too western – and include non-western gay men in the sample. The second was more practical and concerned the need to conduct fieldwork in non-western countries where English was spoken. I had visited India in the mid-1980s and had strong memories of Mumbai as a colourful, friendly, and accessible city – largely because at the time an Indian friend acted as my tour guide. And geographically, it was close at hand. I chose Hong Kong because, like Mumbai, it was relatively close at hand. I imagined also that it would share the values and practices of most port cities and have a history of tolerance and easy-going morals. In the end, it was in Mumbai and Hong Kong that I experienced the greatest difficulties in recruiting potential interviewees, for reason that are explained in the discussion below.

The interviews

Recent advances in interpersonal communications such as e-mail and social networks have made getting in touch with people in other countries easier and more immediate. But unlike when a researcher arranges face-to-face interviews, making on-line connections can be more difficult, time-consuming, and less certain. As anyone who has used either will know, it is easy for a respondent to 'go missing' or simply forget to reply to an interlocutor's requests. In New York, I experienced the demoralising experience of waiting for potential interviewees who did not turn up as arranged. Although it occurred in New York only twice, I did lower my expectations and was pleased when strangers I had arranged to meet on the steps of the New York Public Library or in Bryant Park showed up and we made contact. The only other city where this occurred was Los Angeles. In Auckland, Hong Kong, London, Melbourne, Manchester, Mumbai, and Sydney, I met the men I arranged for interviews as planned. On two occasions, however, I forgot to meet interviewees. The first was on a rainy, summer's day in Washington Square, New York in July 2009 and the second on a sunny day in early spring 2010 in Ponsonby, Auckland. On both occasions, I tried to make alternative arrangements but without luck.

My experience in large cities left me wondering if fieldwork is easier in urban centres than in the Kalahari or Borneo. From my experience, I would say that it is no easier because in vast urban conglomerations like Los Angeles and New York, researchers can get lost and interviewees can forget appointments without loss of face, that is, without experiencing any social consequences for dishonouring an arrangement. Even though Melbourne is a city of almost 4 million people, I never worried that interviewees would break appointments I had made on e-mail or by conventional mail, partly because I was more sure of my place in the city that is home. That said, I was fairly sure also that interviewees would keep their appointments in Auckland, Hong Kong, Manchester, Mumbai, and Sydney, because in each of those cities mutual friends or colleagues had introduced us. There is more about urban fieldwork experiences in the city-by-city accounts that follow.

I have written elsewhere about interviewing and compared my experiences to that which Richard Sennett and Jonathon Cobb described about interviewing automobile workers in the USA 40 years ago.[5] I argued that once I overcame the social distance that my identity as an academic and researcher created between my interviewees and me, the familiarity that I have found to exist between gay men of all classes facilitated an easy exchange. The only time I recalled any difficulties was when I asked a man in his 30s about how his coming out affected relations with his father. The act of recalling his father's response appeared to make the interviewee angry. His reaction to my question led me to examine more closely young men's coming-out stories and using my findings to develop an argument about an aspect of gay men's coming-out difficulties.[6]

Since the early 1970s, when Sennett and Cobb wrote *The Hidden Injuries of Class*, technological innovations such as the advent of the Internet and social sites such as Facebook have changed ordinary people's understanding of their autobiographical selves. In particular, Facebook has encouraged a generation, their parents, and in some cases their grandparents to make more public than ever before the details of their everyday life. I suspect that because so many of us have got into the habit of posting story-like accounts of our lives and daily doings on sites like Facebook, it has become a lot easier for people to reveal their life story when interviewed. While this is the same for gay people as it is for straight people, I would argue that what I call gay men's 'autobiographical ease' – the casual way in which a gay man can talk about the signal moments in his 'gay life' (or the 'new' life that begins after coming out) – derives from first, the experience of coming out, which usually means that the gay man must rewrite his social/sexual life story and second, the long history of confessional narratives that gay men since the late nineteenth century have been obliged to tell the medical and legal professions and which have been recorded in the form of case studies.[7] These two experiences of telling his life story first to friends and family and second, to doctors, psychologists, solicitors, police, social workers or priests, means that gay men have a well-developed capacity to recall important moments in their life history and relate them.

In the next section, I explain how I conducted face-to-face interviews in a variety of urban settings, including large and small parks in New York City and Melbourne; hotel lobbies in Los Angeles, Hong Kong, Manchester, Sydney, and Auckland; my hotel rooms in Mumbai, Manchester, and Auckland; interviewees' homes or nearby cafés in Melbourne and Manhattan. The great bulk of interviews were face to face, which I recorded in the presence of interviewees and later had transcribed. I did use the web-based application called Skype for some of my international interviews. Skype allows people to speak to one another via the Internet. Microphones and speakers built into computers allow spoken communication. For the researcher, an advantage over the traditional telephone is the ease with which an interview can be recorded, as well as the fact that Skype is a free service. I held interviews this way with 10 men from England, Hong Kong, India, and the USA between December 2009 and May 2011. I did not use a web-cam but had I done so, the interviews would have been similar to a conventional face-to-face interview.[8]

In principle, the idea of an interview on Skype would seem fairly straightforward, and it is once arrangements are made and the day and time are agreed on and confirmed. I found Skype interviews time-consuming, however, compared with face-to-face interviews. This was because it was my responsibility (a) to establish my bona fides and (b) to arrange and then remind, cajole, sometimes plead with potential interviewees to finalise the preliminary exchanges and settle on a mutually convenient time for an interview. And then because I did not use a web-cam for the Skype interviews, I had no visual contact with interviewees, the effect of which was that interviews were more like a telephone interview in that I could not rely on facial cues or eye contact to enhance the interview, and so had to depend more on my imagination to bridge the gap that time and distance created. I found Facebook useful for establishing my bona fides and setting up the basics of a trusting relationship with the men who expressed interest in giving an interview for the book, especially in Hong Kong, Los Angeles, Mumbai, and New York.

When interviewing in Manchester (see below), I met an academic who said he would be willing to take part in my study but long-distance and by e-mail. I called this a 'written interview'. More like a survey, I sent the academic in Manchester and another academic in Swansea copies of my interview questions, which they answered in writing and returned by e-mail. Hence the term 'written interview'. While this style of interview tends to produce more studied, less spontaneous answers, I was impressed with the liveliness of the replies they sent.

Nine cities

I made contact with many of the interviewees through personal intro-ductions and recommendations and via tentative links I made on the Internet. In the USA, the website called Craigslist was useful for mak-ing preliminary contacts, but it was a chance connection with another author in the field that put me in touch with the majority of American men I interviewed. After that, my personal e-mail account and Facebook were the means I used to keep in touch and confirm appointments. In Australia, England, Hong, India, and New Zealand, I made contact with potential interviewees through introductions from academics and activ-ists. Again, once contact was made, both my private e-mail account and Facebook were helpful for maintaining contact and setting up meetings for interview. I used a 16-question structured interview schedule for each interview. On average, the interviews lasted 45 minutes. After tran-scription, I analysed them with the help of the basic Microsoft Word software program, looking for narratives about the men's experience of age and ageing as well as evidence of conventional relationships and relational attitudes, and evidence for relationships that followed less conventional, gay life projects. In the following sections, the cities are discussed in chronological order of my visits, beginning in New York in July 2009 and finishing with a return trip to Hong Kong in June 2011.[9]

New York

The first set of interviews for this book took place in New York in July 2009. Before departing Australia, I made contact with potential interviewees through advertisements that I posted on the website Craigslist. Craigslist enables members to buy and sell or exchange goods and services such as furniture, accommodation, tutorials, sex and romance, and neither buyer nor seller is charged a fee. I posted advertisements under the 'community' category, asking for responses from gay men who lived in New York. A number of men replied asking if I paid for interviews. A quick reviews of other advertisements posted in the community category showed that a number of other researchers, mainly affiliated with North American universities, were offering to pay respondents for interviews. I did not pay men in Australia when I interviewed them for *The Changing World* and had not planned to do so for this book, so I replied in the negative. Several people who seemed promising interviewees and with whom I was beginning to establish a research relationship broke off contract with me at that point. Once on the ground in New York, I was surprised also by the number of men with whom I arranged to have an interview who either did not meet me as planned or ceased replying to my e-mails after we had made fairly definite arrangements, including setting a date and place to meet.

In hindsight, one of the shortcomings of trying to arrange interviews on the Internet, whether by e-mail, a market-exchange site like Craigslist, or a social-network site such as Facebook, is the ease with which arrangements can be forgotten or dishonoured. I believe this is chiefly to do with the tentative nature of relationships that individuals can create when they use the Internet. It is easier to miss an appointment made by e-mail when e-mail is the only means of communication with the other person because the consequences of doing so are not as serious as they can be when the other person has your telephone numbers, home or work addresses, or knows your friends or family.

The importance of local knowledge cannot be underestimated when planning fieldwork in international cities like London, Mumbai or New York. And here I am not referring to the type of local knowledge that Edmund White relied on when researching *States of Desire*, that is, on contact with leaders or critics of the gay scenes, though local knowledge of this nature is invaluable and on reflection would have made my work easier in New York.[10] I am referring to local knowledge of a more mundane kind, such as how to use an underground rail system or the community bus service, and how to grasp the lie of the land in short time and at short notice. Should I walk, take a taxi, use the underground to get to the public library or believe the hotel staff when they say that it is only a short walk through the Friday market? – and having to learn all of this while balancing limited time and funds. While these obstacles are nothing compared to the difficulties with which an anthropologist has to contend who is working in Sawarak or Colombia, it is worth noting that fieldwork and holidaying in a foreign city are entirely different activities, and it would be a mistake to assume that, because a city was trouble-free to negotiate when on holidays, it will be so when conducting fieldwork.

On arriving in New York, I had seven interviews logged and hoped that I would leave the city after a two-week visit with at least a dozen completed interviews. Five of the pre-arranged interviews went ahead; two of the men who had agreed to an interview did not show up as arranged. The contingency plan that I had devised before arriving in New York was to recruit the additional five interviews I had planned for by way of personal contacts I had with two friends living in New York. My intention was to ask them to put me in touch with their gay friends, hoping therefore to increase the number of interviewees in the New York sample by making use of an informal network of 'friends of friends'. But before having to resort to this plan, I met by chance an academic who lived in New York who offered to post my recruiting advertisement on the gay and lesbian social network of his alma mater, an East Coast university. This serendipitous connection allowed me to make contact with a number of potential New York interviewees, six of whom I interviewed.[11]

Manhattan resident Scott Davis helped me also recruit gay African-American men as well as men who were recovering addicts. All gave their time freely and provided extremely rich data for this research. During the two weeks I was in New York, I interviewed 11 men in total. Six of the interviews were held in the open air – chiefly in or around Bryant Park in Manhattan – while, of the five interviews that were held indoors, two took place in interviewees' apartments, two were held in cafés, and one was in the office in a university building in Manhattan.[12] The New York sample comprised one man from the old age cohort (60 and over), eight men from the middle age cohort (40–60), two men from the young age cohort (40 and under). Two men from the New York sample were HIV positive. The occupations of men interviewed in New York were in the main middle class and included two senior university academics, one unemployed man, and one clerk. Four of the interviewees from New York were men of colour.[13]

Los Angeles

I spent three days in Los Angeles in August 2009. This was originally intended to be a holiday after my fieldwork in New York but, as a result of the interest I received from the Los Angeles alumni of the same East Coast university whose gay and lesbian social network provided me with such good connections in New York, and because I had left New York with fewer interviewees than I had originally intended, I reorganised my plans and set aside what time I had in Los Angeles to interview another small group of North American gay men. When I flew into Los Angeles, I had fairly firm plans to interview six men, all of whom had agreed to meet me in the lobby of my hotel, which was located in Santa Monica, about 30 minutes by car from the international airport. Unfortunately only three of the six men who agreed to an interview appeared as arranged. Los Angeles can be a daunting city because it comprises one of the largest urban sprawls on the planet and is difficult to traverse without a motor car. 'A city without boundaries, which ate the desert', whose urban landscape is dominated by freeways and flyovers, Los Angeles is a city where the rich live in gated communities and small bands of homeless people are harried by the police and municipal officers.[14] Because of these features and because my time was limited, I was particularly grateful that the men who agreed to have an interview met in me in the lobby of my hotel. In the end, three did so. Another three who had agreed to an interview did not show up, perhaps because they found it impossible to get to my hotel on the day as arranged.

The small sample gay men that I interviewed from Los Angeles comprised two men who belonged to the middle generation and one man from the young generation. I did not interview any men from Los Angeles who belonged to the old generation or the very-young generation (under 30). The men's occupations were varied. One man worked in information technology, one man was a postgraduate student from a rich family, and the third man lived on a disability pension. I had a fourth interview with a man from Los Angeles in February 2010, which was conducted on Skype. He belonged to the middle generation, worked in administration, and was a man of colour. One of the four men from Los Angeles was HIV positive.[15]

Mumbai

As mentioned earlier, I decided to recruit interviewees in Mumbai for two general reasons and two specific reasons. The general reasons for recruiting in Mumbai were, as already described, to include non-western men in my sample and to have access to a population where many would speak English. The two specific reasons for choosing Mumbai were first, a memory of the city as relatively accessible and second, Mumbai's proximity to Melbourne. In preparation for the field trip to Mumbai, I began in October and November 2009 trying to contact by e-mail social organisations that were based in Mumbai whose work involved same-sex health matters such as HIV-AIDS education as well as social organisations that were involved in same-sex ageing and that lobbied for same-sex social and political rights. In particular, I sent e-mails to the Sakhi Char Chowghi Trust and the Humsafar Trust, both of which had offices in Mumbai, as well as the Lakshya Trust because of their interest in same-sex ageing issues.[16] I tried to contact the Sakhi Char Chowghi Trust because of the work they do with hijras and other transgender people, and men who have sex with men. The Lakshya Trust I tried to contact because of their work in Gujarat with ageing gay men and because their chairperson, Prince Manvendra Singh Gohil, is an internationally respected lobbyist on matters concerning gay ageing. Colleagues whose areas of expertise were South Asia and HIV-AIDS respectively recommended that I contact the Humsafar Trust.

Initial attempts to make contact with any of the social organisations in Mumbai were unsuccessful and it was not until I acted on the suggestion of a colleague, who worked in the HIV-AIDS field in Melbourne and had knowledge of HIV-AIDS programmes in India, that I contacted Shivananda Khan, the chief executive of the Naz Foundation International – which has a registered office in London and a regional office in Lucknow – that I began to make some headway. Shivananda provided me with the equivalent of an electronic letter of introduction, which opened the way for what turned out to be a successful round of interviews in Mumbai. He put me in e-mail contact with Prince Manvendra Singh Gohil, the chair of the Lakshya Trust, and Vivek Anand, the chief executive officer of the Humsafar Trust. Both Prince Manvendra and Vivek Anand responded positively to my request for help in finding potential interviewees when I arrived in Mumbai.

I had six days in Mumbai over Christmas 2009, three of which I devoted to fieldwork, collecting five face-to-face interviews.[17] My hotel was in Colaba, an upper-class suburb, five minutes on foot from the Gate of India and the Taj Hotel, the latter being the site of the terrorist attack that occurred in Mumbai in November 2008. Mostly, I used taxis to get around Mumbai or explored on foot the neighbourhood in which my hotel was situated. On Christmas Day, I was invited to an evening meal with friends of Prince Manvendra, a number of whom I later interviewed. Prince Manvendra accompanied me on the train from Colaba to Santa Cruz, which was just as well because I could not speak Hindi and the station attendants spoke very little English. All the men I interviewed in Mumbai spoke English well and comprised two men from the upper class, two men from the middle class and one who was born to working-class parents. All of them were friends of Prince Manvendra or friends of his friends. I strongly believe that because of their association with Prince Manvendra, the Mumbai interviewees were not representative of the variety of men who identify as gay or who have sex with men in Mumbai and elsewhere in India. As a group, they were more than ordinarily aware of gay or 'GLBT' rights and related issues, articulating views that were as well informed as any of the western men interviewed for this book. In part, I ascribed this to the influence of the Internet but chiefly to the men's involvement formally or informally with the Lakshya Trust and the Humsafar Trust.

The Mumbai sample comprised eight men in total.[18] Three men were from the middle generation, three were from the young generation, and two were from the very-young generation. Six of the interviews were conducted face to face in Mumbai and two were conducted on

Skype. The first Skype interview took place in mid-December 2009, before I arrived in Mumbai, and the second was held in February 2011. I continued trying to recruit Mumbai interviewees on my return to Melbourne, chiefly via Facebook connections of friends of some of the men I interviewed when I was in Mumbai in December 2009. Only one man agreed to a Skype interview. A number expressed interest in having an interview but either did not have access to Skype or were discouraged when I sent them copies of my statement of research and ethics statement.

Deciding on what pseudonyms to use for the Indian men interviewed for this book caused a minor ethical dilemma. When I was in Mumbai and reflecting on the matter, I had first thought to use fictitious Hindi names for the Indian men until I realised that to do so would make it much easier to identify them, largely because they would be revealed as a discreet, small, subset of the larger, international sample. In May 2010 and after some reflection, I changed the Hindi pseudonyms I had allocated them and instead used English first names. This seemed a commonsense solution, especially as one of the men I interviewed in Mumbai told me in December 2009 that many Indian men have English first names. For all other interviewees I have used English names, including for a European expatriate I interviewed in Hong Kong.

Hong Kong

I chose to look for potential interviewees from Hong Kong for similar reasons that I chose Mumbai. First, it promised the possibility of including non-westerners in my sample, and second, many Hong Kong citizens had English as a second language. I had also two specific reasons for choosing Hong Kong, First, I imagined that, as a port city, it would share the libertine morals and laissez-faire sexual practices of other port cities, such as existed in Shanghai in the late nineteenth century and continued long into the twentieth century.[19] Second, like Mumbai, Hong Kong was an attractive location because of its proximity to Melbourne. I interviewed in two phases.

In phase one I went to great lengths to recruit Chinese gay men from Hong Kong, but without any success. I posted advertisements on Craigslist and other social network sites, for example Anglo Info Hong Kong. And yet despite the presence of a great variety of advertisements for short- and long-term sexual and/or intimate relations on Craigslist and other websites, which suggested a lively gay world of clubs and bars in Hong Kong, my advertisements for potential interviewees generated nil interest. In the face of this nil response from the advertisements

I posted on the Hong Kong page of Craigslist, I tried posting advertisements for interviewees on its Melbourne page. My reason for doing so was that I hoped that among some of the young Hong Kong residents studying at Melbourne universities there might be gay men who would be willing to have an interview with a Melbourne-based researcher when I was in Hong Kong. This generated nil interest also, which only increased my despondency and anxiety. Over the course of three months I tried to elicit responses to my research from gay men in Hong Kong, and by early December 2009 had all but given up hope. In the last fortnight before I was due to leave Melbourne for Hong Kong and Mumbai, I enlisted the help of a non-Asian gay man who was living in Hong Kong with his North American partner and organised a social group for middle- and upper-class gay men. I also contacted a Chinese academic working in the field and asked him for assistance. The academic's response was that without Cantonese, I would have little chance of recruiting gay men in Hong Kong.

This last prognosis proved correct, for despite a persistent, concerted effort, I was unable to enlist any Chinese gay men to take part in my research. I managed to recruit three expatriates, however, two of whom were from North America, the third from Europe.[20] These men do not and cannot represent Chinese gay men living in Hong Kong. The two men from the United States, both of whom were in their 50s, had spent quite a deal of their adult lives in New York City, and I suspect their views were more representative of affluent East Coast USA than Hong Kong. The European expatriate I interviewed had spent most of his adult life living away from his country of birth. He initially left his country to escape compulsory conscription and homophobia, and then settled into an expatriate's existence in the Pacific and SE Asia. He annually returns to Europe to resume relations with friends. All three of the men I interviewed in Hong Kong represented views of metropolitan citizens who happened to find themselves living in Hong Kong – temporarily in the case of the two North Americans and on a permanent basis in the case of the European man whose partner of 12 years was Hong Kong Chinese.

Their interviews did reveal insights into gay life in Hong Kong that supported the views and arguments of Travis Kong, a Hong Kong academic whose field of study is gay life in the former British colony. Kong has examined the difficulties gay men face in Hong Kong. He considered a combination of historical and personal factors. Among the historical factors he cited were the city state's former status as a British crown colony and the Government's homophobic policies. Personal factors that were likely to keep Chinese gay men in the closet included their preference for unambiguously masculine men and fear of state persecution or social stigma.[21] Concerning the influence of family in Hong Kong, Kong wrote:

> rather than expressing pride in their homosexuality ... [gay men in Hong Kong] want to avoid being labelled a 'sissy'; and they seek family acceptance and behave discreetly in order to avoid the shame that they may bring on their families. They seek to find a 'suitable' gay identity that can be reconciled with the institution of the neo-Confucian family.[22]

A European expatriate I interviewed in Hong Kong, a man in his late 50s, argued that the Chinese government's policy of 'repopulating' Hong Kong helps to explain the hidden quality of gay life in Hong Kong:

> Most of these people are immigrants from the lower classes, without much education and not much university background. You have to consider that culture is not something that is well developed in Hong Kong ... [and] you cannot expect those people from farms ... up country ... will be open to the gay life when in China it is still not open. I don't think the mixing of population, that is, immigrants and expatriates, changes the mentality of those people. (Bernard, aged 59)

Later in his interview, Bernard explained that he had a gay, Asian partner and they had lived together in Hong Kong for 12 years. As the following suggests, fear of offending their parents is a very strong reason gay men in Hong Kong remain in the closet:

> My [boy] friend has a lot of Chinese gay friends. ... None of them says anything to their parents and they are in their 40s and 50s. It is very strict. The parents won't accept it, so it is ... very difficult to be Chinese in Hong Kong and gay.

When I asked Bernard whether he thought things would be different for gay men in Shanghai, on the grounds that it had a long history of being open to the West and western attitudes, he returned to the effect that Chinese government policies have on the lives of gay men:

> I know there is a gay life developing very quickly in China but it is still secret and very closed. In Hong Kong now there are a lot of gay

associations. ... But this is new in the last two or three years. About
five or six gay associations struggle for the right, but this is very new
and they have a lot to do before being accepted by the government,
the law, and the general public. ... You are not going to kiss anybody
[publicly] here [*Laughs*]. You will be arrested by the police.

These factors help to explain the reason why I struggled to attract any
potential interviewees to take part in my research when I was in Hong
Kong in late December 2009 and early January 2010. One thing I could
have done that might have yielded positive responses to my research
was to immerse myself in the thriving club and bar scene that exists in
Hong Kong. But unfortunately at my age and with my experience of the
gay worlds in Asia, Australia, and Europe, I no longer have the stamina
or interest required to go out on the gay scene – where evenings begin
at 11.30 pm and only begin to close around 3 am or 4 am.

My second attempt to recruit interviewees in Hong Kong began in
May 2011 after a chance exchange with a friend in London who put me
in touch with an Australian citizen who with his partner was a resident
of Hong Kong. This led to contact with the Pink Alliance, formerly the
Tongzhi Community Joint Meeting or TCJM. A volunteer-based organisation for people of different sexual orientations, the Pink Alliance is a
clearing house for GLBT ideas and research in Hong Kong.[23] Once doors
began to open in Hong Kong, the only difficulty I found was how as a
westerner to interpret 'non-replies' from the men I contacted by e-mail.
What I learned in this regard was that non-replies often meant that the
times/days I suggested for an interview were not convenient but the
men were unwilling to say so. I found this frustrating (new city, time
constraints) until I realised that perhaps respect for the scholar and the
nature of the interviews I was proposing (about the men's sexuality and
private lives) could affect how the men were interacting with me. When
I did suggest alternate times/days and allowed the men more choice,
that is, when I replied to the non-replies by suggesting alternatives, it
was easier to arrange mutually convenient times for interviews. Not all
my Hong Kong interviewees were Chinese men and included expatriates from England, India, and North America.

In retrospect, an important reason for greater success in phase two
of my attempt to recruit interviewees in Hong Kong was that, despite
the best efforts of the men who went out of their way to find potential interviewees for me in the last quarter of 2009, better connections
exist in Hong Kong through British expatriates than European or North
American expatriates. I suspect this is because of Hong Kong's former

status as a British crown colony and the longstanding business, education, literary, and other cultural connections between Hong Kong and Great Britain.

Melbourne

After interviewing 24 men from New York, Los Angeles, Mumbai, and Hong Kong between July 2009 and January 2010, I turned in March 2010 to look for interviewees closer to home. By chance, a cousin of mine offered to put me in touch with a small group of his friends, all of whom were gay men in their 20s. As well, a young colleague who was interested in my research put me in touch with the gay uncle and partner of one of her workmates, both of whom were over 60. Once I made contact with the couple, they in turn offered to ask men in their friendship network if they were interested in an interview. Through personal and work connections, I was able therefore to recruit men from opposite ends of the life course, where at the time my sample was weak. In November 2010 – and again through the agency of some friends – I contacted and interviewed a small group of six men who were in their 50s, 70s, and 80s, managing again to 'plug' gaps in the sample as they appeared to me then.

My greatest difficulty was in recruiting men over 80. I was conscious of not wanting Melbourne men to swamp the sample but, because I live in Melbourne, I was always able to continue recruiting when it was no longer possible to conduct international interviews by telephone or travel overseas. As already mentioned, face-to-face interviews are less time-consuming and easier to arrange than international telephone interviews, notwithstanding the cost and other advantages of Skype. This stage in the recruiting phase was not accidental but occurred because – aware as I was that the sample did not sufficiently represent very-young men, that is, men born after 1986 or from older age cohorts, that is, men born between 1926 and 1946 – I purposely went out of my way to seek help from people whom I thought could put me in touch with men from the age groups I was seeking. What I found when in the field was that recruiting these two groups of gay men required quite different approaches. The young gay men were initially relatively easy to contact, by e-mail, and responded well to my preliminary inquiries – because my cousin forewarned them. After contact was made, I sent the men copies of my plain-language research outline – as I had done in the United States, India, and Hong Kong – checking after a couple of days if they were still interested in an interview. If they were, I arranged a mutually convenient day and time for an interview. As all but one of the young men in this friendship network were university students and relatively mobile, I was able to meet most of them in a relatively public setting in the vicinity of the State Library of Victoria.

By contrast to what occurred with the very-young gay men in Melbourne, I interviewed the five men from older age cohorts in their homes and only after explaining to the 'lynch-pin' couple the purpose of my research and the safeguards I used to protect interviewees' personal identity. I called the gay couple I first met the 'lynch-pin couple' because after contacting them, the younger of the men asked if I would visit them so they could get to know me before agreeing to an interview. Once I did so and once I reassured them that their stories and identities would be protected, they generously gave up two Sunday mornings and provided me with tea and cake while I recorded aspects of their life stories for this book. The older of the men was born in the 1920s, the younger in the 1940s. By their own account, they had lived quiet, discreet lives, partly because when they met and began their relationship, social opprobrium against homosexuality was considerably more pronounced and partly because one of them had been married and had children and grandchildren. After concluding my interviews with this couple, they provided me with introductions to three of their friends – a couple who had been together for seven years, aged 82 and 65, and a single man aged 77.

Of the men I interviewed from Melbourne, eight belonged to the old generation, five were from the middle generation, three were from the young generation, and eight were from the very-young generation. Seven of the interviewees were retired (all but one of whom were from the old generation) and seven interviewees were university students. The occupations of the men who were in full-time employment at the time of interview were mostly in education, the professions, the arts, or the public service. One Melbourne interviewee was Aboriginal and one was HIV positive. Most of the very-young gay men I interviewed in March and April 2010 were from upper-middle-class families, while, by contrast, the men from the old generation I interviewed in April, May, and November 2010 more evenly represented the middle classes in Australia. Many of the very-young men were still living at home with their parents. Finally, in March and April 2011, I interviewed two very-young men from Melbourne, aged 18 and 19, whom I met through a work colleague. In total, the Melbourne sample comprised 24 men.[24]

London

There were two phases to my interviews with men from London. The first was when I visited England in July 2010 and held face-to-face interviews with two men in London, the second was when through the agency of a friend – who once lived in Melbourne and now lived in London – I was introduced to a group of five men in their 30s, 40s, and 50s, whom I interviewed on Skype. My field trip to England took place in July 2010 and coincided with the annual conference of the British Society of Gerontology (BSG) in London where I presented a paper on the effect of HIV on the identity of ageing gay males. I arrived in London with a handful of interviews scheduled, all of which were with men from Manchester, and a plan to recruit additional potential interviewees from London, first through the Manchester men who had agreed to an interview and I hoped would have friends in London, and second via on-line social sites such as Craigslist, which as mentioned I had used in New York. At the BSG conference, I met an Australian academic who was interested in my research. I duly interviewed him as one of my Australian sample, and he introduced me to a friend of his, a young man in his late 20s who lived in London, whom I interviewed before departing England as part of my London sample. The second London interviewee was a man in his 50s whom an American friend suggested I contact. I was disappointed to leave the UK with only two interviews from men in London but rationalised that I might create an amalgamated UK sample comprising interviews I had with two men from London, four men from Manchester, and the 'written' interviews two men had promised me – one of whom was from Manchester and one from Swansea.[25]

Between July and October 2010, I became more aware that the very small number of two men from London was a serious fault in my sample, and it would make more sense to cull the two London interviews. I imagine one of the characteristics qualitative researchers have in common is a strong dislike of having to delete interviewees from their hard-won sample. I certainly felt this. In the southern spring of 2010, I made contact after 22 years with a friend from Melbourne who moved to London in the late 1980s. Interested in my research, he was willing to encourage men from his friendship network to take part in it. As a result of this serendipitous connection, I increased the number of men from London from two to eight. The additional London men were interviewed on Skype between December 2010 and January 2011.

Manchester

I recruited interviewees in Manchester when I was in England for the BSG conference in July 2010. I wanted to include Manchester because of its reputation as a one of England's 'gayer' cities, a reputation that mostly grew from its being the setting of the British television series,

Queer As Folk. Before I left Australia, I posted an advertisement on Craigslist, Manchester, which yielded one expression of interest. When I replied seeking to confirm where and when we might meet for an interview, the respondent disappeared and would not reply to any of my inquiries. Of the four days I had in Manchester, three were spent in the field. An English academic in his 40s who worked in Manchester agreed to be one of my interviewees, and then introduced me to three gay men in their 60s who agreed to be interviewed as well.

I departed Heathrow Airport in July 2010 with six interviews from gay men in England – four from Manchester and two from London. In addition, I had promises from two men to send me written interviews. By March 2011 and after considerable effort on-line and via e-mail, the England sample comprised 14 men, of whom eight were from London, five were from Manchester, and one was from Swansea. Of the England sample, eight men were in their 40s and 50s, and six were aged 40 or less. Men aged over 60 and 30 or less were absent. Ten of the interviewees were either middle or upper-middle class; two were working class and two upper class. The occupations of the men from the middle and upper-middle classes tended to be in the law, education, media, or business.

Sydney

Sydney is the 'gayest' of the capital cities in Australia, both because of the international reputation of its gay and lesbian Mardi Gras parade and festival, and the large number of gay men attracted to its well-developed gay 'scene'.[26] In 2006, it was still the most populous city in Australia.[27] It would be foolish therefore to examine gay life stories in Australia and not include the voices of Sydney men. Help for the Sydney stage of my research came with the assistance of Mr Peter Trebilco OAM, who offered to pass on my call for interviewees to the Pride history group, Sydney.[28] As a result, I received invitations for interviews from six men associated with Pride in Sydney. I visited Sydney in mid-October 2010 en route to Auckland, and over a weekend interviewed seven men.

The Sydney sample consisted of eight men, six of whom I interviewed there in October 2010, as well as an Australian academic I met at the BSG conference in July 2010, and a retired member of the legal profession who agreed to have an interview with me when I contacted him through a mutual friend in November 2010. Of the eight men who comprised the Sydney sample, four men were from the old generation, one was from the middle generation, and three the young generation. By comparison with other city samples, interviewees from the middle generation were poorly represented in the Sydney sample; also, not one

Sydney interviewee was from the very-young generation. Two of the men from the Sydney sample belonged to the upper class. The remainder were either middle or upper-middle class; the majority being middle class. Most the middle-class men from Sydney were employed in education and a couple in business.

Auckland

In October 2010, I flew to Auckland to interview gay New Zealand men. Given our proximity, it seemed silly not to include a sample of gay men from one of Australia's closest English-speaking neighbours. Preparations for this field trip began early in 2010 when I contacted Michael Stevens, the mutual friend of a colleague.[29] I contacted Michael in October 2009, and then again in the southern autumn to ask if he would help me find potential interviewees when I was in Auckland. In the six weeks before flying to Auckland, Michael put me in touch with two people who prepared the way for my field trip: Jacqui Stanford a writer and subeditor at GayNZ.com, a gay and lesbian website, and Vaughan Meneses, the manager of OutlineNZ, a GLBT support agency based in the Auckland suburb, Ponsonby. Jacqui wrote a piece alerting gay New Zealand men to my arrival, and Vaughan kindly offered me the use of an office at OutlineNZ. I also posted an advertisement on Craigslist Auckland and, unlike my experience in New York but similar to my experience in Hong Kong, received nil replies.

New Zealand men who responded to notice of my research trip publicised by GayNZ.com and OutlineNZ included three men in their 70s, three men in their 50s, and three men in their 40s. Thus I was able to restore some age balance to the sample. As well, three of the Auckland men were Maori and four were retired. Having an office from which to work at OutlineNZ in Ponsonby, a fairly central, inner-city suburb of Auckland, made interviewing straightforward and one of the easiest field trips. Like my research experiences in Hong Kong (phase two), Manchester, Mumbai, and Sydney, my fieldwork in Auckland was made possible and easier with the assistance of locally based gay organisations and/or academics or activists.

Conclusion

Pre-planning is crucial if the researcher intends fieldwork of this nature. I hope that what I have described of my adventures in the nine cities where I recruited and interviewed 97 gay men shows the advantages of having a local guide or contact person, especially in non-western countries or in large, international cities. Also, I hope that my accounts of fieldwork underline the importance of allowing plenty of time, having reserves of funds for when things go awry – for they always do – as well as acknowledging the importance of making arrangements as water-tight as possible before departure while at the same time knowing that people will cancel at short notice or not show up for an interview as arranged. And finally, it is worth noting that the contemporary form of a letter of introduction, which today comes in the form of an e-mail copied to a person known to only one interlocutor, is as vital now as it was in Hamlet's day, perhaps even more so given the ubiquity of the Internet and the many unwanted requests for assistance to which it gives rise.

The locations from which the men interviewed for this book were recruited consist therefore of two megalopolises (New York and Mumbai), two metropolises (Los Angeles and London), two large cities (Sydney and Melbourne), two smaller cities (Auckland and Manchester), and a port city (Hong Kong).[30] All interviews were safely arranged in advance. I did not explore gay ghettoes with my digital recorder in hand and collect the voices of gay men that way. Eliminated therefore from this sample was a range of gay men that would have been more commonly found in the samples sociologists collected in the 1960s and 1970s in large, western cities before the advent of gay liberation.[31] To my knowledge there were no hustlers or male prostitutes in the sample. Absent from the sample also were transsexual men, who now are a separate sexual identity but who for many decades mixed with gay men, shared the same bars and clubs, and were often subsumed in the slang epithet, 'queer'.[32]

The only observations I feel qualified to make about the effect of place on the sort of lives gay men lead is that in Hong Kong and Mumbai where homosexuality is not yet as open and accepted as it is in many western cities and where high rents mean single accommodation is available only to the very rich, gay men have to lead slightly different lives. In Hong Kong, for example, a man in his late 20s told me that he and his partner have to rent a hotel room or go to a sauna to have sex, and that this was so because both men still lived at home with their parents. Anecdotal evidence from informal conversations with men in Hong Kong suggested the city had an extremely busy gay sauna and sex club sector. In Mumbai, as Jeremy Seabrook has shown, sex between men can take place as publicly, as it once did in New York and other western cities in the early twentieth century.[33] One of my interviewees from Mumbai explained that he and his boyfriend would find a secluded seat on the harbour (far away from the sex workers) to maintain their intimate life.

I interviewed gay men from all classes and a variety of ethnic backgrounds, and, in the cases of some men, on extremely sensitive topics to do with their sexuality, health, and life-threatening illnesses. Among this last group were men who had been recently diagnosed with HIV and others who had lived with it for more than 30 years. I interviewed men who had personal histories of drug and alcohol addiction, men who had spent time in prison, as well as men whose lives had been relatively trouble-free and men who had successful careers and relationships. Included in this sample of gay men were men who shaped their lives around the sexual adventurism that longstanding institutions of the gay world make possible. On the other hand, it includes also men who have lived monogamous or serially monogamous lives. There is also a substantial minority of men in this sample who have lived single but not necessarily lonely lives. Men interviewed for this book include those who lived double lives in the decades before the 1970s, some of whom then left their wives and established relatively open gay relationships. And still others there are in this non-representative sample who continue to live discreet, somewhat closeted lives – employed as they are in senior management positions. These are some examples of the varied material included in the next six chapters. In them is evidence also of consistent themes in the men's lives, such as their capacity to practise well the single life, friendship, and fatherhood, and their ability to maintain long-lasting relationships and continue to seek social recognition and relational equality for their relationships and 'everyday experiments'.[34]

2
Single Men

My mother and father had a friend ... when I was
very young. They decided to invite him to dinner ...
because poor Barry was single [and] would be missing
out on good, home-cooked food. ... One of my fears
about being gay was that it meant you were single
which meant that you did not get to eat as well as
everybody else did.

(Isaac, aged 56, Melbourne)

Introduction

At least two different narratives have circulated at different times in the
West regarding the single life and how it is valued. On the one hand,
there is a narrative that depicts the single life as incomplete and single
people as invariably lonely. On the other hand, there is another, possibly more powerful narrative, its origins dating from the 1950s and
1960s, in which the single life is represented as exotic, perhaps even
threatening because the presence of single people challenges the conventional path from teenage, heterosexual romance(s) to married life
with its associated duties and familial responsibilities.

In their discussion of single lives in the 1990s, husband-and-wife sociologists Ulrich Beck and Elizabeth Beck-Gernsheim paint a cruel picture
of lonely singleness, which they argue is one of the consequences of
increasing individualisation:

Everything is planned round avoiding feeling lonely: all kinds of
contacts making different demands on one's time, daily habits, a

37

well-filled calendar and carefully planned moments to recover from social life, all designed to alleviate any fear of being left out.[1]

The image their description conjures is of an individual too aware of his/her aloneness to derive any meaning or joy from the unoccupied spaces in his/her weekly life, and who has more spare time than s/he knows how to use. The time that hangs heavily on the hands of single people is presumably not experienced in the heteronormative world where it is put to good use by the person's partner or children. Beck and Beck-Gernsheim argue also that, the more accustomed to a life alone the individual becomes, the less likely he/she is to achieve success in the quest to secure a partner:

A private cosmos can be created around one's own ego with its idiosyncrasies, strengths and weaknesses. The more successful this effort proves, the greater the danger that is will prove an insurmountable obstacle to any close partnership, however much one longs for one.[2]

According to Beck and Beck-Gernsheim, the likelihood of more people leading lives such as the one they describe will only increase if both sexes continue to demand equal rights. 'This road does not lead to a happy world of co-operative equals but to separateness and diverging interests.'[3]

As the quotation that heads this chapter suggests, there is a similar but possibly more destructive myth about gay men that has been circulating for at least 60 years in Australia, and I suspect also in similar western countries, which is that they are destined to spend their later years alone and lonely. I would argue that this myth is more destructive than the myth about the single life because of the assumption on which it is based – that to be alone and lonely is the gay man's inevitable destiny. In an earlier work, I began questioning this myth and provided fairly compelling evidence from an all-Australian sample that on the whole gay men aged 60 and above lived relatively well-rounded, contented, and positive lives, whether single or not.[4] As I explain below, this chapter continues that work, challenging the myth that gay lives lived alone *at any point* in the life course are destined to be eked out in a sad, pathetic state such as the one suggested in the Beck and Beck-Gernsheim sketch.

The myth of the single person as exotic and a threat to the settled normality of married life in the West was perhaps strongest in the decades following World War Two, when the state worked very hard to

persuade men who had been soldiers to take up peacetime roles as husbands and fathers, and to coax women from paid, wartime work in fac-
tories and on farms to accept the unpaid role of wife and mother. North
American historians John D'Emilio and Estelle Freedman argue that a
connection exists as well between valorisation of the exotic, single life
and the hyper-commercialisation of sex that began in the United States
in the 1950s.[5] This narrative of the single life was paradoxical and over-
laid with a very basic, double standard. In the first place, the single life
for women was presented in love stories and soap operas on radio and
television as a much less validated alternative to that of housewife and
mother; in the second place, 'single women' occupied a dubious position as a central focus of heterosexual men's sexual fantasies – which
Hugh Heffner's *Playboy* magazine empire exploited and popularised.
The single heterosexual male was often depicted as a loner and preda-
tory, and in need of feminising. Single women threatened the couple
ideal as much as did single men because their presence had the potential to unsettle the fidelity and trust on which pair couples depend for
their success.

The single homosexual male was and is a different type of single person. His presence did not upset the dominant place of straight couples
but could threaten the couple bonding that took place in the gay world.
The hyper-commercialising of sex that occurred before the outbreak of
HIV-AIDS was possibly more widespread in the gay world than in the
straight world, and the market and facilities it created for easy, anonymous sex, such as sex clubs and back rooms, helped solidify the image
of (single) gay men as licentious and sex-obsessed. Australian theorist
Denis Altman argued in the mid 1980s that the market for the com-
mercialisation of sex was extremely large and would only continue to
grow, for, 'as the emphasis in capitalism moves more and more towards
consumption, sex inevitably becomes big business'.[6]

I have discussed elsewhere the nature and practices of the gay commercial 'scene' and that the Australian gay men I interviewed had
mixed views about their worth, many describing them as impoverished
and sexualised.[7] In much the same way, the single men interviewed
for this book were divided over how they regarded gay bars and clubs.
They connected with them in varied ways, in much the same way that
straight men's relationship with institutions vary. Some of the men said
that they contributed to their enjoyment of full and active social lives,
while other men said that they avoided them altogether.

The stories that single men from the international sample told of
their social lives are the focus of this chapter. In all, 41 men from the

international sample (or slightly more than 40 per cent) were single at the time of interview. In this chapter, I continue to question the myth of the old, gay man as alone and lonely, and propose in its place an alternative narrative, which is that gay men are as able as any other group of people to live gregarious and socially fulfilled, single lives. They are only one of many subsets of a growing number of one-person households that western demographers and scholars have identified over the past two to three decades as an increasing, notable trend. While the attention of policymakers has often been on the number of elderly people living alone, data from countries like Australia, Germany, and the UK show also that greater numbers of people in their 20s, 30s, and 40s are living alone and that this trend is only likely to increase. In the UK, for example, official data showed that in 2011, more than seven million people lived alone, of whom more than 1.5 million were aged between 25 and 44. In Australia, while there are not directly comparable statistics, government data showed that the proportion of one-person households increased from 16 per cent of households in the 1976 Census to almost a quarter of households in the 2006 Census, and that the Australian Bureau of Statistics has projected that by 2031 one-person household will represent more than one quarter of Australian households.[8]

While these changes suggest that more people will be single in the twenty-first century, the trend might represent a return to the long-standing patterns that existed in the twentieth century before the post-war baby boom, when marriage was often delayed and when single people were a more common sight and less stigmatised identity. At the height of the baby boom in the 1950s in the West, there were unusually high rates of marriage and in particular youthful marriage.[9]

When writing about gay men's communities in the West in the late 1970s – before the advent of the HIV-AIDS epidemic and when gay men were beginning in greater numbers to enjoy of the benefits of increased individualisation – Michael Pollak noted that many young people were willing and able to take part in life experiments that combined 'fleeting sexual relations with a social and affective life based on a variety of relationships, not necessarily destined to last long'.[10] Edmund White is an American novelist and social commentator. He is also a man who has been living with HIV-AIDS for a very long time. White's explanation for the separation of affective life and sexual life to which Pollak referred is that it is a function of negotiated intimacy that people who live in big cities are required to make. He writes of the style of life that he observed in New York in the late 1970s, and which I would argue continues today among certain classes of people in New York, as well as in other megalopolises, such as London, Los Angeles, and Mumbai:

> [T]he conventional conflation of sex, romance and friendship into marriage has been exploded and the elements separated out. Sex is performed with strangers, romance is captured in brief affairs, friendship is assigned to friends. In this formula ... the only stable element is friendship.[11]

White does not distinguish between gay people and straight people in his account of the way that sex, romance, and friendship were compartmentalised in New York. What Pollak and White observed in the late 1970s among communities of gay men later became the research interest of Beck, Beck-Gernsheim, and Giddens, as well as Zygmunt Bauman, whose attention focused on the shape and nature of contemporary intimate and personal life. In later chapters in this book on long-lasting relationships and gay marriage, there is more detailed discussion of some of the defining features of contemporary relationships, including discussion of Giddens's work on what he calls the 'pure relationship'.[12] Elsewhere, I have argued that apart from celibacy and episodic sexual encounters, the pure relationship is the intimate relationship most practised by gay men and that friendship is the relationship they most value.[13] If White and Pollak are correct – and the work of Beck, Beck-Gernsheim, and Giddens suggests they are – and young people in advanced western democracies are experimenting more and more with the relationship, getting involved in partnerships of varying length and meaning when it suits them, they must accept also that there will be times when they are single, as well as those times when they are in relationships.

Theorist Henning Bech argues that coming out creates difficulties for gay men in sustaining friendships. In order to become who and what he wants to be, the gay man must leave behind what Bech describes as the warm familiarity of his previous life. 'The homosexual ... must leave the safe and self-evident socialness he has otherwise become embodied in.'[14] According to Bech, a gay man's world is turned upside down when he comes out; he must re-examine and reassess his relationships and affective relations. Some of these will not bear close scrutiny: some friends will rejoice, others will disappoint. Some relatives will support him, others will be indifferent. And then there will be others who call him a 'poofter' or 'faggot' to his face or behind his back. Bech explains what he understands as the effects of coming out and how it can cause social relations to rupture:

> He can never be one with ... friendships. He carries around the basic experience that togetherness can come to an end, that it is not covered by a guarantee. He can be thrown back on 'himself'; this empty 'self' remains outside. To this extent, he is doomed to be alone.[15]

This grim prognosis was not borne out in my previous research on Australian gay men. What I found instead were stories showing that men of all ages valued friendship above other relationships including pair relationships. Among the reasons they gave for the value they found in friendship were (a) the social interaction it provided and (b) the mutual exchange of care and support it afforded.[16] I have drawn similar conclusions from the research for this book, and found in the main that friendship was the crucial, signal relationship for gay men. One of the focuses in this chapter is on the friendship networks single men foster as part of first, an active involvement in the gay scene and second, the social distance they actively maintain *from* the gay scene. I identified two groups of single men from the international sample who said they had full and active social lives. The first group said their social life was full and active because they regularly went out on the scene; the second group said that theirs was so because they avoided contact with the scene.

Who were the men from the international sample who were living their lives alone and singly at the time of interview? As mentioned, slightly more than 40 per cent of men from the international sample were single when I interviewed them.[17] The single men came from all nine cities where I held my interviews.[18] The age group with the highest proportion of single men was the 70-plus age cohort.[19] This is not so surprising because as life expectancy for men in the West is 78–82, men aged over 70 are more likely to be living alone because of the death of a partner.[20]

In summary, increasing individualisation in the West has allowed for greater choice about when and how people conduct couple relationships, as a result of which we now see more single people. Gay men have been experimenting with a form of intimate life that combines casual sexual encounters and couple relationships of varying durations and intensity since at least the 1970s – and probably, as I suggest elsewhere, for a lot longer because their relationships were until recently the subject of mockery if not scorn.[21] My argument is that gay men who experiment thus have to experience times when they are in pair relationships and times when they are not and must live singly, just as do heterosexuals who experiment similarly.

There are two parts to the chapter. In the first part, the stories that a group of 18 men told are examined for their evidence of full, active social lives. In the second part, the stories that a group of 14 men told are examined for their evidence of contracted social lives. The 18 men who recounted stories suggesting full, active social lives were predominantly aged 23–53; the majority were in their 40s and 50s. The 14 men whose accounts suggested contracted social lives were aged 38–81, and the majority were over 60.

Full social lives

I found evidence of full, active social lives in the stories that 18 men told me when explaining the effect that growing older had had on their social life.[22] If the men said or signalled that they had well-developed friendship networks, I assumed that their social lives were full and active. The majority of these men were in their 40s and 50s, with a smaller group aged less than 40. The 18 men comprising this group used two narratives to explain why their social lives were full and active and had not been affected by age. The chief narrative was that their social life was full because they regularly went to gay bars and clubs, circuit parties, and mass events, in other words, were strongly scene-focused.[23] The second and minor narrative, mostly preferred by men under 50, was that their social lives were full and active precisely because they avoided gay bars, clubs, and mass events, were not scene-focused.[24] The evidence these two groups provided of gay men's varied engagement with the scene does not cancel out or negate the value of the two sets of stories they told. Rather, what it suggested is that gay men connect with the scene in varied ways, just as straight men's relationships with institutions vary.

Seven men used the chief narrative, showing a strong scene focus, when they described their social life.[25] Seventy-two-year-old Colin from New York was the oldest man in this group. In our interview in his Manhattan apartment, which was not far from Christopher Street in Greenwich Village – where gay bars and businesses have operated since the 1920s and the location of the Stonewall Inn – he declared that he had had 'five husbands' and was a reformed alcoholic.[26] He was a vibrant, provocative interviewee, who when we talked explained how he had overcome addictions and prejudices of various kinds and now felt much closer to other men:

> You see a lot of love between gay men and straight men in Alcoholics Anonymous, a lot of connection because ... we have all crashed, so a lot of prejudice gets taken away. I have come to appreciate a lot of straight men beyond the stereotype ...

> At Body Electric ... we would have these circles. You would spend two or three minutes with each man and you had no choice. Some would be young; some would be old and fat. I had always had a horror of touching somebody I wasn't attracted to. But that all changed. As soon as I started touching all these men and making some sort of personal connection, it was different. It's a horrible prejudice in gay men. They don't want to touch someone who's not beautiful. I don't know. It's like [they are worried] they will catch it.

Colin reckoned that at 72 his life was better than it had ever been and, as this extract above suggests, also he was particularly proud of the relations he developed with straight men at Alcoholics Anonymous. Colin was proud also of the relations he made at Body Electric – a self-help group that focuses on erotic and physical improvement – with men from different social and sexual backgrounds, overcoming as well some of his fears about body shapes and types.[27] Elsewhere in his interview, he boasted also of varying relations he maintained with gay men of all ages through the S&M world in New York. His recently acquired views on men's fears of saggy skin or old bodies directly challenge powerful gay narratives in which youthfulness is valorised, as a consequence of which, with the exception of the leather and S&M scenes, men over 50 can be marginalised in gay social spaces.[28]

Included in this group were four men in their 50s. Fifty-three-year-old Ryan from London said that he had formed a large group of friends through travelling, sex, and work, and that maintaining his extensive friendship network was not easy:

> I travel a lot and ... I have got more and more friends. I also meet people sexually and they become friends and I also meet people through work. ... At the same time, I'm getting to the age where I am really wondering how long I can maintain this, and that is one of the problems I'm going through at the moment because I am still quite promiscuous and have been for the last three years, a bit less now, but now I am beginning to feel I am getting older and I cannot quite keep up with this.

Ryan said he thought his friendship group had become so large that he might have to shed ephemeral friendships:

> If I decided to cut down my friends ... I would just have to make the decision with some people who are not really as good friends and who ... [have] not responded to me in the same way. I would keep all my old friends, a handful of new friends but all my old friends are largely the ones who are actually most faithful.

Because I did not ask him a follow-up question at the time, I wonder in retrospect if the concern Ryan expressed about the size of his friendship network and the inconstancy of some friends was an inevitable consequence of a life lived on the move. His very thorough interview suggested a highly mobile life. The constant movement that was a standout feature of his life took the shape of being physically on the move, as result of his regular travelling and psychically/sexually on the move, as a result of his fairly persistent hunt for new sex partners.

Hilton, who lived in New York, was also 53. His interest in younger men was the cause of his full social life. In the following extract, Hilton explains that while he liked and was attracted to younger men, he knew that they were not always reliable relationship prospects. He was aware as well, however, that in Manhattan there were and always have been young gay men seeking older men for social or sexual relations, which might explain his continuing interest:

> I know a lot of gay men who are mature enough not to be fixated on wanting younger men as partners. I have not reached that stage yet. I am still fixated on 20-somethings and 30-somethings, and the older I get, the more I realise how tenuous that can be, although not always. There's still guys out here looking for older guys.

Hilton's dilemma regarding young men is, as I have discussed elsewhere, peculiar to gay life in very large, international cities where young gay men appear prepared and willing to put on hold ageist prejudices that can be common in young people's friendship circles in exchange for the material advantages that often accrue from relationships with older men.[29] There is nothing new about the nature of this exchange for intergeneration relations between same-sex-attracted men have a very long history. Henning Bech says that in Ancient Greece, 'at least in the sixth to fourth centuries BC it was customary ... that men had relations with "boys" or "young men"'.[30] Stephen Murray argues that courtship rules for 'age-stratified homosexuality' were formal and clearly understood, and operated according to a social script where the role for the older man was to desire and for the younger man to feign interest, which if successfully done would often attract from the older man 'interest and worldly goods, ranging from presents and payments to long-term support'.[31]

From the 1970s until quite recently, the gay world in New York had a reputation for its highly specialised, commercial scene where, according to one of my interviewees,

> you used to go to a bar and knew exactly what the bar was for. You want a black guy and you are a white guy, you went to this bar. You want a Latin, go to this bar. You want a chubby, you go to this bar. But I'm not sure that exists anymore ... youth have become more diverse so when you go to a bar, it has a bit of everything, straight in it, women, lesbians. In New York, everything [once] had a specialty so you could avoid some of that stuff. (Parry, aged 63, New York)[32]

The two remaining men in their 50s were from Melbourne. Both men regularly went to bars and clubs in inner-city suburbs where there were gay venues that catered for older men, particularly the baby boomers, as well as the leather and S&M set. Mike, who was 52, said that, as a result of developing a less judgemental attitude to other people, his social life was richer than it had been when he was in his 20s:

> I would have to say the circle of people I know is as eclectic ... as any gay man in Melbourne and ... [some] people allege that I know every gay man in Melbourne by one degree of separation. ... I [now] open myself to engaging with people much more comfortably and I find it's just amazing who I meet.

The other man in his 50s from Melbourne was Calvin (aged 51). Like Mike, Calvin was gregarious, with an open, accepting approach to strangers. He was aware also that at his age he no longer had the stamina of a man in his 20s or 30s, and that as a result could no longer participate as fully as he once did in mass parties and other events that are fixtures in the gay social calendar of any city the size of Melbourne:

> Nowadays, for social activities, I still go to the venues, I still go to dance parties. I still go to the sauna if I want to. In terms of not going

to situations, ageing has not affected me. It may when I am in my 60s but at the moment it has not.

It was clear from Calvin's interview he had no intention of allowing ageing to affect his involvement in the gay scene. It was evident also that he had adopted strategies to allow him to continue his participation, such as taking part less often and more carefully husbanding his physical energy levels, diet, and consumption of alcohol and recreational drugs. Like many gay men over 35, Calvin was aware of the balance needed to participate in the youthful activities of the gay scene and to work nine to five on weekdays.

One principal narrative connecting the stories that these men told of their full, active social lives in the context of regular participation on the scene was that its bars and clubs provided all that men needed who sought social/sexual contact with strangers, a practice with a long history in the West.[33] It was clear that the scene enabled the oldest interviewee (Colin from New York) to continue making less fearful connections with other men, of all ages. His ability to do so came as a result of the psychic healing he undertook of his own accord with AA and Body Electric. The stories from the men in their 50s revealed a similar tale of enjoyment to be had from contact with strangers. Where the scene can be most useful is in its ability to draw together a wide variety of men interested in having sex and/or social intercourse with other men, and this facility is of greatest benefit for men who like to do so with strangers.

Strongly woven in the narratives of the men in their 50s was a refusal to be affected by ageism on the scene, to continue to use its bars and clubs as a place for social/sexual exchange. For gay men who enjoy anonymous relations with men and do so by compartmentalising their lives as Edmund White saw sexually active people doing in New York in the 1970s, the scene, with its sex clubs, saunas, and back rooms, caters for all their needs.

An interesting aspect I noticed in the men's stories was that those who structured their lives in order to enjoy social/sexual contact with strangers lived highly organised lives. It could be argued that their highly, even over-organised lives suggested a need to fill empty spaces – in line with the argument made by Beck and Beck-Gernsheim; an equally valid argument is that the demands of a compartmentalised life require a high degree of planning and organisation. These findings about the social practices of a group of men chiefly in their 50s, from a variety of backgrounds and locations, contrast with what Arlene Stein found regarding the social practices of middle-aged lesbians. She argued that as the lesbians she studied grew into middle age, their attachment to the non-heterosexual sub-culture changed, and they tended to lead what Stein calls more 'decentred' lives.[34]

> As certainty about their lesbian identity grew, they ... feel 'at home' in the community with which they mainly identify, but also in numerous other contexts in which they participate and with which they feel some sense of identification.[35]

One reason for the difference between gay men's and lesbian's social practices might lie in the men's avowed interest in a gay scene-oriented social life for the sexual encounters it promises and their continued interest in these.

Six men, almost all of whom were under 50, provided accounts of full, active social lives that largely or entirely avoided contact with the gay scene.[36] Two of these men actively shunned it;[37] three of them were acutely aware of its limitations and mostly stayed away from gay bars and clubs;[38] and one man had no need of it because of an extensive network of friends and how he socialised.[39] Earl was 51 and lived in New York. He turned his back on gay bars and clubs after the death of his older partner, and shaped a private social life with men who lived in and around fairly exclusive parts of Manhattan.

> I don't go out ... late-night clubbing. I stay out late but don't go out to the same places. In terms of my public social life ... I think I do more sophisticated things [like] smaller parties in richer locations [such as] Park Avenue apartments. Even though I always had access to very wealthy venues, now it is more [the case] that my friends are older and have these places.

The other man who shunned the gay scene was Charlie, who had just turned 40 and lived in Hong Kong. He said that because he was satisfied with his friendship circle, he had no need for more friends: 'I don't really want to meet strangers for the sake of knowing more people.'

Elsewhere, I have written on the nature of the social venues that have been available to gay men since the 1950s, and even earlier in the West when homosexuality was illegal. Two conclusions I drew about gay bars and clubs were first, that they have a strong youthful orientation and second, as their chief purposes were the consumption of alcohol and recreational drugs and as a site of sexual exchange, meaningful social interaction was unlikely, especially between different generations of gay men.[40]

Three single men from the subset of this sample said that they were aware of the scene's limitation and so largely avoided gay bars and clubs. Two men in their early 30s gave very similar reasons for their dislike of gay social sites. The first man was Anton, who said that he avoided gay venues in London because he did not like 'going to noisy, crowded, gay bars full of 12-year-olds in muscle vests', that he preferred being able to speak to his friends and hear what they were saying.[41] In addition, he said that, as he was now earning a better salary, his idea of socialising had changed: 'very often my social life revolves around going to rather nice restaurants'. The second man, Leo, who was from Sydney, made a connection also between the change in his material circumstances and how he socialised:

> I earn more money as I have got older so I can afford to go out a little bit more and also do some nicer things like go to nicer restaurants or can afford tickets to a show or something that I could not afford before. ... I think I'm moving into a different phase where I tend to go out more for dinner with friends rather than partying in a nightclub. I get more out of spending fifty or a hundred dollars on a really nice meal, good company and some nice wine than fifty or a hundred dollars on beer and gin and tonics [*Laughs*] at the pub.

Like Anton also, Leo was both aware and critical of the loud, noisy presence in gay venues of a new generation of young men. To illustrate the sense of social obsolescence he felt, Leo described his experience at a mass music event in Sydney where at 31 he had the impression that he was one of the oldest people there, both in terms of the age and behaviour of many of the people in the crowd:

> I am getting to the point where if I attend some events, I actually feel a bit old for this now. In January this year ... I went to a straight music festival ... and there were lots of kids ... lots of 16- 17- and 18-year-olds on ecstasy and running around like idiots. ... They have announced the line up for next January's gig but I would not consider going again. ... I am a bit bored with them but also a little bit old amongst the crowd.

The fact that both these men were in their early 30s and not ten or twenty years older indicates the speed at which social obsolescence is now taking place. While it might have taken twenty years or more for the baby-boomer cohort to feel that young people were invading their social spaces, taking their place, if the accounts of these two men living in London and Sydney are any indication of a more general perception and/or experience, the age cohort who are now in their 30s might already be aware that they are losing social place to younger people.

The sole man who showed little interest in or need for the gay scene was 47-year-old Teddy from Mumbai. He worked as the senior manager of a community-based organisation, and through his links with gay men's organisations in the West and western colleagues, was aware of how the gay scene operated in the West as well as in Mumbai. During our interview, he explained why he believed a strong friendship network is crucial if gay men are to maintain a strong sense of self and to ride out life's emotional storms:

> Whether men like it or not, you cannot only rely on your relationship or your lover. Your life goes beyond that. We have friends who have had relationships for 15 years now, and they are together yet they rely on the support system. They need friends because in the straight world, their relationship is not accepted so this [network of friends] is the family from where they gather their emotional support.

The value Teddy recommended gay men place on friendship as a foil against relying too heavily on a pair relationship to meet their needs supports the findings from my research on the importance of friendship to Australian gay men.[42] Teddy's comments are significant also because they suggest an awareness of the effect increasing individualisation can have on pair relationships.[43] When a straight friend asked Teddy why he was closer to his gay friends, he explained how friendship operated in his circle:

> If I am feeling a little down and out in the night, I can just pick up and call one of my close gay friends and he will come home and spend the rest of the night talking to me, and I will do the same for any gay friend of mine. But if I am going through rough weather at two in the night ... I would think twice before calling you because you have a wife sleeping next to you and two children. ... It is how we are made. ... These [gay friends] are my brothers, my children and that is my family so I have this support system around me. ... We fight, we scream, we shout, we yell ... and yet we manage to stick to each other, be with each other.

In the Indian context, it is not surprising that Teddy used a family metaphor to explain how gay friendship networks operate in Mumbai. With the exception of ruling-class families, in most western countries an individual's birth family is now far less important as a source of identity than it once was. In India and other South Asian countries, such as Bangladesh, Pakistan, and Sri Lanka, it remains one of the central sources of an individual's identity. 'In South Asia, a person's position in the joint and extended family, marriage and children, are central to social definition and personal identity.'[44]

Although not a single man, an Indian contemporary of Teddy, Edmund (aged 44) referred also to understanding gay friendship circles as modelled on the traditional extended family. In the following extract from his interview, Edmund added another level of meaning when he compared friendship circles that gay men arrange to hijra, or transgender, networks in India:

> Pseudo family is a unique thing in India which has been borrowed from the transgender system, is developing relationships between the older and young men, in a sense of having a mother, having a father, mother–daughter relationship, then aunts. For instance, if you take my own example, I am a mother to several daughters. I am 44 now and have daughters as young as 18 years. I have nieces because I have sisters, and I am the aunt to their children. ... This networking is unique in India, and this bonding has brought the community closer to each other, and in this we don't see who is old and who is young. There is actually a ceremony performed where the mother makes a younger gay man his daughter in Gujarat.

In using the transgender or hijra system in India as an analogy for gay friendship circles, which he called pseudo families, Edmund most likely had in mind the local social organisation of hijras, which Serena Nanda describes as follows.

> The effective working group of the hijra community is the local level communal household, consisting of anywhere from 5 to 15 members ...

> Each house within a region has a leader, called a *naik* (chief). ... For any important occasion within a locality, whether the initiation of a new recruit or the resolution of a dispute, the naiks ... get together in a *jamat*, or a 'meeting of the elders'.[45]

The organisation of hijras by households makes perfect sense in India where communal groups and groupings are central to the country's social organisation. 'The person has a family and community identity in which personal identity is subsumed.'[46] Among the characteristics that the pseudo family to which Edmund belonged share with the hijra household are a mixture of people of different ages and a hierarchy that is based on age. Even though Edmund says age is overlooked – 'we don't see who is old and who is young' – it is clear from his account of its familial structure (he is both a mother and an aunt, has daughters and nieces) that a mentoring role is implicit in the relationships that exist between family members.

When Teddy was describing relations in his family of friends, it was clear also that a hierarchy operated and that the mother was the most powerful figure: 'We are known as family. ... If mother decides to crack the whip, then all the kids have to shut up.' Teddy made clear also in his interview that he was free to call on members of his family whenever he was in need of support or aid. The family he described and the nature of their affective relations were similar to a form of alternative family that non-heterosexuals have created in the West – which British historian Jeffrey Weeks has called 'family of choice'.[47] An important similarity between the family that Teddy described and the western family of choice is that in each case the surrogate family provides gay men with a haven and defence against homophobia in the straight world. One of the more important differences between the Indian and western version of the non-heterosexual family is that, whereas the western family of choice can include an individual's former and/or current sexual partners, Teddy was quite clear that this was not and never the case for his family of friends in Mumbai: 'We are a family. We do not believe in incest. We do not sleep with each other.'

Three narratives were common to the stories the six men told whose full, active social lives included nil or only fleeting contact with the scene. The first narrative related to a preference for spending time with friends, not strangers. It was captured in Charlie's brief statement that at 40 he did not need to go out to meet more strangers, and was implicit in the other men's observations. A second and related narrative concerned friendship and its importance to the men. Charlie said that he had no wish to meet more strangers because he was content with his friendship circle, and for him the bars and clubs of the scene were places mostly populated with strangers.

The importance of friendship and practising the art of friendship well was most apparent in the stories that Edmund and Teddy told of how they sustained their private lives in Mumbai. Their accounts of pseudo families pointed to how differently gay friendship can operate in different locales. Their concept of friendship and friendship circles modelled in the first place on the Indian family and in the second place on the hijra communal household were to a certain degree comparable to the western idea of families of choice, with the notable exceptions that the Indian pseudo family does not include current or past sexual partners, that it operates hierarchically, and actively provides more security and support for the younger and weaker members.

The third narrative these men drew on is one that I have examined elsewhere in the Australian context, and related to men's dislike of the impoverished physical environment of the scene. The men who were in their 30s and 40s explained that they disliked the noise and juvenile behaviour of younger gay men, and in doing so revealed also an unsettling experience for people so young – of accelerated social obsolescence.

Contracted social lives

Fourteen men described contracted social lives when they explained if age had affected their social life. Eight of these men were at least 60, while six men were under 60 years old.[48] The men drew on one principal narrative when explaining why their social lives had contracted. Used by men in their 70s and 80s and (almost counter-intuitively) also by men in their 30s and 40s, this narrative was that things simply slowed down at their age or stage of life. The men over 60 said that a contracted social life was normal for their age because they had fewer friends and fewer opportunities for socialising with them. The men under 60 said that a contracted social life was normal for their age because of the increasing importance of careers and changes in the social practices of their straight friends. Finally, both age cohorts said that they were less socially active because gay bars and clubs had either changed or lost their appeal, and they had no interest in socialising there. In neither group – the over 60s or the under 60s – was there any evidence of the men being alone and lonely or sad or overly affected by pathos. In other words, there was no evidence to support the myth of single men as sad and alone even when they gave evidence of contracted social lives.

Two age groups of men said that a less active social life was normal for their age. The first group comprised men in their 70s and 80s, and the second group men in their 30s and 40s. Interestingly, the men did not always regard a contracted social life as a less fulfilled one. The men in their 70s and 80s seemed both reconciled to it, as a natural part of the ageing process, and accepting of it and what their life comprised – possibly because of their greater life experience. Eighty-one-year-old Godfrey from Sydney said without drama or any hint of self-pity that 'one's social life of its own accord slackens off. ... I'm quite happy to be at home and to go to bed at half-past nine and read my book.' At the same time, Godfrey pointed out that his social life was not wholly home-bound, that he had been out the night before our interview, and has fairly regular dinners with friends:

> I have a ... subscription and was at a concert at the Opera House last night. But that is really my only social life in a way, unless I have dinner with friends periodically, and then that's always an early affair out of deference to me, I think in some cases. There's no imperative. It's just the way it goes. You don't go out as much, you don't need to go out as much and you have less friends, you know.

Godfrey's account of how and why his social life had contracted is significant for three reasons. First, his use of concert subscriptions suggested a degree of self-awareness, that is, that living on one's own requires external structures such as pre-arranged social events to avoid feelings of loneliness or apathy. Second, his reference to dinners with friends was another example of a semi-formal external structure. The fact that he believed his friends arranged dinner at an early hour to make things easier for him suggested their friendship was based on mutual regard and consideration, which I have discussed elsewhere as a valued feature of friendship, or the moral economy of giving and receiving.[49] Third, Godfrey's common-sense observation that a person's life invariably contracts with age as her/his friends decline in number suggested an acute, lived understanding of the life course and his place in the penultimate stage of life, an often painful transition that Norbert Elias described as follows:

> Most people in our society have before retirement formed affective ties not only within their families by with a larger or smaller circle of friends and acquaintances. Ageing itself usually brings with it an increasing withering of such ties outside the narrowest family circle.[50]

The second of three 81-year-olds from the international sample was Clancy, who was also an Australian and lived in Melbourne. His experience of a contracting social life differed from Godfrey's in that Clancy had learned relatively early in life to shape a social life that would suit him into old age. His embrace of a less socially active life began when he was relatively young: 'I learned that the theatre and dining and all those things were important in my social life.' As a young man, Clancy sought to advance himself socially. He found an influential mentor, which was crucial in his view if a young man expected to get ahead in the camp world of the 1950s and 1960s in Australia. Still cautious and discreet, Clancy described his former mentor in the following terms:

> I was mentored by a beautiful person who was in love with me but I was not in love with him. ... He was older, not that much older though. It would have been about 12 years. ... He was a down-to-earth, intellectual, high-up person. I won't go into any more detail, though.

On the social status of mentors, Clancy said a young man had to choose carefully: 'A lot depends on your mentor as to which way you go. If I had have been mentored by a wharf labourer, I might have been a bit different.' As it was, Clancy spent most of his working life as manager of a clothes shop for men.

Along with Godfrey and Clancy, four other men aged over 60 said that their social life had become more home-based as they aged. Ambrose who was 75 and, like Clancy, lived in Melbourne, said that while his younger friends visited him, friends his age rarely did so because they were no longer confident or willing to travel out of their suburb. A New Zealander who was 75 and whose life was more home-based said the exception was when he went out to classical music recitals, and a 61-year-old Melbourne man (Anselm) said that his social life was now more solitary because gay venues were not welcoming: 'growing older has contracted my social life in that I don't feel as confident as I might have even ten years ago about going out by myself'. Anselm belonged to a small group of men who explained that their social life had contracted because they were not longer willing or able to participate on the gay scene. Their accounts of a social life that contracted because of the nature of gay bars and clubs are examined in the next section.

A widespread assumption concerning ageing is that a person's life slows down as he/she ages because he/she has less energy and mobility and, if living on the state pension, less opportunity to engage with the outside world. As a general statement, this picture mostly applies to people after retirement or people in their mid to late 60s and 70s. I was surprised therefore when a man as young as 38 and others in their 40s and 50s said that life had slowed down for them, almost as a matter of course, and that their social lives were now less full and active.[51] Three men from this group explained that their social life slowed down as they and their friends began to concentrate on their careers and they assumed more prominence in their life.

Everett, a 49-year-old man from New York, told me that he had less time for socialising with strangers (by which I assumed he meant men at gay bars and clubs), because he spent more time with this work colleagues outside work, and because he believed that as a person's personality becomes more defined he/she has less time or interest in meeting strangers. In the context of gay socialising, Everett added that he was increasingly aware that apart from sex he had very little in common with men in their 20s.

Another man from New York, Timothy (aged 46) said that while he had not gone through a period of 'heavy socialising' on the gay scene, growing older meant he went to bars and clubs much less often, perhaps only once every six months. Interestingly, he did not say that he yet felt too old to go 'clubbing'. In his interview, Timothy emphasised also the importance of career in contributing to a change in his social life, as well as the time of life changes that his straight friends were experiencing, such as marriage followed by children:

> And then the other thing is myself and other friends investing more in careers. A number of my friends are either in long-term relationships, married, or some have children so our collective social life is different.

Forty-year-old Kyle lived in Auckland and came from a family of Pacific Islanders. While still relatively young in terms of the gay life course, he said that because of his job, which involved dealing with people in different settings every day, he was no longer interested in meeting strangers.[52] He now rarely went on the scene and was fairy content with the company of family:

> I have probably closed it up myself. I have closed off. I find it easier. For instance going out, I hang out with my family. It's easier. I don't have to explain. Going out and meeting new people, I just can't be bothered.

Of the three remaining men from this group, the first, who was 56 and from Los Angeles, said he had withdrawn from the sex-based social life because it was a waste of time. The second man, who was 40 and lived in New York, said that life in New York could become wearing and that he had retreated from actively socialising in order to maintain his equanimity. The third man was 38 and came from London. He said that like Timothy (above) his social life had changed because his straight friends were having children and therefore socialised less often.

It is significant that most of the men who noted a change in their social life said it represented a withdrawal from the world of gay bars and clubs – whether this withdrawal was a reason for or symptom of their contracted social life was not clear from their oral testimonies. The age range of the men in this group was 38–81, including five men aged over 60.[53] A paradoxical aspect of the commercialised gay world is that while ageist attitudes mean that some gay bars and clubs are not welcoming of men over 45, there are venues where men in their 60s can feel quite at home. In particular, this applies to gay men who belong to the bear or leather scenes, which are far more accepting of men over 40 and men in their 60s and older. One of the oldest men from the sample, 81-year-old Godfrey, had once been a fairly regular participant on the gay scene in Sydney but now doubted how he would be received:

> I wonder what would happen if I rocked up to Oxford Street one night and tried to get into one or other of the gay bars. They would probably knock me back as an oldie, you know.
>
> *Author: some bars are more accepting than others.*
>
> I wouldn't know because I just don't do it now, but I used to love going to the bars.

For those age cohorts of gay men who came out before or during the gay liberation period in the West, bars and clubs were as important as meeting places and sites of social change as were 'gay lib' consciousness-raising meetings at universities and work places. This political aspect of gay socialising during the era of gay liberation explains the signal importance the bars and clubs held and continue to hold in the memory of gay men who were in their 20s or 30s between the late 1960s and early 1980s. Before homosexuality was legalised, the bars and clubs provided both a sanctuary from a hostile world and a venue for dissemination of alternative beliefs and practices, social and sexual.

I interviewed 72-year-old Jeffrey in his home town, Auckland. Like Godfrey, he had enjoyed going to bars and clubs in his youth as well, and until quite recently:

> I used to enjoy them ... [but] it is different now to what it used to be. When I first came out, there was the *Alex Hotel* which was a bar

we could go to. It closed at ten and then we'd go from there to the *Staircase* and stay til 1 am or 2 am which was a different social atmosphere, totally. It's different now. *Urge* is okay but it is not the same as what the *Alex* was, which was lights on, open talking, chatting. *Urge* is lights out and I cannot hear anybody for the noise and there is no real dance club like the *Staircase* where you could go somewhere and talk to people. But anyway, if I go to *Urge* now, I seem to be left standing in a corner.

This extract from Jeffrey's interview suggests a layered experience of gay bars and clubs in Auckland. First, there is evidence that he had been on the scene at various points in the recent past and had knowledge of changing fads. Second, it is clear that in his view the bars and clubs that once operated were superior to those that now comprise the scene, because none of the current ones allows 'open talking, chatting' or is a dance club. It is worth noting that despite my findings elsewhere that ageism in gay bars and clubs often dissuaded older men from participating in the scene, Jeffrey at 72 was still willing to go to a gay bar on the odd occasion even if the experience was neither welcoming nor particularly enjoyable: 'I seem to be left standing in the corner.'[54] That Jeffrey and other gay men in their 60s and 70s are willing to risk rejection in this way underlines the signal importance of bars and clubs as convivial locations in the eyes of many gay men, for the reasons I mentioned above, that is, that they were sites of foundational importance in the men's youth when they formed their identity as gay men amidst regular social/sexual encounters with other men like them.

The final account of the mixed appeal of gay bars and clubs came from Connor, a 41-year-old Londoner. His experience of gay bars and clubs in London combined elements of what the men preceding him had said. Like Kyle (above), Connor was still relatively young in gay terms when interviewed. He explained that in his late 20s and again in his mid-30s, he and some friends had gone out on the scene:

I used to go clubbing a lot. I did two stints of the clubbing scene. One was relatively later on. I suppose I would have been about 27 or 28. It was around about 1996–7, when my two good gay friends both discovered the scene ... and we would go out clubbing probably almost once a week. But you cannot do that for very long. I think we did that for ... about a year and then we had other things in our lives. ... But then through an on-line networking thing called Jake, which was a social and professional network ... I met another circle of friends and with a couple of those I had another little stint of clubbing in the mid-2000s, again, for a relatively short period of time.

Nowadays, Connor does not go on the scene, largely because, as he explained, its appeal waned and other things became more important. Interestingly, his second experience of the scene occurred when he was in his mid 30s and as a result of meeting another group of friends via an on-line social site called Jake.[55]

> Now, I really could not think of anything worse than in the wee small hours of the morning, when I would want to be tucked up in bed, bouncing up and down to mindless banging music in a brightly-lit strobe lighting environment. It chills me now. I couldn't imagine doing that any more.

Connor's first experience of the scene in London occurred at a time when was in his late 20s. He would therefore have been socialising with men who were younger by about ten years and older by as many as 20 years. His second experience occurred seven or eight years later. On each occasion, it would seem that he and his friends went to gay clubs and bars briefly and intensively. At 41, his view of the scene was, however, of barely concealed disdain. Unlike Jeffrey, the 72-year-old New Zealander, who was still willing to test his luck in an Auckland gay bar, Connor showed no sign of wanting to do the same in any of London's gay bars or clubs, chiefly because, as he said, he preferred being asleep after midnight.

The principal narrative common to the accounts these men gave was that a slower social pace was to be expected at their time or stage of life. Included in the stories the men over 60 told were (a) the importance of an organised structure to a person's social life, such as concert subscriptions and regular contact with friends and other social outings; (b) an acceptance that a person's social life invariably contracts as his/her friends reduce in number; (c) the realisation that the gay scene operates at hours that are not convenient to older men.

The group of men under 60 made a different set of observations about a slowing social life, which they understood as being appropriate to their stage of life. Included in their stories were the following. First, their social life began to slow down as their careers assumed more importance. Second, those men for whom it was important to socialise with their heterosexual friends found that their social life naturally slowed down in their 30s or thereabouts when their friends began having families. Third, for a number of reasons the men found that they were less interested in socialising with strangers at bars and clubs, though, as mentioned, there was a 72-year-old New Zealander who persisted with the gay scene, even when disappointed by his experience.

Conclusion

In this chapter, I have examined the stories of 41 men from the international sample who were single at the time of interview and did so in the context of, first, increasing numbers of people in their 20s and 30s living single lives, and second, two powerful myths about intimacy in general and gay intimacy in particular. The first myth is that gay men are destined to live alone and be lonely, and the second myth is that the single life is deviant and a threat to normative adult behaviour. The fact that single gay men are depicted either as lonely, both in popular image and by researchers such as Henning Bech, or as deviant and therefore dangerous because their single status challenges the norm of 'settled' gay couples, are features of a homophobia that transforms to counter the new circumstances of non-heterosexuals and the homonormative push from white, affluent, gay men in the West (and their counterparts in developing countries as well) who see secure couple and property relationships as desirable expressions of gay intimacy. 'The dominant signs of straight conformity have become the ultimate measure of gay success.'[56]

Beck and Beck-Gernsheim argue that individualisation will make couple relationships harder for everyone; hence we are seeing more singles or more people being single more of the time. They do not predict more loneliness, but the image they painted in their discussion of singleness was not a happy one, suggesting single people spend most of their spare time (*spare* because they do not have partners or children) making excuses for their existence and trying to fill empty hours. Their claim that fewer people are starting couple relationships might be less significant than they claim because it could instead be evidence of a return to what was more usual before the intense pair coupling that occurred after the end of World War Two. Increased individualisation might make coupling less straightforward, but some of the changes Beck and Beck-Gernsheim identify could suggest a return to longstanding patterns of delayed marriage. Couples' decisions to delay marriage and childbirth are often affected by any change toward increased job or income insecurity; these in turn are brought about by the type of changes to local and global economics that have been destabilising the world of work since the 1990s.[57] Job insecurity affects gay men as well as straight men and women, but is less likely to affect couple formation because, as I have argued here and elsewhere, gay men began experimenting with short-term relationships alternating with singledom in the 1950s and 1960s, in other words, some decades before the trend became more common among their heterosexual counterparts, and for reasons that specifically related to their need to remain closeted and keep safe their identity.

This chapter yielded three findings of interest. The first was that a group of men representing almost half of the single men said that their social lives were full and active. A smaller group of slightly more than a third of the single men said their social lives had contracted. The second finding was that age was not a crucial factor in the men's experience of being single, avoiding loneliness, or practising friendship well. The older men demonstrated a resilience and competency in whatever social sphere they circulated. The picture of gay men as lonely is therefore more mythic than real because the men practised the art of friendship well and conscientiously in their full private lives. The third finding was that where there was evidence of friendship operating and being practised differently in different locales, and there was a nice comparison here between the stories men from Mumbai told of gay friendship circles, for example, Edmund's pseudo family, and the stories that men from New York and other western cities told of their friendship networks or families of choice.

Finally, I think the place the gay scene assumed was of interest in explanations men from the two groups gave for the quality of their social life, whether full and active or contracted. The men who had full, active social lives and continued to engage with the scene mostly did so because they enjoyed the prospect of social/sexual exchange with strangers. Those men who had full, active social lives and avoided the scene together with those men whose social lives had contracted and avoided the scene also mainly gave two reasons for doing so. First, they were not interested in social/sexual exchanges with strangers, and second, the impoverished physical environment of the bars and clubs of the scene held no allure and positively discouraged their participation. What this shows is that the men connected with the scene in varied ways, in much the same way that straight men's connections with institutions vary, and that only some of them had developed the decentred lives that Arlene Stein found among ageing lesbians. The next chapter explores the stories told about long-lasting relationships – the direct opposite of the single lifestyle.

3
Long-Lasting Relationships

> We are one and the same person I think now. ... We
> have turned into the same person – grumpy, difficult,
> intolerant [*laughs*] shouting at the TV.
>
> (Bryce, aged 63, Manchester)

Introduction

This chapter looks at the life stories of a group of 24 men whose long-lasting relationships resemble the companionate marriage in all but name. It is remarkable that, despite persistent, public stereotypes of youthful promiscuity or loneliness in old age and despite a long history of minimal social recognition of or support for gay, couple relationships, a substantial minority of a quarter of the men from the international sample (*n* = 97) provided evidence of gay men's capacity to conduct stable, long-lasting relationships. It is remarkable also that these men's relationships should so closely resemble the companionate marriage when in the five decades since the 1960s the couple relationship has undergone radical changes, becoming at the same time more flexible and subject to change and more fragile, less permanent.

That such a substantial minority of men with experience of enduring relationships was present in the international sample is remarkable again because I did not purposely set out to recruit men whose life stories would demonstrate histories of long-lasting relationships. As I explained in the Introduction, my original plan was to collect stories from a wide age-range of same-sex-attracted men living in nine international cities in the hope of gauging their experience of age and ageing. It is worth mentioning at this point that the 24 men in long-lasting relationships, who are the subject of this chapter, were part of a larger group of 55 men, or almost 60 per cent of the international sample, who were in relationships at the time of interview. This relatively high proportion of gay men with a high level of pair relationship experience compares favourably with earlier findings from an all-Australian sample regarding the proportion of gay men in relationships.[1]

The central argument of this chapter is that a significant minority of men from this sample provided evidence of gay men's capacity to commit to stable, long-lasting relationships. This runs counter to an increasing tendency in the West toward less durable, more fragile couple relationships described by Zygmunt Bauman, Elizabeth Beck-Gernsheim, and Ulrich Beck, among others, as due to increasing individualisation.[2] From my analysis of their stories, the relationships the men described closely resembled the companionate marriage, which until quite recently was a fairly widely accepted model for marital relations, based as it was on an understanding that the couple would be companions, friends, lovers, and sexual partners, even if the household division of labour remained strongly biased in favour of the male partner.[3]

Evidence to support the argument that long-lasting gay relationships closely resembled companionate marriage was found in men's relationship stories revealing two prominent companionate traits – companionship and partnership. As well, there was evidence in the men's accounts of fairly conventional storylines about sexual relations and relationships. The first storyline concerned the place of sex in long-lasting, monogamous relationships, and the second referred to the space that some men negotiated in long-lasting relationships for one or each partner to participate in adventurous sex. The companionate traits and the sexual storylines are examined in two separate sections of the chapter. Introducing these sections are two preliminary sections. The first preliminary section deals with the couple relationship, a brief survey of relevant literature, and the second preliminary section provides a brief sketch of the couples who provided the data for this study.

Couple relationships

Dating from eighteenth-century England, where it first developed among the upper classes and was then taken up by the middle and working classes, the companionate marriage broke from the impersonal, functional style of marriage that preceded it because of its emphasis on the love and companionship that a couple could expect to experience in marriage. Before this marriage was a social institution principally providing for the transfer of property with varying provisions for the security of wife and children.[4]

It is important to note that companionate marriage did not and does not exclude a romantic or sexual dimension, and is not a euphemistic term to describe marriage when sexual relations have waned or are absent. In her study of contemporary personal life, Carol Smart observed a tendency among scholars working in the field to distinguish between four categories of love, namely, romantic love, sexual love, maternal love, and companionate love. She argued, however, that these distinctions were not helpful because the boundaries between the four types were fluid and that people understood that sexual love and/or romantic love generally preceded companionate love.[5] Before the western sexual revolution in the 1960s, the companionate marriage was recommended as the appropriate place for sexual relations between a woman and a man. For example, when it was revived and popularised in the USA after World War One, social conservatives accused advocates of the companionate marriage of encouraging loose morals in the general population because sexual satisfaction in marriage was one of the arguments they used to recommend it. 'Men and women sought happiness and personal satisfaction in their mates; an important component of ... [which] was mutual sexual enjoyment.'[6] And, as Andrew Cherlin noted in the North American context and John Murphy in the Australian context, during the 1950s companionate marriage was the only socially acceptable place for couples to enjoy sexual relations.[7]

> Although some of ... [its] features had antecedents in nineteenth century ideals ... the companionate marriage ... [was] recognizably modern: a female sexual desire as strong as, even if different from, that of the male; the need to have it satisfied; the availability of birth control so that couples could enjoy sex without the worry of unwanted pregnancies.[8]

Of course, not everyone conformed to convention, and in the 1950s and 1960s there were couples who defied social norms by cohabitating instead of marrying. Cherlin argues, however, that while this was the case, cohabitation was not widespread, that only the poor or avant-garde practised it, and that it was not until the 1970s and later that cohabitation became a widely accepted alternative or prelude to marriage in western countries.[9]

One of the more persuasive arguments concerning changes that have taken place in personal intimacy and relationships since World War Two is that because of declining traditional attachments and community obligation – consequences of increasing mass individualisation – couple relationships are subject to forces that tend toward their disintegration.[10] The first disintegrating force is the abundance of choice individuals face in personal lives and a tendency toward obsolescence that this can produce. Eva Illouz describes this as a '"shop-and-choose" outlook' and Zygmunt Bauman uses the following terms: 'since present-day commitments stand in the way of the next day's opportunities, the lighter and more superficial they are, the less is the damage'.[11]

Almost a decade before Bauman observed the effect of obsolescence on couple relationships, Anthony Giddens identified a similar trend, which he argued was brought about as a result of the separation of love and sex in intimate life. Separating love and sex in relationships meant that couples were engaged in what he called 'pure relationships'.[12] Giddens's definition of a pure relationship was one that was

> entered in to for its own sake, for what can be derived by each person from a sustained association with another; and ... continued only in so far as it is thought by both parties to deliver enough satisfactions for each individual to stay within it.[13]

The second disintegrating force that can affect couple relationships is an expectation that partners will meet personal needs that in former times would have been satisfied by interpersonal exchanges with a variety of people, both closely and distantly related, such as priest, siblings, relatives, friends, work mates, neighbours, and colleagues. '[O]ne is supposed to seek and find in the macro-microcosm of life with the beloved everything that society previously assigned to various professions and often different parts of town.'[14] In the face of increasing individualisation, the companionate marriage ceased some time ago to be the most common form of pair relationship, but continues to be one among a number of models for marriage and, as this chapter shows, was the prevailing model for long-lasting relationships among a significant minority of gay men interviewed for this book.

Since the 1980s, when research on gay and lesbian private lives was in its infancy, scholars have cited a tendency toward short-term, temporary relationships as a typical, though not universal feature of gay relationships.[15] A summary of the literature suggests three reasons for this. First, as same-sex relationships were not recognised until recently in the West, gay men were forced to experiment with relationship types that were different from the heterosexual norm.[16] A second, related reason was that the separation of love and sex that Giddens observed in contemporary couple relationships was a feature also of gay relationships, which hostile commentators have used to label gay men as 'sex-obsessed' and incapable of conducting committed relationships. Third, if gay men preferred to conduct short-term relationships it was often because of strategic decisions they made to cope with social opprobrium. 'The most effective defense [sic] against oppression lies in fleeting and clandestine relationships which do not attract attention or provoke suspicion.'[17]

If there is truth in Beck and Beck-Gernsheim's argument that a principal feature of couple relationships today is the expectation that one's partner will meet all one's affective and sexual–social needs, then I would argue that while this continues to be the case for some gay men now, it was especially so for many gay men in times of social hostility, when their partner became trusted confidant, little brother, as well as lover, closest friend, and sexual partner.[18] In light of the fragility of modern-day relationships and the conditions under which gay men have arranged and conducted couple relationships in times of varying social acceptance, it is notable that a significant minority of 24 men from this sample of 97 men showed clear evidence of managing successful, long-lasting relationships. And in addition, that these relationships of 10 years and longer should so closely resemble the companionate marriage in terms of commitment and longevity.

The couples in my study

For the purposes of this study, I defined a 'long-lasting' relationship as one where the couple has been together for 10 years or more. On the basis of this definition, 24 men, or one-quarter of the international sample of 97 men, were in long-lasting relationships. Of these, seven were in relationships of more than 30 years' duration;[19] eight men were in relationships of between 20 and 30 years' duration;[20] and nine in relationships of between 10 and 20 years' duration.[21] As mentioned, the 24 men were from a larger group of 55 who were in relationships at the time of interview.[22] It is worth mentioning also that of the 42 men who were single at the time of interview, 30 had previously been in relationships of on average six and a half years' duration. Included in each of the age cohorts mentioned above was a small number of couple pairs, that is, pairs of men in relationships together. Their stories are occasionally discussed separately, without reference to what their partner said and sometimes jointly so as to compare what each partner said about the same topic.

This main body of the chapter has two parts. In the first part, I look at the evidence in the men's relationship stories to support the argument that their relationships closely resemble the companionate marriage. In the second part, I consider the place of sex in the men's stories of their relationships. Its relative absence from the men's stories suggests that long-lasting gay relationships are no different from long-lasting heterosexual relationships and marriages where similar stories are told of the relative insignificance of sexual relations after time.

Togetherness, companionship, partnership, and love

The focus in this section is on the relationship stories of eight men that showed traits of companionate marriage. Three of the relationship stories were from men in the 30-plus group,[23] four were from men in the 20–30 group,[24] and one was from a man in the 10–20 group.[25] My analysis of these eight relationship stories suggests two principal narratives, the presence of which I argue is evidence of companionate relationship. First, there is evidence in the stories of a togetherness and companionship that suggests a sense of equality.[26] Second, there is evidence of a regard for the personal qualities in the other man, suggesting a partnership that is not necessarily merely economic, that takes the shape of a mutual sharing of the load both metaphorically and literally. Underlying each of these narratives is evidence of the men's capacity and willingness to commit to their partners and their relationships. In the following sub-sections, the two principal narratives I identified as features of a companionate relationship are discussed in turn, that is, (a) togetherness and companionship and (b) partnership, before considering a third and minor narrative, which is about love and the means by which the men expressed feelings of love toward their partner.

Togetherness, companionship

For the purpose of the discussion that follows, I have understood 'togetherness' to describe that close, personal, almost animal-like intimacy that develops between two people who have shared lives together from young adulthood until late middle age or older. I have understood the term 'companionship' to mean a mutual understanding between two individuals such that each is willing to sacrifice his/her time to keep the other company. It is a relationship where affection is often present that is not only sexual and where each person has a reasonable expectation that the other will come to his/her aid, is accepted for what he/she is, can be relied upon, and is dependable.

Evidence of togetherness was found in the life stories of three men, two from the 30-plus group and one from the 20–30 group. Two of the men referred to sleeping together – that is, that they still shared the same bed after all those years – as a sign of the success and quality of their relationship. The first man to cite the fact that he and his partner still slept together as evidence of the success of their relationship was Ashton (aged 70) from Sydney. The second man to do so was Bryce (aged 63), who was from Manchester and before retirement had worked in the entertainment industry. He had lived 'tolerably happily together' with his partner, Alfie (also 63), 'for 39 years':

> We're quite happy to go to bed each night comfortably and snuggle up ... [and] if people were ever to ask me what I see in the relationship, well, you care for one another. And, if we've been together such a long time, it's because we continue to care for one another. We're anxious about one another's welfare.

Not only was the fact that they still went to bed together to 'snuggle up' a sign of the companionate nature of their relationship but also and importantly that they cared for each other and were anxious about the other's wellbeing. In many ways, these two men maintained an old-fashioned relationship where the other's wellbeing was each partner's prime concern, an essential ingredient of a companionate relationship in both theory and fact.

Importantly, Alfie and Bryce's relationship was a civil partnership:

> We both said quite clearly that we don't see it 'as marriage as such' [because] we've lived together long enough to not have to do it but ... it is significant in terms of inheritance and rights. We are one another's next of kin and that is very important. And certainly in terms of pension considerations, you know. ... We only asked about a dozen friends. ... The majority were straight.[27]

When describing their relationship, Alfie said that they had become 'one and the same person', that when they went on holidays, people often asked if they were 'brothers'. To confuse his fellow holidaymakers, Alfie would refer to Bryce as his 'next of kin'. A popular, negative view of gay relationships is that they are invariably narcissistic because, in looking for another man to be his partner, the gay man must be seeking his 'mirror image'. This is not what Alfie meant when he said he and partner had become 'one and the same person'. What I found in his account of their close relationship was evidence of the natural growing together that occurs in many relationships when the partners have shared lives from youth to early old age.

In the next part of the discussion, I draw on the accounts of five men for evidence of the importance of companionship in their couple relationships. One of the men was from the 30-plus group; three were from the 20–30 group; and one from the 10–20 group. Christian (aged 72) was from Sydney and had been with his partner for more than 40 years. The only man to refer to his partner as his 'companion', he said that he regarded him as 'a wonderful friend ... and lover': 'It is a very blessed thing in my life. ... I have been very lucky to have ... [received] such wisdom and support [from him].' In the eyes of 70-year-old Ashton, one of the two men (above) who cited sleeping with his partner as evidence of the success of a long-lasting relationship, the companionship that he and his partner shared could be measured by the absence of abuse in their relationship:

> And the most amazing thing is that we have never had a punch up. ... I have never hit him and he has never hit me. We still sleep together but that is about it. But we have never had an out-and-out, screaming, nasty, unnecessary fight.

Ashton's partner was a younger man by at least 20 years and they had been together for 25 years at the time of interview. Ashton struck me as a manly man. His career had been in agriculture and small business, and he was used to working around men and horses. That he should boast that he and his partner had never had 'a punch up' said a great deal about the unspoken care and concern that he understood to exist in their relationship. When I asked him why his relationship worked, he said, 'we go our different ways to a certain degree' and then noted the absence of 'punch ups'.

The third man whose life story contained evidence of companionship in his long-lasting relationships was Zachary (52), an expatriate working in Hong Kong. He and his partner, also an expatriate living in Hong Kong, had been together for 22 years. In his account of their relationship he explained its success in the following terms.

> [W]hen I talk to younger people today ... I feel ... they are very impatient with relationships. They want it to be perfect and want their partner to be perfect and have little patience with humanity with ... learning to live with another's quirks and are in too much ... [of a] rush ... [to] move in together

For Zachary, the quality of the partnership that he and his partner had achieved was as a result of patient acceptance of each other's personal flaws. And that, while they did 'fall into a very natural long-term relationship', it had occurred over time, developing as the result of a mutually cautious approach.

Buck (aged 51) was an expatriate also working in Hong Kong when interviewed. The relationship he had with his partner of 22 years, also an expatriate living in Hong Kong, Buck described as, 'not perfect but ... for the most part ... everything I have dreamed of'. Expanding on the worth of their relationship, Buck said he was surprised at the ease with which couples, straight and gay, fall out of love: 'I run into people who after a couple of years of marriage ... [are getting] a divorce.' And he was puzzled why couples with emotional difficulties do not 'stay in love and overcome the problems' they have. Finally, he explained the reason for the success of his relationship, citing in the following what he felt for his partner.

> I admire my partner very much. I respect him and when I have to do ... [important] things ... I ask him what ... [he] thinks of it, just to get his opinion. It is ... the chivalry that comes out because whatever I do affects him, so it is important that he is part of it.

Buck has a traditional view of the responsibility of the companion in a relationship. He hints that he owes his partner a chivalrous obligation and vice versa. When he seeks his partner's view on important matters, he does not see this as a sign of dependency (which it might also be) but as a courtesy.

The fifth man whose life story includes evidence of companionship and its qualities is Eddie, aged 45, from Manchester. He and his partner had been together for more than 18 years, and in the following quotation he provides an honest, nuanced account of their relationship:

> We get on ... we fight ... not physically but we argue and are combative. ... I think you get like that when you get older, when you've been together so long. ... It's a loving relationship ... based on getting on with each other and chatting but ... also based on independence.

The robust companionship that Eddie and his partner enjoyed does not include physical violence, and is similar in this respect to the companionship that Ashton from Sydney described (no 'punch ups', in Ashton's language) but Eddie goes further than Ashton. He admits to a combative relationship, arguing that verbal jousts are a feature of any long-lasting relationship and then, after reassuring me that he and his partner have a loving relationship, goes one step further to point out that their bond comes from the open communications they enjoy 'getting on with each other and chatting' and also, crucially, the independence they allow each other. For many men, independence or the idea that they may exercise or enjoy a degree of independence is a crucial part of being male, which Eddie made clear in the story of his relationship.[28]

The extracts I examined from the life stories of five men aged 44–72 suggest the following about companionship in long-lasting relationships. First, that it exists where a partner is a supportive advisor (Christian, 72,); second, that it exists where abuse is absent (Ashton, 70); third, that it is present where there is mutual respect and consultation (Buck, 51); and fourth, that it is present where communications are good and each man enjoys a degree of independence (Eddie, 45). If the characteristics of male companionship include the mutual exchange of qualities such as acceptance and dependability as well as affection, I would argue that, from the accounts of their relationships, these four men seem to have experienced it in part or in full and with varying degrees of emphasis.

On a related question, I am not sure whether gay men are more likely to experience companionship in their relationships than heterosexual men are in their friendships, that is, that gay men experience a closer male bond in their relationships than straight men do in their friendships. A great deal has been written about the social construction of masculinity, competitiveness between males in general, and how the demands of hegemonic masculinity affect relations between straight men – they may get close to their friends but not too close in case it is misconstrued as homosexual attraction, which is taboo.[29] Gay male relationships are not devoid of conflict or competitiveness, however, but the erotic, emotional, and sexual closeness that gay men often achieve in their relationships can mitigate the need to dominate, which Pierre Bourdieu argued is the learned behaviour of most males.[30]

Partnership

I have understood partnership to connote a joint enterprise or mutual effort, a sharing of the load (emotional and material), suggesting a willingness and ability on the part of each person to work together for the good of both. It was in the story of one man, Duncan (aged 47), that I found strongest evidence of the partnership that I argue connotes a companionate relationship. Duncan was an expatriate living in Hong Kong when interviewed. His business career had included work for companies in Europe and the Middle East, and he and his partner of 21 years had had a fairly 'mobile' or peripatetic private life, the international travel it involved largely influenced by the demands of multinational corporations for whom Duncan has worked and the separate demands of his partner's career.

The way Duncan and his partner managed frequent long periods apart, as each pursued his career, strongly underlined the partnership aspect of their companionate relationship. In spite of long periods of separation, beginning when they were in the full flush of youth, Duncan and his partner conducted their relationship on the understanding that its future was guaranteed and that each separation would come to an end. I would argue that a couple's ability to manage separation as Duncan and his partner did is evidence of an enduring partnership, especially, as the following shows, enforced separation created difficulties for their private life and did not necessarily get easier with experience:

> After six or seven years together, I assumed ... that two years apart would not be difficult. I underestimated how difficult it would be. We survived it ... but it was traumatic.

An associated problem their international careers caused was that they were no longer sure where they felt most at home: 'we have lived in lots of different places but neither one of us wants to fully live [in any of them]'.

At the start of this section, when discussing the elements of companionate relationships, I argued that for partnership to exist there must be evidence of a joint effort or mutual enterprise. Duncan's story of his relationship of 21 years suggests how important it is that each partner is willing to conduct relations with his partner on the basis of partnership, especially where separation is involved or is to be expected because of the competing demands of separate careers. The practical difficulties that separate, global careers can cause underlines also another narrative that is familiar in the published accounts of life stories of gays and lesbians, which is that, like increasing numbers of straight couples, they too are capable of 'living apart together' and maintaining affective bonds while physically separate.[31]

Presence of love

When discussing the nature of companionate marriage, historians such as John D'Emilio and Estelle Freedman and Lawrence Stone argue that it is the presence of love and companionship that distinguishes the companionate marriage from its pragmatic, functional predecessor.[32] What, then, did the stories of the 24 men who were in long-lasting relationships say about love? Its presence, which can be expressed in practical terms as well as in poems and love songs, was the crucial, new ingredient of the companionate marriage when it emerged in the late seventeenth and early eighteenth centuries, evolving as it did when love began to speak its name, claim its place in marriage.[33] Eight men from the group of 24 who were in long-lasting relationships used the word 'love' or something similar when recounting their relationship stories. While this finding is better than findings from my all-Australian sample of gay men – where only one man out of a sample of 80 Australian men said his relationship was important because of the love he experienced with his partner[34] – it is still the case that the men whose relationships stories were the subject of this chapter were reticent to refer to love when speaking of their relationships.

When analysing the all-Australian data, I inferred its presence in relationships if the men spoke of companionship or intimacy. In regard to the data used for this chapter, I would argue that the accounts of companionship or partnership the men told in their relationship stories were practical expressions of love for their partner. When, for example, Ashton (aged 70) announced (above) that his relationship was on a firm footing because of the absence of 'punch ups' or when Buck (aged 51) said (above) that he sought his partner's opinion whenever he had to make an important decision, I believe they were expressing those deep, affective bonds for their partner that are generally known as love. The bigger question of men's fear of expressing their feelings, with which women in heterosexual relationships are all too familiar, can be compounded in same-sex, male relationships. But fear of expressing feelings does not mean that those feelings are absent, and evidence of love can be found even if people do not use the word.

Analysis of the men's relationship stories revealed that eight men (or one-third of the 24 men in enduring relationships) spoke of love in their relationships. The first was Christian (aged 72) from Sydney, who said (above) that having his 'lover' in his life for 42 years was 'a very blessed thing'. The second man was Parry (aged 63) from New York, who explained love as commitment and loyalty, both of which were tested quite considerably when his lover was sent to prison:

> That relationship has been full of all sorts of things I would never think of ... [it has] been a challenge for me but also a challenge for me to see how committed I am to loving someone ... when he was

gaoled and going through all this stuff, when my friends were asking, 'Why are you bothering?' And you know I'm too loyal.

Although Parry affected a casual response when speaking about the time his partner was in gaol, I would argue that his decision not to discard his partner or break off the relationship was a fairly dramatic expression of love and loyalty, in anyone's terms. The third man was Hugh (aged 62) from Melbourne, who said the strong spiritual and emotional bonds he felt for his partner were a type of continuing 'in-love-ness'. The fourth man was Eddie (aged 45) from Manchester, who said (above) that he and his partner had a 'loving relationship'. And the remaining four men referred to love when they distinguished between romantic love and sexual relations in their relationship.[35]

In short, there was evidence of one or all of the traits of companionate marriage in the men's stories. I found examples in their relationship stories of togetherness, companionship, or partnership. In addition, I have argued that the accounts the men provided of companionship or partnership in their relationship stories were evidence of love's presence, as it also was if the men used the word 'love' in their stories or a similar word or phrase.

Sex and the long-lasting relationship

Earlier in the chapter, I observed that the term 'companionate marriage' was not a euphemism for a marriage where sexual relations had waned or were non-existent and that, on the contrary, the couple's sex life was seen as an important element of the companionate marriage. The focus of this section is the sex life of the men in long-lasting relationships that resemble the companionate marriage in all but name.

In total, only six men, or a quarter of this sample of 24 men, referred to sexual relations when telling their relationship story.[36] On the surface, this might seem to suggest that sexual relations occupied only a relatively minor place in the men's relationships, with the notable exception of a small number of men who conducted their long-lasting relationships as open relationships at some point. Of course, the absence of a sexual storyline does not mean that sexual relations were absent from the long-lasting relationships under study. Perhaps some of the men were shy about discussing this aspect of their relationship in an interview, or some of the men had low sex drives and sex did not play an important part in their relationship. Perhaps also some of the interviewees overlooked any mention of sexual relations because it was a taken-for-granted aspect of their private life, and I did not probe sufficiently tenaciously or the place of sexual relations in the relationships had diminished – as it does over time in most relationships, straight and gay – and occurred only occasionally. In any case, its relative unimportance was instructive and contradicted powerful, public narratives that portray gay men as primarily sexually oriented if not sex-obsessed.

The six men who spoke about sex in their relationships fell into two groups, drawing on two familiar sexual storylines. The first group consisted of three men, who when they spoke about sex referred to (a) an early period in their relationship when they had a lot of sex, or (b) the fact that their relationship was now not solely based on sex or had evolved so that sexual relations were only one of the means through which they expressed their affective bond. This is a fairly conventional narrative about the waning but not extinguishing of the sexual fire that can occur in monogamous relationships. The second group of three men who referred to the sex in their relationship did so in the context of the sex that they or their partner had with other men, that is, when they gave details of their open relationship. This is a less conventional yet familiar storyline, reminiscent of the swinging couples of the 1960s or key parties which, before the onset of herpes, were a feature of the suburban avant-garde in the 1970s when married couples incorporated a degree of extra-marital sex into their sex lives, without jeopardising their marriage. It is a storyline that permeates gay relationships as well and suggests gay men's capacity to incorporate a transgressive element in their sexual/social lives without putting at risk their primary relationship.

All three men who belonged to the first group were in their 40s, from Britain, and had been in relationships of between 10 and 20 years.[37] The three men did not describe their relationship as 'open', and I did not ask them if they had sex or were having with anyone other than their partner. What they did say about their relationship is instructive for what it reveals about distinctions people make between affectionate and sexual relations. Fred (aged 47) said that his relationship began sexually, 'we met illicitly and shagged, had fantastic sex', slowly evolving into a romantic relationship, after which it became companionate in nature when they 'moved in together the following year and have been together ever since'.[38] His partner, Jonathon (aged 45) agreed with Fred's recollection of the early days of their relationship: 'we saw each other in a sexual but not in a romantic sense'. The romance in their relationship began, in the story each told of the relationship, between 18 months and two years after they met.

That the romance in their relationships followed an initial period of sexual fervour confirmed what Michel Foucault observed in the early 1980s about gay relationships. In the following excerpt, Foucault distinguishes between sex and the romantic longing a person weaves when his lover has departed. While the distinction between a period of frantic sexual attraction and activity and a period of quieter romantic contemplation is common to most couples, Foucault's point was that, in the late twentieth century and before homosexual law reform was achieved, it could be especially poignant for gay men considering the circumstances of their meeting (clandestine, at short notice, for example) and whether a second meeting was guaranteed:

> For a homosexual, the best moment of love is likely to be when the lover leaves in a taxi. It is when the act is over and the guy ... is gone that one begins to dream about the warmth of his body, the quality of his smile, the tone of his voice.[39]

The third man from this group, Eddie (aged 45) was interviewed in Manchester. He and his partner met in 'a sleazy gay bar'. It was nice in his view because they just got on and 'it wasn't just based on sex'. Although I did not interrogate Eddie further at this point in our interview, I now suspect that what he meant by the shorthand, 'we just got on; it wasn't just based on sex', is that their relationship came into existence because they knew one another more than sexually.

The second group of men that spoke of the place of sex in relationships comprises three men. The oldest one in this group is Drake (77) from Melbourne; the next in age is Parry (63) from New York; and the youngest is Ben (52) from Manchester. As mentioned, all three men spoke of having conducted or of still conducting an open relationship. Drake is from the group of men whose relationships were 30 years or longer, and Parry and Ben from the group whose relationships were between 20 and 30 years in length. The reason and the occasion when each man opened up his relationship differed and reveals that there is no standard pattern as to why, when, or how gay men in long-lasting relationships agree that one or both may have occasional casual partners. In Drake's case, he and his younger partner had recently agreed that the partner could meet for casual sex with 'fuck buddies', and for two reasons.[40] First, while Drake and his partner were interested and capable of having sex with each other, they could not, according to Drake, 'get it together at the moment'; second and more importantly,

Drake was concerned that his partner might struggle to find a new partner after his death:

> At my age, I could drop off any day or any year and … [my partner]
> can't be left … at, say 60, wondering how he finds a friend. I'd rather
> it were smoother in that area, which is pretty important for … us.

Allowing his partner to have casual sex was not a new arrangement for,
according to Drake, during the course of their 31 years together, they
had been 'sexually active … while having other partners'. This time,
however, the agreement was strongly altruistically motivated, inspired
as he said it was by a desire to ensure his partner would not have to
lead a life alone after his death, suggesting Drake's companionate connection to and regard for his partner. Drake's assumption was, of course,
that he would predecease his partner who was 21 years his junior. He
made it clear, however, that he would not allow a friendship with a
casual sex partner to threaten their relationship:

> I don't want him to fall for anybody. I'll fight him about that but
> having a range of 'fuck buddies' or whatever you want to call them
> would be more social for him.

In Parry's case, his open relationship arose from a desire to have more
satisfying sex than he was able to have with his partner. At the time
of interview, Parry had been with his partner for 25 years, the first 14
years of which they lived together; while for the last 11 years, they had
been living apart. When Parry sought more satisfying sex outside the
relationship, it was because his partner meant a great deal to him, or as
he said in his own words, 'I couldn't give up on our relationship':

> It's 25 years of growing old with someone … I absolutely adored from
> the moment I saw him. The night I met him at a cocktail party, I said,
> 'he's the person I want to spend the rest of my life with', and I am
> still committed to that.

After having casual sex three or four times over a period of about six
months, Parry met a man who wanted to start a relationship with him.
Because he regarded his original relationship as enduring, Parry decided
to conduct a separate relationship with the second man. In order to
make this possible, he made arrangements with his first partner to

continue their relationship, obtaining his partner's permission to begin a parallel relationship with the second man. He and his first partner began living apart together when Parry began this second relationship.

An unusual aspect of Parry's account of the two relationships is what I understood to be his genuinely stated belief in monogamy: 'I was monogamous for so many years and I believe in a monogamous relationship.' One possible explanation for the disjunction between his belief in monogamy and his affective practices is that Parry understood that each of his relationships, which he conducted separately with each partner, to be monogamous and that, by keeping the men apart and their affective lives separate, he was being faithful to each. It was clear to me at the time of interview and later when listening to the recording of the interview and analysing the data from the written transcript that Parry genuinely believed he was conducting two independent and monogamous relationships. His partners knew of the other's existence but this was not a *ménage à trois*. The three men kept two separate establishments in order for Parry to conduct his relationships separately and, I suspect, maintain the impression that he was being monogamous when in fact each of his partners was having a monogamous relationship *with him*.

Barry Adam's study of the relationship scripts of a non-representative sample of Canadian gay men provides another possible explanation for the apparent disjunction between Parry's beliefs and practices. Adam argues that gay men will often use monogamy for building trust in the early phases of relationships. He argues also that a tension can exist between the gay 'relationship trajectory' of romance and monogamy and gay men's pursuit and enjoyment of 'outlaw sex', or what Adams calls 'male-gendered scripts of sex as adventure, pleasure, and exploration without commitment'.[41] In other words, it is possible to understand Parry's decision-making in the following terms. He practised the monogamy of which he spoke in the first 14 years of his relationship with his first partner. At that point, he sought more satisfying sex outside the relationship on the understanding with his partner that in his words, he 'would not give up on the relationship ... [even if] we seemed to be going sexually in different directions'. On meeting a man with whom he found satisfying sex and who wanted a (possibly monogamous?) relationship with him, he negotiated to continue one relationship, which had operated monogamously, and to start another, which he conducted on a similar basis.

I did not interrogate Parry about the sexual dissatisfaction he had experienced with his first partner, so it is not possible to know if the setting up of the second relationship occurred because he could not reconcile the tension that Adam identifies between romance and monogamy and the pursuit of outlaw sex. From my understanding of Parry, gleaned over the course of two hours only, I suspect he honestly believed that he can and does conduct his relationships without seriously compromising a belief in monogamy.

The third person in this group of three men who spoke about sex in his long-lasting relationship is Ben. He was 52 and had been with his partner for 21 years when interviewed. Ben related the conventional story of the open relationship – where he and his partner agreed to open their relationship after they had been together five years so that each could have separate casual sexual encounters outside their primary relationship. Their decision to do so at that point supports Barry Adam's argument that in some gay relationships the purpose of monogamy is to build trust in the early years, and also his other argument that monogamy can conflict with men's pursuit of sex as a recreational pastime, an adventurous, pleasurable hobby or interest.

Ben and his partner took a while to adjust to their open relationship: 'It was difficult at first. We still felt jealous and fearful that the other would abscond with someone else. We still do!' An interesting sideline to the story of Ben's open relationship is that at one point his partner had a relationship with another man that ran for three years, with Ben's consent. It ended, however, when, said Ben, 'the other man decided that he really wanted a monogamous relationship'. An aspect of this sideline story is reminiscent of Parry's second relationship, except that the man Ben's partner was seeing did not have the power, was not in a position to insist on a monogamous relationship, and Ben and his partner were no longer conducting their relationship monogamously.

A fairly standard story of open relationships is as follows. Two men start seeing one another regularly; in line with Barry Adam's study of Canadian gay couples, the two men conduct monogamous sexual relations, often living apart until they decide to live together. In most cases, it is once they have lived together for a period of time – five years in the case of Ben and his partner, 14 years in the case of Parry and his partner – that they will discuss how and when to open their relationship. In his Canadian study, Adam found one of the more common arrangements was 'two plus one', where a third man is invited to have sex with the primary couple, and that these third parties were often only a temporary addition to the primary relationship, thus helping, he argues, to distinguish between sex with love and recreational sex.[42] I found no evidence of 'two plus one' in the stories that Drake, Parry or Ben told of their open relationships, but again this could be because

I did not interrogate them intensely when they were telling me about their sexual relations.

Ben's open relationship more closely conformed to the conventional understanding of an open, gay relationship because each partner made use of the new arrangement to seek sexual variety outside the primary relationship. By contrast, Drake and Parry's stories of opening their relationships were a variation on this theme, involving only one partner from each relationship. Drake said, while telling his relationship story, that both he and his younger partner had had casual sexual encounters ('fuck buddies') 'on the side', and that recently they had reached an understanding that his partner could continue having sex with 'fuck buddies' because doing so might increase his circle of friends. Drake made it clear, however, that he would not allow a friendship with a 'fuck buddy' to threaten their relationship and that he had agreed to or suggested (his meaning was unclear) the new arrangement because he wanted his partner to avoid loneliness in the event of his predeceasing him, a reasonable and altruistic motive given the 21 years that separate them in age.

Parry, on the other hand, was conducting two separate and possibly in his mind simultaneously monogamous relationships when I met him for an interview in his lower Manhattan apartment. In a sense, he was doing as many men before him have done and maintained two separate households, one for the wife and one for the mistress, which understanding is underlined in the quotation from Parry's interview that heads this chapter. What made Parry's story so interesting was that sex outside his primary relationship had not become routine when he arranged with his partner to look for more satisfying sex with other men, and that within six months of making that arrangement he had met a man who wanted a relationship with him. As mentioned, it was at this point that he set in place arrangements to conduct separate relationships with two men who, in his words, 'bring out ... different parts of me'.

In summary, then, what these three accounts of open relationships suggest is that there is no one uniform or universal tale of polyamory in the gay world. And that like heterosexuals freed of the restraints of marriage banns, gay men can invent a variety of creative sexual/social relationships to suit their erotic needs, about which there is more in the chapters that follow later in the book on fatherhood and then on gay marriage.

Conclusion

Based on an analysis of the stories of 24 men in couple relationships of 10 years and longer, I have argued in this chapter that the companionate marriage is the model for long-lasting, gay relationships. This subset of 24 men from the international sample comprised men aged 47–87 who were interviewed in Auckland, Hong Kong, Melbourne, Manchester, New York, and Sydney in the years 2009–12, and included men who had been previously married or in relationships with women, men who were in civil unions, and men who were gaily married. It is significant that a quarter of the 97 men from this international sample showed evidence of sustained, long-lasting relationships, especially so in light of published research that shows that, as a result of individualisation, the couple relationship is subject to forces tending toward its disintegration – evidence for which can be found in divorce figures and rates of remarriage. One possible reason for this achievement is that same-sex couples can have a greater capacity for companionship and partnership in their relationships because relations between partners are more inclined to equality and more closely approximate Anthony Giddens's notion of the 'pure relationship'.

The 24 men whose long-lasting relationships were the focus of this chapter were from a larger group of 55 men who were in relationships at the time of interview. To provide a clearer picture of relationships practices among gay men, I explained that of the 42 men who were single at the time of interview, 30 had previously been in relationships of on average six and a half years' duration. The picture this sample paints is of gay men's strong propensity to enter into and maintain relatively stable relationships that are subject to similar forces affecting heterosexual relationships, with the companionate marriage as the pervasive style for those couples in long-term relationships. In light of the political pressure for 'marriage equality' that is occurring in many western countries, it is worth remembering that one factor that might help explain the success of long-lasting gay relationships is that they have never been subject to the same level of public expectations that affect heterosexual marriage, and as well are often free of the gendered assumptions about roles and divisions of labour that can affect many straight relationships.[43]

In support of the argument that long-lasting gay relationships closely resemble the companionate marriage, there is evidence in the men's relationship stories of companionate traits – identified as companionship and partnership. Evidence for companionship was found in men's accounts of the emotional support their partner provided, which one man gauged by the absence of physical violence, their ability and willingness to accept their partner, to tolerate his personal flaws, and to sacrifice time to keep him company. Partnership connotes a joint enterprise or mutual effort, a sharing of emotional and material loads, and a willingness and ability of each person to work together for the good of both. Evidence for this was found in the relationship story of one man in his late 40s whose relationship of 21 years included periods of separation when both partners were working on different continents and/or working out how to live together. Such stories of enforced intimate separation are not uncommon among people who work for large, global corporations. I have argued also that accounts of companionship or partnership were evidence of love's presence in the men's relationships, as it also was if they used the word 'love' in their stories or a similar word or phrase.

The relative insignificance of sexual relations in the stories the men told of their relationships was the subject of the final section in this chapter. This finding is notable for two reasons. First, it is often assumed that sex plays a prominent role in gay men's relationships, that gay men are highly sexed and sexualised. For example, when I told a class of final-year students that one reason many older gays and lesbians feared having to go into nursing homes was because it would mean they would have to go back into the closet, one student said that was only as it should be because sexual relations were problematic for all residents of aged care facilities. Her assumption was that gays and lesbians were highly sexed and sexualised individuals, and she equated celibacy with going back into the closet. Second, the relative insignificance of sexual relations in long-lasting, gay relationships reflects the experience heterosexuals have of long-lasting relationships and marriage, suggesting a similar experience over time for couples who are determined and committed to remain together 'until the bitter end'.

Two groups of men did speak of the sex in their relationships. The first group spoke about sex when referring to an early period in their relationship when they had a lot of sex or to the fact that their relationship was now less sexualised or had transformed so that sex was only one means of expressing their affective bond. There is a fairly standard story in the literature of gay and straight couples that points to a tension between sexual love and romantic love; the former is often seen as excessive, if not destructive, and certainly at odds with the need to conform to the routines and rhythms of the adult world of work, while the latter represents affect of a calmer, kinder nature. The second group of men referred to sex in the context of their relationship as an open relationship. And here evidence from three men's stories showed three distinct, different approaches to polyamory, suggesting that no single narrative of open relationships can be said to exist in the gay world and reflecting gay men's capacity to incorporate a transgressive element in their intimate life without jeopardising their principal relationship.

4
Fatherhood

I probably slightly envy straight men because ... being
a parent is one of the richest experiences in my life
and one I would not have missed. ... I would like to
have had more children.

(Hector, aged 81, Melbourne)

Introduction

This chapter examines the fatherhood settings and fatherhood stories
of 14 gay men from the all-Australian sample and eight men from the
international sample.[1] When these 22 men spoke about relations with
their children, they mainly did so by first, explaining the means by
which they came to be parents, which I call 'fatherhood settings', and
second, describing in more detail the nature of relations with their
children, which I call 'fatherhood stories'. My analysis of their stories
revealed two fatherhood settings and four main fatherhood stories. The
fatherhood settings and fatherhood stories the men told are examined
in the context of generation difference, where applicable, and in light
of gender assumptions about masculinity and care.

I identified two fatherhood settings in the stories the 22 men told
about being fathers. The first setting was that which occurred when
17 of the men were married to or in a relationship with a woman,
later transforming when the men came out and, in the case of most,
embarked on gay relationships. This fatherhood setting, which I have
called 'heterosexual fatherhood', and which represents the experience
of the majority of men interviewed for this study, was also the usual
means by which gay men experienced fatherhood for the greater part
of the twentieth century – as a result of the double life many led in

response to fairly widespread homophobia in the West.[2] The marriages or heterosexual relationships of these 17 men ranged in duration from 7 to 55 years. The second fatherhood setting ('non-heterosexual fatherhood') occurred in the case of five men whose fatherhood arose *not* as a result of a heterosexual relationship. In the case of the five men interviewed for this study who experienced fatherhood in a non-heterosexual setting or context, two men became fathers when they arranged to have children with lesbian couples; two men did so as foster parents, and the fifth man became a father by adoption. Similar settings have been discussed in relation to the fatherhood experiences of British and North American men.[3]

When the men described the quality of their relationships with their children, they related four fatherhood stories, which I distinguished by the level of closeness they maintained with their children. The first story was used by a group of 13 men who said they kept very close relations with their children,[4] and in doing so demonstrated what researchers call 'involved fathering'.[5] The second story was used by a group of four men who were in regular contact with their children.[6] A third story was used by a group of three men who spoke of fairly distant relationships with their children.[7] And a fourth story, which was in fact a negative fatherhood story, was related by two men who made no mention of their children at all.[8] None of the interviewees expressed their parenting closeness quantitatively, that is, in terms of daily, weekly, three-monthly contact, for example, and I did not ask them to quantify their relationships with their children. The four fatherhood story types are discussed in the section below under the following headings, 'Very close relations', 'Regular contact', 'Distant relations', 'No contact'.

The sample used for this chapter differs from the sample I have used for the other chapters in the book because it comprises two sets of data that I combined so as to locate a sufficient number of men who had been fathers. As mentioned in Chapter 1, the two data sets consist of an 'all-Australian' sample of 80 gay men that I interviewed in 2001–3 and an international sample of 97 men that I interviewed in 2009–11.[9] In this combined data set of 177 men, there were 22 men who had been fathers; 14 of these men came from the all-Australian sample and eight from the international sample. The 14 men drawn from the all-Australian sample were aged 33–75 and, with the exception of one Aboriginal man, were of Anglo-Saxon or Anglo-Celtic descent. The eight men drawn from the international sample were from all social classes and a variety of ethnic backgrounds, and were aged 43–87.

I argue in this chapter that gay fatherhood is tied to heteronormativity because the majority of men whose interviews were analysed for this chapter came to be parents in heterosexual settings. They tended to be older men who were young adults in the 1970s and most likely married as a result of social pressure, uncertainty about their sexuality, or because marriage was the conventional place for adult sexual relations. Their parenting was 'involved' or less involved, and often this related to their experience of coming out and the behaviour of other family members when the news was received. A minority of men whose interviews were analysed for this chapter parented in a homosexual setting, in the context of the 'everyday experiment'. These men tended to be younger and relatively advantaged.

Fatherhood settings

The men used two settings or contexts when speaking about their experiences of fatherhood. The first setting was one with which most males are familiar, coming about as it did when 17 of the men from this sample got married to or began a relationship with a woman and became fathers as a result of sexual relations with their female partners. These marriages or de facto relationships later transformed when the men came out and then began gay relationships of one sort or another. Not surprisingly, I have called this setting, and the form of fatherhood it represents, 'heterosexual fatherhood'. It was the experience of the majority of gay fathers interviewed for this study and was the usual means by which gay men became fathers for most of the twentieth century and earlier – as a result of a double life many had to lead because of varying levels of homophobia in the West. Oscar Wilde being one of the best-known examples of a same-sex-attracted man who came to fatherhood this way. The second setting occurred when men became fathers *not* as a result of sexual relations with a woman but instead by artificial insemination, foster parenting, or adoption, in other words, by everyday experiments. These two fatherhood settings are discussed in order.

Heterosexual fatherhood

Seventeen men said that they their experience of fatherhood began when they were married or in a relationship with a woman, that is, as a result of heterosexual sexual intercourse and then childbirth. The families of choice the men then established varied according to how and when they came out, the nature of the gay relationship(s) they created, and their children's place in them. Aged between 45 and 87 at the time of interview, the heterosexual relationship histories of these 17 men can be divided into three groups according to how long they were married or in a relationship with a woman. The first group comprised six men who were married for more than 30 years, and included a man who had been married for more than 50 years and still was at the time of interview.[10] The second group comprised four men who were married between 20 and 30 years.[11] And the third group consisted of seven men who were married less than 20 years.[12]

For me, two questions immediately arose from these data. The first was, Why did the men marry in the first place? And the second was, When and how did they cease being married and begin their gay intimate life? In answer to the first question, social pressure to conform to the heterosexual model of marriage was the principal narrative they used to explain why they married or began a heterosexual relationship. It is significant that men from all classes said that social pressure caused them to begin a heterosexual relationship in their youth, which in a number of cases lasted into middle age. Coming out late in life does not necessarily mean that the men purposely exploited the women they married or with whom they conducted a relationship. It is possible for men who are homosexually attracted to continue an emotionally significant relationship with a woman because of their shared, intimate history and, if parents, the bond that they formed with each other when bringing up their children under the same roof.

It is significant also that the period during which these men conducted their relationships with women stretched from at least the 1940s until the early 1980s – with the notable exception of two men who were still married at the time of interview.[13] In other words, the compulsion the men felt who came out later in life to conduct heterosexual relationships was not confined to the period of acute homophobia in the West, which occurred in the 1940s and 1950s, even into the 1960s,[14] but extended well beyond it, underlining Norbert Elias's argument that reduction in shame affect and increased social tolerance do not occur uniformly but in spurts as people become more tolerant of behaviours their parents or grandparents would once have shunned, been too ashamed to practise or admit practising.[15]

When explaining why their heterosexual relationships came to an end, the men said that either their relationship broke down irretrievably or they experienced a gradual drifting apart that led to separation and/or divorce. A small number made no mention of how or why their marriage or de facto relationship ended, and the majority described amicably separating from their wives or female partners or being still married at the time of interview. Accounts from five men suggested that they had had difficulties bringing to an end their marriage or relationship. Two of these men spoke in fairly general terms about the termination of their marriage, implying that the breakdown in relations involved more than incompatible sexual preferences. Gerald (aged 75) said: 'We were married for 31 years until various circumstances broke that marriage irretrievably,' and Henry (aged 50) explained that he and his wife had, 'a series of family deaths and traumas, and the combination of these and my [sexual] ambiguity ... was enough to break up the marriage'. For at least two men, their heterosexual life came to an end when their wife died. A third man described more traumatic events surrounding the breakdown of relations with his former wife. Drake said that he had wrestled with his emerging sexuality and, after a period of intense personal self-examination, helped by lots of alcohol and poring over Dennis Altman's *Homosexual*,[16] he came out to his wife. It was the early 1970s and he was in his late 30s. Their separation was dramatic partly because, like many men in his situation, he felt guilty about being gay and betraying his wife, and partly because he discovered that his wife was having an affair.

Non-heterosexual fatherhood

The idea of non-heterosexual fatherhood presupposes a number of things, the most important of which is that gay men are ready and willing to take on fatherhood, that it is one of the many everyday experiments in which they, along with others, are involved in the suburbs of large cities the world over. To check the strength of the narrative underlying these everyday experiments, that is, that gay men were willing and able to take on fatherhood, to parent children with lesbian couples, by surrogacy or adoption, for example, I examined the answers the men from this combined sample gave to the question, 'How would your life be different if you were not gay?' It is both a simple question and an extremely significant one. Slightly fewer than half (81 men) of the combined sample of 177 men said that they *would have had* children if they had not been gay. The remaining men did not mention children, or indeed heterosexual marriage or a relationship with a woman, but commented on the qualitative differences between their gay life and an imagined life as a straight man. Their answers varied between those who said life as a non-gay man would be less interesting, more interesting, boring, easier, less adventurous, more socially aware than as a gay man.

What was significant about the men's answers is that almost all of them associated parenting and fatherhood with heterosexuality and

heterosexual couple relationships. Only one man, a 25-year-old from
Melbourne, said that being straight would have made having children
easier, in other words, that he intended having children but that
doing so would have been easier if he had been heterosexual.[17] Of the
81 men from the combined sample who mentioned having children,
99 per cent associated it with the heterosexual married ideal.

If this non-representative sample in any way mirrors the intimate and
parenting desires and practices of gay men, I would argue that alternative parenting narratives are not yet widely incorporated into narratives
of the self by which they understand themselves or the relationship
possibilities available to them. While alternative parenting practices
might be common knowledge in some districts of Manhattan, some
parts of north London, as well as in some pockets of some suburbs in
Auckland, Los Angeles, Manchester or Melbourne, it is likely that only
small cliques of privileged gay men share a similar awareness of fatherhood choices and possibilities in the major cities of the developing
world – in Hong Kong or Mumbai, for example. The strong impression
I have from analysing these data in light of other published research is
that alternative fatherhood is a practice only available to certain groups
of gay men in some parts of the First World.

Five men experienced fatherhood in settings *not* as a result of
sexual relations with a woman. These comprised three different non-
heterosexual settings. Gabriel and Tony belonged to that subset of gay
couples who arrange to father children with lesbian couples. Joseph
and Neville fostered children, and Bernard adopted a son. These three
non-heterosexual fatherhood settings are discussed in the context of
five men's stories of fatherhood. Three of the men were in their 30s, and
their stories are discussed in turn.

The first non-heterosexual fatherhood setting is the 'everyday experiment' that Weeks, Heaphy, and Donovan identified as one of the 'stories of choice' available to gays and lesbians today. This is where a gay
couple and a lesbian couple conceive a child by insemination (other
stories of choice include surrogacy).[18] From my sample, two men,
Gabriel (aged 43) and Tony (aged 33), arranged to have children with
lesbian couples. Gabriel was from Auckland and worked in the health
sector. During the course of our interview, he mentioned his son only
in passing, and did not give the impression when he did so that he
regarded gay fatherhood as exceptional. When analysing his transcript,
it occurred to me that his relationship with his son might have been
complicated by a number of factors. Looking over Gabriel's account of
his working life and relationship history, I got the impression that at least

three factors would have affected his parenting, and these were: (1) his relationship with the boy's mother(s) – for example, he did not mention access or any of the other sorts of shared arrangements that one would normally expect to hear about in cases of this kind of joint parenting; (2) whether he was in a relationship at the time his son was conceived and born and what involvement, if any, his former partner had with his (their) son; (3) he did not say and I did not ask him to tell me if he had been a sperm donor only and/or only marginally involved in his son's life.

Gabriel was well into another, stable relationship when I met him. His relationship with his son would have been affected therefore by his relations with the boy's mother(s), his former partner, and his current partner. Blended families such as this are becoming more common in some parts of some cities in the West and, as they do, they will affect conventional understandings of family and familial relationships.

Tony (aged 33) was the second man to have parented a child with a lesbian couple. As I have discussed elsewhere, Tony and his partner, who was 38, had been together nine years when they and a lesbian couple began making arrangements to have a child together. The detailed arrangements they made included plans for conception, birth, and the upbringing of their daughter – the seriousness of their intent starkly contrasting with the casual ordinariness in which so many new infants are conceived and born each year. Tony and his partner had been together for nine years when they were introduced to a lesbian couple who were interested in co-parenting a child. Both couples took some time to commit, and both agreed they wanted full involvement in their child's upbringing. As other research has shown, some gay men are content simply to be sperm donors and have nothing more to do with the child they helped conceive. Tony and his partner and the lesbian couple spent months getting to know each other and took part in joint couple therapy to make sure they shared common parenting values. Only after this extensive orientation process did they then formally document when and how often the parents would see their child, how holidays would be shared, and where the child would go to school.[19]

The second non-heterosexual fatherhood setting was that which two men and their partners had as foster parents. The first man was Joseph (aged 35). Together with his ex-partner, Joseph had looked after two teenage boys for three and a half years. The nature of the parenting and the manner of the care they provided the boys is discussed in the next section on fatherhood stories. The second man was Neville (aged 37), who had a fatherhood experience that was similar to the foster parent relationship of Joseph, except that the children Neville and his partner were fathering were related by birth:

> I tend to have a lot of my family living with me at various points of time. We have got a couple of young girls that have lived with us for most of their lives, from when they were three years old. ... The oldest girl spends every second weekend with us, and it's essentially a parental relationship. They are my nieces.

As an Aboriginal man, Neville described the relationship he had with his nieces and other relatives as familial, but 'not in a white-fella sense'. He did not describe it as foster parenting, which is my term, but simply as 'parental'. In Neville's view his relationship with his nieces was parental because he was able to provide and care for them in a relatively conventional family setting. Elsewhere I have described as 'gay nuclear' the type of family Joseph and his ex-partner and Neville and his partner provided for the children living with them.[20]

The third and final non-heterosexual fatherhood setting was revealed during the course of my interview with a 59-year-old expatriate living in Hong Kong. Bernard had a partner of 12 years, and when discussing the changed circumstances many gay men now enjoy, compared to how things were in the 1960s and 1970s, Bernard told me about his adopted son:

> It was very easy to adopt even as a single man and ... I hope it will become law very soon in open [-minded] countries. I adopted him when he was three weeks, so he grew up in a gay environment which had no influence on his [sexual] identity.

Bernard's experience of adopting, as a single man, was relatively trouble-free, and his musing was apposite as to whether the same could be said for the situation gay men now face who want to adopt a child. On this, George Chauncey writes that, while polls taken in the late 1990s in the USA showed fairly consistent opposition to gay marriage, they were beginning to show increasing support for the right of same-sex couples to adopt children. Popular support for non-heterosexual adoption has not always been reflected, however, in court decisions in state jurisdictions in the USA. Martha Nussbaum cites, for example, the case of a lesbian who lived with her daughter in a committed relationship with another woman. On the grounds of 'fitness' to be a parent, a Virginia court awarded custody of her child to the child's grandmother.

In the UK, Weeks *et al.* observe that non-heterosexuals may adopt but only as single parents,[21] while, in France, the situation is set to change. As mentioned in the following chapter on gay marriage, in 2012, the French government signalled its intention to introduce legislation in 2013 to allow same-sex couples the right to marry and to adopt children.

Fatherhood stories

I divided the men's fatherhood stories into four categories on the basis of the closeness of their relationships with their children. The first group of men maintained very close relationships with their children, and in doing so demonstrated what I call 'conscientious fathering'.[22] In the stories that these men told of their conscientious fathering, they revealed two things. First, they revealed the ordinary, everyday nature of fatherhood as they understood it, and second, they revealed a dedication and commitment in doing it well for the sake of the children in their care.

The second group of men was in regular contact with their children.[23] On the whole, these men were as interested in their children as were the men from the first group, but saw them less often because their children were adults and had their own familial responsibilities and duties.

The third group, which comprised two men, spoke of fairly distant relationships with their children.[24] They did not see their children often for two quite distinct reasons. In the case of the older man, his adult children had not warmly welcomed his coming out to them as a gay man, and in the case of the second man, who was living a double life, it suited him to keep his children at a distance so that he could conduct his clandestine gay relationship without undue surveillance.

The fourth group of men either made no mention of their children at all or said they never saw them.[25] It was difficult to be absolutely certain that two of the three men from this group were estranged from their children. Their interviews were remarkable, however, for the absence of any mention of their children, except to say that they existed. The third man had a sad story to relate of being prevented by his divorced wife from seeing his children before they reached adulthood.

Very close relations

The group of 12 men whose stories revealed very close parenting relationships included four of the five men who were non-heterosexual fathers, at least one of whom (Tony) showed signs of having developed very strong, long-lasting bonds with his new-born child – 'I want her all the time. I want to be a full-time parent' – thus exhibiting what Anthony McMahon calls the 'joys of fatherhood'.[26] For Tony, familial relationships had always been important and he, 'never imagined ... [he] could not be a parent'.

Joseph too valued familial relationships, as experienced in his birth family and his 'family of choice':[27]

> My biological family, that is, my parents and my sisters have always been important people to me. ... But I see my family as broader than that. I include in it some of the heterosexual friends I have had for decades.

The remaining eight men who had very close relations with their children became fathers in heterosexual settings. Included in this group of eight was a man in his 50s who despite the break-up of his 20-year marriage, 'had really nice relationships with ... [his] kids'. There were also two men who not only had very close relationships with their children but also maintained good, strong relations with their former wives, and a man who had resumed very close relations with his children after a separation his wife forced on them.

The first example of a gay father who had very close relationships with his children and also his wife was 64-year-old Clive from Canberra, who provided the following description of his merged family:

> It's curious because ... my wife from whom I have been separated for many years now, is a lesbian and living in a lesbian relationship. We have between us five children ... [and] having seen aspects of my life ... they seem to be remarkable and accepting of it.

In a brief story about relations with his children, Clive related how the family had gathered to mark his teenage son's premature death. All the members of Clive's merged family took part in preparing for the event and were present on the day:

> It was very sweet. There was no great ceremony. We just gathered. We had our lunch and ... my granddaughter watered the plant and we parted. I was happy and felt contented. When relations with my family work out ... I am happy.

Elaborating on the chance nature of good relations with his family, Clive explained how the imminent birth of another grandchild had affected him:

> My son and his wife are having another baby next week, and I have got a mobile telephone for the purpose, which I never had before, so they could call me when the baby is due, so I can go and look after their granddaughter. I think this is very nice. I also worry about it and think, 'Will I do it okay and how will I feel about it?' This is the cautiousness [I experience] even though they are loving towards me. As I described before it's curious because of the nature of my family. ... It is not your barbecue-in-the-backyard family, which is what the heterosexual life might have been.

The stories Clive told of the relationship with his children and wife were not of uniformly close relations. They did suggest, however, that good relations with family members were vital to his sense of self and wellbeing. Moreover, the transformation that they reveal – from heterosexual family man to gay father and a member of a fairly well-functioning, merged family – suggest a degree of mutual love, regard, and support between family members, as well as significant personal evolution and maturity on his part, especially in light of a confession Clive made in his interview about being a member of Alcoholics Anonymous.

The second example of a gay father who had very close relations with his children and former wife was Hector, an 81-year-old man from Melbourne. Hector was self-employed when I interviewed him, and in the 25th year of a same-sex relationship. He was not divorced from his wife and, as he explains below, regularly saw her on Sundays. Together they had had a daughter, who was in her 30s. At one point, Hector's wife had wanted to start divorce proceedings but, as he said, 'she's quite gone off the idea. And I never wanted to get a divorce. I didn't care. I didn't want to go off and get married to anybody else.' Relations between the members of Hector's merged family were both friendly and polite, as this extract shows:

> [My wife] has got a better brain than I have. ... She comes here most Sundays and ... always brings a computer which is sitting on her knee. As soon as we get busy with a job somewhere else or down in the garden she just goes on with her own work. ... She and [my partner] mercifully get on very well together ... and they have similar tastes in flowers and interest in and knowledge about flowers and

plants. They're both very good cooks and ... have conversations about flavour that I go to sleep in because I don't know what they're talking about. ... I haven't got the palate to perceive the subtleties that they're talking about.

As the quotation from Hector's interview that heads the chapter makes clear, relations with his daughter was the great joy of his life. 'Being a parent is one of the richest experiences in my life and one I would not have missed.' All things considered, Hector must be considered a lucky man. At 81, he had a daughter whom he loved, a wife with whom he had maintained a close and harmonious relationship, and a male partner of 25 years who, according to Hector, went out of his way to keep good relations with Hector's wife and daughter. The picture he paints is of a quaintly old-fashioned, affective triangle that persists and has meaning because of the goodwill of three people in their 70s and 80s.

The man who resumed close relations with his children after a separation that his wife forced on them was Austin who lived in Auckland. Austin said that as a 20-year-old man, he had no choice but to get married. The pressure to marry that he faced as a young man in rural New Zealand in the 1970s, he explained as follows:

My old man was a Korean [war] veteran. He would watch *Are You Being Served?* on television and say ridiculous things like, 'Look at that queer there! Shoot the fucker!' ... Was I going to come out to him? The hell I was ... 'You got balls boy! Use them! I want a grandchild!' ... So I married this woman.

Austin's marriage fell apart when news of his same-sex desires became public in the small, country town where he lived with his wife and children. He was taunted and threatened with violence at work. When he came out to his wife, she forbade his from seeing their children:

Their mother got a bit angry when I jumped out of the closet, but time went on and sometimes I think life's about Karma. It comes round and bites the person who is so nasty. ... They have nothing to do with her now because she was so nasty and kept them from me as they grew up. Anyway, she has to live with that.

Austin's life story was punctuated with experiences of cruelty and rejection at the hands of family members and in the workplace. When his children became adults, however, they sought him out and re-established good paternal relations. Now, according to Austin, the bond he has with his sons is very strong:

> I now know the meaning of care, love, support now ... from where it matters. Yeah, one hundred per cent. I was with them in the weekend. They are all boys. Yep. Well-rounded. I didn't see them for 12 years.

There is a strong redemptive theme in Austin's story. After many experiences of rejection and mistreatment, he was able nonetheless to rebuild his self-worth via renewed relations and regular contact with his sons.

Regular contact

Five men maintained regular contact with their children. These included one man who had been married for 20 years and in a same-sex relationships for more than 20 years (Terrence, aged 64), and two men who were married for more than 35 years and had been in same-sex relationships for 20 years respectively (Leslie, aged 74 and John, aged 65).

Terrence said very little about his adult children, but what he did say was significant: 'My children are important. They saved my relationship.' There are occasions in any interview when in retrospect it would have been beneficial to ask the participant to pause. This was one such occasion, but I did not interrupt Terrence's narrative. From memory it was because he had taken charge of the exchange and was explaining who or what were important in his life. He mentioned his children, explained that they saved his relationship, and in the next sentence said that their friends were important as well and, without drawing breath, told a brief story about their frequent get-togethers with their friends.

Leslie described his relationship with his children as positive and supportive, which he attributed to 'coming out over a number of years'. John was still in touch with his wife and children: 'I am very lucky because ... there is a lot of friendship there.' If the relationships these men had with their children were less close than those of the men from the previous group, this can be explained by the men's age. Their children were adults whom they saw regularly but not frequently. In the natural course of events, adult children are more removed from their parents than are young children, teenagers, or children in their 20s – this greater distance most often being as a result of their own familial or relationship obligations and duties. In many families, it is often grandchildren that become the compelling reason for increased frequency of contact between first and second generations.

Distant relations

Two men saw their children only occasionally. The first of these, 75-year-old Gerald, told a poignant story of his children's mixed reaction to news of his homosexuality. One of Gerald's daughters at first responded aggressively:

> She cross-examined me, 'Am I gay? How long have I been gay? Why did I not tell the family? And, if I was gay, how could I father children?' And questions like that, which was unbelievable.

In the end, and after more acute difficulties with his son, Gerald reconciled with all his three children. The response of Gerald's daughter underlines the fatherhood difficulties of earlier generations of gay men, many of whom were forced to choose between a double life and marriage in order to maintain relations with their children, or separation and divorce and the risk that they might see their children only occasionally – life choices that Weeks, Heaphy, and Donovan call 'stories of impossibilities'.[28]

The second man who kept only distant relations with his children was Douglas, a 63-year-old who lived in Melbourne. His intimate life was not straightforward. Divorced from his first wife, Douglas was still married to his second wife and had children from both marriages. His same-sex partner was a man in his 30s who lived in a flat that Douglas had bought for him. As mentioned in an earlier footnote in this chapter, Douglas identified as gay. When I asked him about relations with his children, he thought for a while, and then cautiously and carefully explained that one daughter suspected him of being gay, had asked some probing questions, and that on the basis of that experience he was determined to keep his sexuality hidden from them. Running twin households and keeping one of them secret as he was; being more emotionally and sexually involved with his same-sex lover as he was; and having adult children from two marriages, it is understandable that Douglas maintained only distant relations with them.

No contact

A fourth group of three men made no mention of their children or had no contact with them. Two of the men, Roy (aged 58), who was from Hobart, and Trevor (aged 49), from Melbourne, made no mention of their children during the interview, and I have assumed that because of this they had only minimal if any contact with their children. The third man, Hilton, who was aged 53 and lived in New York, spoke about his children and former wife. Hilton was 53 when interviewed and surprised me with his story of a relatively late-in-life coming out, short period of drug addiction, and a prison sentence.

When I met him, Hilton was working as a social worker in a predominantly African-American neighbourhood of New York. In his former career he had worked in the finance sector and enjoyed a successful life as a high-achieving white male, married with children. When he came out to his wife, she, like Austin's wife, stopped their children from having any contact with him. Coming out relatively late in life, Hilton was particularly aware of the fact that the new life he was leading was more varied and interesting than his former life as a married man:

> When I go back to college reunions ... I would see a lot of very bored straight men in ... very affluent situations ... I mean with all the crazy stuff I've done and all the places I have been, I have met really a far more interesting group of people.

He was aware also of missing out on seeing his children and being able to develop a relationship with them:

> I have not seen them in four years, and we have never really had a conversation about me being gay ... [and] one thing I fear is growing old and dying without ever being able to reconcile with them.

Hilton's fear of being estranged from his children for the rest of his life was not a melodramatic claim for I suspect that his recent experiences of drug use, prison, and becoming HIV positive had painfully coloured his outlook on life and inner calculations about his life expectancy.

What the fatherhood stories revealed of the men who maintained very close parenting relations with their children were their ordinary, everyday nature and the men's explicit understanding of what fatherhood entailed and their determination to undertake it as well and diligently as they could – for the good of their children or the children in their care. The evidence the men's stories revealed of a high level of conscientious fathering is in line with other published research.[29] The stories of regular contact, distant relations, and no contact revealed a number of different types of stories. The men who maintained regular contact with their children often showed an interest that varied only slightly from the close contact the previous group of men demonstrated. The reason I categorised the second group of men as being only in regular contact with their children is because their children were adult and, as I argued, it is a fairly accepted social fact that adult children see their parents only infrequently because they have their own lives to lead and often their own children to look after. The two men with what I described as 'distant relations' with their children provided their own idiosyncratic explanations for the relations they had with their children. The first man saw his children infrequently because they had not easily accepted his coming out as a gay man. The second man led a double life, and it suited him for that reason to keep the children of his two marriages at a distance and to see them at significant family functions only, such as Christmas or birthdays.

It was difficult to come to any strong conclusion about the three men whose relations with their children I described in the negative, that is, who had no relations with them. Two of the men, both of whom were from Australia, did not mention their children in their interview except to say that they had children. My assumption was that they rarely saw them, either because the children had not accepted their father's gayness or because the children were estranged for some other reason, as often occurs after divorce. There was a third man, however, who did speak about his children and his yearning to reconcile with them after divorcing their mother. This man lived in New York and had been through a confronting time, which included extensive drug use, a prison sentence, and a diagnosis that he was HIV positive. His longing to repair relations with his children was both natural and possibly also a consequence of the extreme life-changing events he had experienced since coming out.

Conclusion

Heterosexual fatherhood represented the experience of the majority of the 22 men interviewed for this chapter. The heterosexual relationships that these men began when they were young men most likely occurred as a result of social pressure to conform to heteronormative values, being unsure about their sexual identity, or because marriage was the conventional means for channelling sexual desire. The omnipresence of heterosexual fatherhood was in evidence when a substantial majority of men from the combined data set said that having children would be easier if they had been straight. If these findings are representative of the average gay man's views on fatherhood, they suggest that alternative fatherhood narratives have not yet won widespread acceptance and that a strong, pervasive story continues to associate parenthood with the heterosexual married ideal.

It is reasonable to assume, however, that the incidence of non-heterosexual fatherhood will increase, representing as it does everyday experiments on which young gay and lesbian people are increasingly prepared to embark in advanced, western democracies like Australia, Britain, and the USA. The speed at which this change will occur is unclear. There will be pockets of rapid change, neighbourhoods or suburbs in major cities in the West, for example, where a greater preponderance will be found of non-heterosexual couples engaged in alternative parenting arrangements. Findings from the research for this chapter showed that the men most likely to engage in everyday experiments involving conception with a lesbian couple or through surrogacy or artificial insemination were from the younger age cohorts and relatively advantaged, and that the men who were fathers as a result of previous heterosexual relationships tended to be from the older age cohorts, who had come out relatively late in life.

The fatherhood stories that men interviewed for this chapter related ranged from accounts of intense, involved fathering – including those from four of the five non-heterosexual fathers, as well as men in their 50s and one in his 60s – to relationships that were regular and close, to more distant relationships and no relationship at all. Factors that affected the men's level of involvement with their children included, for example, experiences associated with coming out and the behaviour of other family members. The accounts the men related of intense, involved fathering reflected an explicit dedication and willingness to commit to fathering, which is in contrast to two prevailing stereotypes: that men are generally unwilling to devote time to caring for their children unless asked to do so by their wife or female partner, and that gay men are notable for their self-centredness. The men's accounts were remarkable also for the evidence they showed of their casual acceptance of the ordinariness of their involvement in and commitment to their children's care. Finally, what the stories analysed here show is that the growing number of successful non-heterosexual fatherhood experiments are opening up all sorts of gay fatherhood possibilities that were not available to previous generations of gay men.

5
Marriage

As friends my own age who are heterosexual get less
and less into the idea of traditional marriage ... the
gays have really embraced ... [the] bluestone church
and black and white tuxedo. ... Gays are pretty much
the only ones who really care about marriage these
days. If you took away the right of marriage from heterosexual twenty-somethings, they would not care.

(Denis, aged 27, Melbourne)

Introduction

In an earlier chapter on long-lasting relationships, I referred to evidence
showing how in the West, as well as in cities like Mumbai and Hong
Kong, gay men were capable of conducting stable, long-term relationships resembling the companionate marriage in all but name, and had
a history of doing so. This chapter and the next are paired because
they both consider the views of the men from the international sample
regarding the push for marriage equality or formal recognition of same-
sex relationships. In this chapter, I examine the arguments of those men
who favoured marriage equality, and in the chapter that follows will
examine the arguments of the men who opposed it. These two chapters
most clearly reflect aged-based differences of opinion among gay men.
As the discussion in this chapter shows, it is men aged 31 and younger
who most uniformly support marriage equality; while, by contrast, in
the next chapter, the strongest arguments against gay marriage are to be
found in the views of men aged 51 and older.

The evidence presented in Chapter 3 to show gay men were able and willing to maintain relatively stable relationships, resembling companionate

marriage in all but name, contrasts with the picture of the fairly radical change sociologists Zygmunt Bauman, Ulrich Beck and Elizabeth Beck-Gernsheim argue has taken place in the couple relationship since the 1960s and 1970s. The change these authors identify in couple relationships, of increased flexibility and fragility, they argue, was brought about by mass individualisation and its twin consequences, rising rates of divorce and rates of remarriage. The paradox here is that despite the serious structural changes that have affected heterosexual marriage, a substantial minority of men from an international sample of 97 men showed strong evidence of a capacity to commit to and maintain companionate-like relationships. In this chapter, I consider the arguments that men from the international sample made in favour of gay marriage or civil union and civil partnership, in the context of (a) the greater freedom that western heterosexuals now have to make and break relationships and then to try all over again, and (b) the enthusiasm with which young men regard gay marriage – men like Denis who is quoted at the head of this chapter.

Social agitation for same-sex marriage rights gained momentum in the mid 1990s when the worst of the HIV-AIDS epidemic was over in the West.[1] Canadian historian Angus McLaren argues that at that time, the 'havoc of AIDS' created for many gay people in North America a 'nostalgia for family life', and US historian George Chauncey maintains that it was the lesbian and gay baby boom together with the AIDS crisis that provided the impetus for the gay marriage project in North America.[2] Regarding the effect of HIV-AIDS on gay men's personal and communal lives, I would argue that the experience many gay men had during the HIV-AIDS crisis in countries like Britain and New Zealand – of being shut out from their lover or partner's funeral or when hospitals gave priority to members of dying men's birth families and not their partners – contributed to the determination of gay-marriage activists to seek legislative certainty and security for same-sex-couple relationships. A Melbourne man in his 50s said during his interview that as a result of gay men's experiences in the 1990s he learned that gay people must influence the movement for same-sex marriage:

> When AIDS was about … I saw some very ugly family behaviour around money and property then. … I saw people move in on the partners of people who had died. And to me that's a big part of what the whole [gay marriage] argument is actually about, and I … wish the gay and lesbian community would keep making that point.[3]

The Dutch historian Gert Hekma makes a stronger political argument, which is that, as the HIV-AIDS epidemic created what he calls a 'struggle for monogamy', the irony for gay men was that, being denied the right to marry, they were thus shut out of the 'institution that belongs to monogamy'. It was this realisation in the 1990s that spurred on the movement for marriage equality in Europe.[4] As has often been the case when social reform has been required in the West, it is the Nordic countries that lead the way, followed by more socially enlightened countries elsewhere. In 1989, for example, Denmark passed legislation to provide 'registered partnership for same-sex couples'–which was followed by Norway, Sweden, and Iceland in the 1990s and Finland in 2001. In 2005, Britain did the same, creating 'civil partnership' status for same-sex couples. The first country to provide for same-sex marriage was Holland, which did so in 2001. By 2008, the following countries had passed legislation allowing same-sex marriage – Belgium, Canada, South Africa, and Spain.[5] In 2013, the same rights will apply to same-sex couples in France, who will have the right also to adopt children.[6]

In countries where neo-liberalism has a stronger hold, such as Australia and the United States, the response has been to pass legislation restating the heterosexual nature of marriage and its primacy. For example, according to Canadian historian Angus McLaren, when Scandinavian governments passed laws in the late 1980s and early 1990s to allow same-sex unions, 'the United States House of Representatives proposed a Defence of Marriage Bill which strictly defined marriage as the union of one man and one woman'.[7] This moral panic that same-sex marriage aroused in parts of the USA was, in the view of anthropologist Gilbert Herdt, the result of deeply felt concerns about social change as well as political expediency in Washington. Herdt argues that the resistance that developed to the push for same-sex marriage occurred because of (a) middle America's fears about changing gender roles in marriage and the pace of social reform and (b) a game of 'wedge' politics that former US President Bush played with his liberal opponents:

> The great fear of 'gay marriage' in the United States is associated in many people's minds with ... President George W. Bush's January 20, 2004, State of the Union address ... [in which] he ... referred to the 1996 Defense of Marriage Act (DOMA), that restricts marriage to a man and a woman, as 'the most fundamental, enduring institution of our civilization'.[8]

In addition to political and social factors in the USA, historian Nancy Polikoff argues that the legal status of the family there presents an obstacle to marriage reform. She explains that a central reason for the difficulties same-sex reformers face in the USA is that in that country a set of important legal rights are exclusively attached to marriage and the married couple, namely, 'retirement and death benefits, healthcare … family leave, immigration, taxation, and dissolution of relationships'. Unlike the USA, in a number of other western democracies legislation is in place to provide couples in civic partnerships with equivalent rights to married couples. In Canada, for example, same-sex couples are now permitted to marry and cohabiting couples of all variety, according to Polikoff, have 'virtually all the legal consequences of marriage'.[9]

The situation in New Zealand and Australia is different from the approach the Canadians adopted in relation to same-sex marriage. In New Zealand, same-sex couples and heterosexual couples can enter civil unions, but only heterosexual couples may marry. In contrast to what applies in the USA, cohabiting couples in New Zealand enjoy virtually the same legal rights as do married couples. Same-sex marriage is not legal in Australia, but Federal laws allow cohabiting heterosexual couples the same rights as married couples and state laws recognise same-sex couples on the same terms as cohabiting heterosexual couples.[10] In 2009, after the matter was referred to the Australian Parliament, a committee of the Senate recommended against allowing the legalisation of same-sex marriage and that the original definition of marriage be retained as between a woman and a man.[11] This decision disappointed many, as does the fact that both major political parties in Australia seem afraid to support gay marriage for fear of a negative electoral response at elections. The Honourable Michael Kirby, former justice of the High Court of Australia, summed up the situation in Australia as follows:

> Whilst so many countries have leapt ahead to 'open up' marriage to same-sex couples, Australian governments have refused even to contemplate civil unions and civil partnerships. Even Spain and Portugal and Argentina have same-sex marriage. But in Australia we've banned civil unions and civil partnerships. This is a humiliating and outrageous denial of civil equality. According recognition in matters of pensions, money and material things is good and fitting. But denying equality in a matter that concerns the dignity and respect due to precious long-term relationships is hurtful and against society's interest. Money is not enough. Dignity, recognition and acceptance are precious in their own right.[12]

When in 2012 members of both major political parties in Australia voted against a private member's bill to legalise same-sex marriage, it was defeated in the Australian Parliament.[13] The defeat of this bill means that federal law in Australia will not change and that marriage firmly remains as between a woman and a man. Legalisation of same-sex marriage might yet occur in Australia, however, because some state governments are preparing to introduce same-sex marriage legislation.[14]

By 2011, seven European states, namely, Norway, Spain, Belgium, Portugal, Holland, Sweden, and Iceland allowed gay couples to marry, and civil partnerships or civil unions were legal in Britain and Germany.[15] In Britain, the public debate was complicated by opposition same-sex marriage proposals aroused from churches, other religious bodies, social conservatives, and some gay and lesbian groups, while attracting support from traditional conservatives such as the Tory Party leadership and metropolitan newspapers including *The Times*.[16] When, for example, the Scottish Parliament decided in 2012 that it would legalise gay marriage, allowing gay couples to marry in civil ceremonies or religious ceremonies, where religious institutions allow such ceremonies,[17] a spokesperson for the Catholic Church in Scotland said same-sex relationships were dangerous and should not be encouraged:

> We ... believe that same-sex relationships are profoundly harmful both physically, biologically, mentally, emotionally and ... spiritually to those involved.[18]

And yet, despite the considerable opposition from churches and social conservatives in the UK, in February 2013, the House of Commons voted by a considerable majority to pass a bill legalising same-sex marriage.[19]

In contrast to the push for gay marriage in Australasia, Europe, and North America, and the public debates it has generated, a recent study of Chinese gay men suggests that in Hong Kong, a significant international metropolis and financial centre, gay men are less interested in same-sex marriage than their western counterparts and more intent on enjoying the many other relationships types and/or sexual scripts with which gay men in the West have been experimenting since the early 1920s. According to the study, this is largely because Chinese gay men are neither willing nor prepared to upset the power of the traditional Chinese family, which continues to prevail in Hong Kong.[20]

Broadly speaking, three principal arguments are made in favour of legalising same-sex marriage, all of which relate to equality in terms of property, relational, and ceremonial rights. The first of these arguments concerns equal property and legal rights, and is a strong feature of the work of North American legal scholar Martha Nussbaum. Nussbaum argues that a common-sense approach to marriage equality ought to lead reasonable people to accept that gay men are entitled to access to the same financial benefits that married heterosexuals enjoy. In the USA, these benefits are connected with an individual's marital status, so, she argues, it is inequitable that gay people are denied them because their relationships are not recognised in law in the same way as marriage.[21] From my analysis (below) of the interviews of many of the young men in this sample, it is clear that this discourse has seeped into debates in western countries other than the USA.

The second argument centres on equal relational status and recognition and has its genesis in the work of the sociologist Georg Simmel. Simmel wrote that marriage's chief purpose was for the care of children. He argued also that by its existence as a privileged social institution, marriage creates a hierarchy of relationships, 'a direct superiority of the [married] group with respect to a group without marriage'.[22] As mentioned, Gert Hekma argues that marriage has pre-eminent status because it is the institution of monogamy, while Martha Nussbaum maintains that legalising gay marriage would validate gay relationships, thus countering the stereotype that gay people live transient, promiscuous lives. In addition, it would encourage them to form what she calls, 'stable domestic units', ordinarily associated with marriage.[23] Support of the kind that Hekma and Nussbaum make in favour of same-sex unions is what Michael Warner calls the 'normalized movement', which other commentators describe as 'assimilationism'.[24]

The third argument in favour of legalising same-sex marriage concerns the sense of ceremonial prestige that has come to be associated with marriage in the eyes of many young straight couples, and by extension many young gay couples. Andrew Cherlin argues that since marriage has been transformed into a status symbol, the ceremony is no longer organised by and for the family, and that 'the wedding ... has become an important symbol of the partners' personal achievements and a stage in their self development'.[25] I would argue that in a desire to register by marriage the success of their relationship achievement, gay couples are no different from straight couples. As well, I would argue that this desire – to make public the success of their relationship – is likely to be even stronger among gay people for the very reason that they have had to achieve it often in the face of public apathy, antipathy, and, in some cases, hostility.

On this last point, there is plenty of evidence below in my discussion on the 'ceremonial' argument that men in their 40s and younger make for gay marriage to support Cherlin's argument that marriage is now regarded as a marker of prestige and status, and my argument that this applies equally to gay couples and straight couples. In the sample I used for this chapter, it was among men aged 31 and younger that I found strongest support for gay marriage, while men over 51 were most likely to oppose it. These generational differences between gay men's attitudes to gay marriage are an important, recurring focus of this chapter and the next.[26]

Everyday lives and gay marriage

My analysis of the men's interviews showed that gay marriage was of greatest importance to young men, in particular men aged in their 30s and younger, and was less important to men aged 51 and older. Each interviewee was asked if he was married, intended to marry, or would like to marry. Set questions notwithstanding, I allowed the men to explain their views on gay marriage very generally, and did not insist that they answer each part of each question separately. At times, their answers included a short explanation as to why they favoured formal recognition of same-sex relationships but not marriage; sometimes they did not. On other occasions, some men conflated gay marriage with civil union (as it is known in Australia, India, New Zealand, and the United States) or civil partnership (as it is known in Britain and Hong Kong).[27] And then again, there were times when men spoke specifically against marriage because they associated it with Christianity or religion and were agnostic, atheist, or anti-religious because they were disenchanted with formal religion, which was particularly the case with men from this sample and others with whom I have had informal discussions who were brought up Catholic.

The breakdown of men's views on gay marriage is as follows: 62 men, or almost two-thirds of the sample, said they were in favour of formal recognition of same-sex relationships, including gay marriage.[28] For the purpose of analysing the data, I divided these 62 men into three age cohorts on the basis of their views on gay marriage.[29] The first group comprised men aged between 18 and 31, who turned and will turn 21 after 2000; all these men reached and will reach social maturity at a time when HIV-AIDS was relatively contained in the West. Almost all of these men favoured gay marriage. The second group was made up of men aged 32–51, who turned 21 between 1980 and the late 1990s, and thus reached social maturity when the HIV-AIDS epidemic was at its most virulent and socially stigmatising. The third group consisted of men aged between 51 and 87, who turned 21 between the mid1940s and late 1970s; what these men shared in common is that all reached social maturity before the advent of HIV-AIDS.

I have used the HIV-AIDS epidemic in the West as a cohort marker because, as I discuss in more detail in Chapter 7, apart from the gay liberation movement in the 1960s and 1970s, it was the single most important, life-changing event for hundreds of thousands of gay men and its effects are still being felt. In the sections that follow, the views of each group are discussed in turn.

In brief, three main themes arose from my analysis of the men's arguments about legalising same-sex relationships. The two younger cohorts mainly drew on two narratives when explaining their support of gay marriage. These were a strong desire for first, relational and legal/property equality, and second, recognition of relationship success along similar lines to the affirmation that young heterosexual couples receive when they marry. The men from the old cohort drew on these narratives as well but also included a third narrative to explain their support for gay marriage, which was the continuation of an involvement in social politics that began in the days of gay liberation.

Men aged 31 and younger

A total of 22 men, or slightly more than one fifth of the international sample of 97 men, were aged 31 and younger at the time of interview.[30] Of these, 19 said they favoured formal recognition of same-sex relationships, two men were unsure, and one said he opposed gay marriage; in other words, a significant majority of younger men favoured formal recognition of same-sex relationships. A breakdown of the 19 men who supported formal recognition of same-sex relationships showed 14 unequivocally favouring gay marriage and five men supporting civil union or civil partnership, but not marriage.[31] More than two-thirds of these men were in relationships when interviewed, and seven were single.[32] None of the men was in a civil union or gay marriage, and none was formerly married to or had been in a relationship with a woman or was a parent.

A majority of men aged 31 and younger were therefore in relationships, which, by their duration, suggested they were fairly successfully experimenting with couple relationships. Because none of these younger men was in a civil union or gay marriage, their views on and attitudes toward formal recognition of same-sex relationships more strongly represent expectations and beliefs than lived experience.

The rest of this section is devoted to the three principal narratives that the 14 men drew on who supported gay marriage, which are as follows. First, the men referred to a rights discourse. The second narrative concerned a less frequently stated desire for ceremonial equality, while the third narrative concerned the extent to which marriage equality was linked to social rights. Each of these narratives is discussed in turn.

Legal and property rights

The practical benefits of marriage ran through the reasons four Melbourne men in their 20s gave for gay marriage.[33] All four men had been to elite, private schools, were enrolled in university courses and were from upper-class or upper-middle-class backgrounds. The social practices they revealed elsewhere in their interviews were markedly different from those of earlier cohorts of gay men, who tended to be more fully involved in the social institutions of the gay world and to include gay friends in their friendship group after coming out.[34] As the stories of the four show, only a small proportion of their close friends were gay; most of them avoided the gay scene, and their preference was to socialise with straight friends.

Underlining these men's arguments for marriage equality was a keen awareness that they should not be denied the same rights and privileges that their heterosexual siblings or cousins could expect to enjoy or that their sexuality should affect the privilege of class – about which they were well aware, as the following extract from Garth's interview shows:

> I can see the benefits [of gay marriage] for tax purposes and division of estate ... if someone dies ... [which] makes it completely understandable as to why you'd want to. And if two people want to show that they are committed to each other like that, then they should be able to.

One reason young men from middle- and upper-class backgrounds can be so aware of property and legal rights is because these are likely to be topics of conversation when they are living with their parents or in houses shared with friends as they move into adult life. Garth's argument in favour of gay marriage neatly combined the legal/property strand and the relational strand of an equal-rights narrative, referring to as he did considerations relating to tax and property (inheritance) as well as an expectation that same-sex couples were entitled to marriage equality when they 'show that they are committed to each other'.

Ceremonial

Four men from the young cohort made a special point of arguing in favour of relationship equality because they wanted to be able to have a marriage similar to their parents' and/or a white wedding or ceremonial occasion similar to a wedding. All these men were in their 20s. Three were from Melbourne, and one was from Hong Kong. The two youngest men – who were from Melbourne – were at university; the third man from Melbourne worked in the entertainment industry, and the man from Hong Kong worked in health.[35]

Denis (aged 27) worked in entertainment in Melbourne, and was positive about his life and future prospects as a gay man. His coming out had not been easy, but his parents now accepted his gayness. He travelled when he was in his early 20s and had a group of supportive friends, gay and straight alike. Denis was very pleased that he might be able to marry and, as the quotation from his interview that heads this chapter shows, he believed that gay men's enthusiasm for marriage contrasted with the declining interest of young heterosexuals. Published research shows that today in western countries, cohabitation is more popular with people in their 20s than it was for their grandparents' generation and possibly their parents' generation, and that heterosexual couples are marrying later, which means that while it might appear to a person like Denis that his straight friends show no sign of wanting to marry, the reality in 10 years' time could be quite different when they begin to marry in their mid to late 30s.[36]

Curtis (aged 29) lived in Hong Kong and worked in Health. In his spare time, he worked as a sex educator, spending Friday and Saturday nights doing the rounds of nightclubs and saunas to hand out condoms and spread advice about safe sex to gay men. His views on gay marriage were multi-layered. In the first place, he said that gay men in Hong Kong regarded gay marriage as the 'gold standard'. In the second place, while as a document on its own, the marriage certificate was of little importance to him, he was strongly attracted to the ceremonial aspect of marriage. 'I like the wedding ceremony,' he said, 'and a party and the couple promising a life in the future together.'

Two university students from Melbourne, Todd (aged 21) and Jarrad (aged 23), shared similar views about wedding ceremonies. Like other men his age who were interviewed for this study, Jarrad was excited by the prospect of his own marriage, drawing on an age-old story of love and romance when he said: 'I would like to find someone and get married and spend the rest of our lives together.' His reason for so keenly wanting the opportunity to marry appeared also to have its origins in the relationship history of his parents and grandparents, which he revered: 'I come a family where both my parents are together, my grandparents on one side just had their 60th wedding anniversary and ... are still very much in love.' Jarrad seemed to assume a link between the longevity of his parents and grandparents' relationships, their relational happiness, and the fact that they had married. Implicit in his assumption was a link between marriage and the promise of a life-long romantic and sexual relationship.

Jarrad's views and those of Curtis touch on twin themes associated with the ceremonial aspect of marriage as one of the reasons young gay men so strongly favour gay marriage. The first theme is the picture of a white wedding representing the romance and love components of successful, life-long, couple relationships. The second theme is that, white wedding or not, marriage is important to young people for the reasons that Cherlin outlined, as marker of prestige and achievement.

Social rights

Two men referred to broader social change when explaining why they supported marriage equality. Both the men were in their early 20s; one was from Mumbai, the other from Melbourne.[37] Their views are notable for two reasons: first, because of the belief that the man from Mumbai expressed in political activism as a means to effect social change, in this case, to bring about greater acceptance of homosexuality in India, and second, an associated belief, which the man from Melbourne expressed, in the inevitability of change toward greater acceptance of gay men in the West.

Giles was a 23-year-old university student who lived in Mumbai. Following a holiday in a northern city, where he had a brief affair with a political activist, he had returned to Mumbai and resumed his studies. In the following extract, Giles explains why gay marriage is important to middle-class, educated, Indian men his age:

> If you want people to change and accept you, you have to accept that marriage is the only way to change the perception ... that if you are gay or lesbian, you only want to sleep around, go partying, you just want to hook up, you just want to do one-night-stand, you just want to fuck around. They [heterosexual people] think like that if you are gay. But if you really want to change your image in front of the straights or your community, you have to accept you are gay and you have to marry a guy. Then they will accept that you are a normal-life

guy who will be with one guy only. I am totally into the marriage scenario. I am one guy who believes we have to marry.

Not all the Indian men in their 20s made the same connection as did Giles between gay marriage and the project to achieve greater acceptance of homosexuality in India, but all that I spoke to were aware of the size of the task they faced in working toward greater acceptance of GLBT people in India. It is notable also that no western gay man (of any age) made the same connection between marriage equality and the struggle against homophobia. I believe the acute awareness that Giles revealed can be explained by the unique historical situation in which Indian men who identify as gay find themselves in the 2010s. They are uniquely placed because of a conjunction of three important changes taking place in how same-sex desire and same-sex relationships are understood in India. First, same-sex-attracted Indian men are living at a time when the Indian middle classes are increasingly aware of homosexuality as a personal identity and way of life. Second, educated Indian men are well aware and informed of gay liberation as it occurred in western countries in the 1970s, including its histories, ideologies, and practices. Third, educated men in India who identify as gay are well aware of the political agitation for marriage equality that is taking place in countries like Australia, Britain, New Zealand, and the USA, news of which is spread via the Internet and the large number of same-sex support groups and information websites that it hosts. All the Indian men interviewed for this book demonstrated a sophisticated knowledge of gay liberation rhetoric, ideologies, and current web-based discussions and debates affecting same-sex-attracted people.

Zane (aged 22) was living in Melbourne when I interviewed him in 2010; like Giles from Mumbai, he too was a university student. In the following extract Zane explained why he believes gay marriage is inevitable in Australia.

In another five years, it will be so accepted and if the law hasn't changed here by then I'll be very surprised. And even under the current government ... [there are] Penny Wong ... in cabinet ... [and] she's an 'out' lesbian ... [and] people like Bob Brown ... in the Senate. ... This is something that will change and it is literally just got to take another ... five years worth of deaths up the top for it [opposition to gay marriage] to fall down. I am at one of the best universities in Australia, studying with people who all share the ... same opinion as me. ... These are the people that are going to get power next, so there's no way that this is going to stay the way it is.

Zane's understanding of marriage equality in Australia is based on two assumptions. His first assumption is that because two prominent politicians in Australia – the Hon. Penny Wong and Senator Bob Brown – have made public their homosexuality, marriage equality will follow.[38] His second assumption is that marriage equality will occur because people like him, who are 'at one of the best universities in Australia', favour it; in other words, social change is both generational and likely to occur when it is supported by people who belong to the privileged classes.

At the time of writing, the only Australian political party that supported marriage was the Australian Greens, the leader of which was Senator Brown. The two major political parties in the country, the Australian Labor Party and the Liberal Party of Australia, formally opposed gay marriage and were on record as stating that they understood marriage to be a union between a woman and a man. One notable exception to this is the Hon. Malcolm Turnbull, former Leader of the Opposition and former leader of the Liberal Party who as Shadow Minister for Communications gave a speech in July 2012 in favour of legalising civil unions for gay people.[39] As mentioned, state governments in Australia have already legislated to provide same-sex couples with equivalent rights to those enjoyed by de facto (cohabiting) heterosexual couples.

In summary, then, a majority of the young men (31 years and younger) favoured formal recognition of same-sex relationships. Support for gay marriage evoked three main narratives: the right to legal and relational equality, the ideal of the wedding day, and marriage linked to social change. It is significant also that no one from this group argued for marriage because they wanted to have children. I mention parenthood in this context because research into heterosexual couple relationships suggests that couples are more likely to consider moving from cohabitation to marriage when the prospect arises of pregnancy or childbirth.[40]

Men aged 32–51

A total of 34 men, or slightly more than a third of the international sample, were aged 32–51 at the time of interview, the bulk of whom were in their 40s.[41] In this group 24 men said they supported formal recognition of same-sex relationships, five said they opposed gay marriage, and five men were unsure. In other words, slightly less than three-quarters of this group favoured formal recognition of same-sex relationships – a lower proportion than for the previous group, but still a majority. Of these 24 men, 16 unequivocally favoured gay marriage and eight men said they would support a civil union or civil partnership, but not gay marriage.[42]

Half of the men in this age cohort were single, and half were in relationships at the time of interview.[43] Three of the men were in a civil union or civil partnership, and three men were in a gay marriage.[44] Two of the men were formerly married, and one man had an adopted child. In other words, half the men aged between 32 and 51 were in relationships. The duration of their relationships suggested a strong degree of relative permanency, which it is reasonable to assume would be the case for people this age. And, of the 17 men in relationships, slightly more than a third were in either a civil union, civil partnership, or gay marriage.

The remainder of this section is devoted to the two narratives these mainly middle-aged supporters of gay marriage drew on. Like the younger men, their first narrative concerned a belief in the right to relationship equality with heterosexuals, and the legal and property rights attached to heterosexual marriage, which they said underlined the need for gay marriage. Their second narrative centred on the type of ceremonies appropriate to a same-sex marriage or civil union. In contrast to what the younger men said, the options the men from this group considered did not include a 'white wedding'.

Legal and property rights

Three men spoke in favour of marriage equality and associated legal and property rights; two of these three were in their 40s, and the third was in his early 30s. Two of the men were from Hong Kong, one was from London, and all were born in Asia or South Asia.[45] Ethan, who was 49 and lived in London, said that if he owned property and were in a relationship, he would be want to be married: 'just for the sake of inheritance and ... next of kin, things like that'. His preference was for same-sex marriage because it promised each partner the same rights that came with heterosexual marriage:

> I would want to be the same, not equal and different. ... I think there should be just one thing and that's it ... [because] if I were to get married, I would want it to be the same as my heterosexual neighbour.

One possible reason for Ethan's preference for marriage and not civil partnership might be that, as he had been born outside Britain, he was more attuned to the rights the British government guaranteed a married couple: 'the UK doesn't insist that ... [civil partnership] is recognised by the rest of the world, which it does with marriage'.

Felix, who was 41 and lived in Hong Kong, was fairly pragmatic also about how marriage would be of use to Chinese gay men his age. He discounted the link between romance and marriage, and instead focused on the rights that married couples enjoyed, arguing that if gay marriage were introduced in Hong Kong, 'or any kind of ... civil union, if it does not have equal rights, it does not mean anything to me'. Alexander, who was 34 and also from Hong Kong, put forward a neo-liberal reason for supporting gay marriage. He first said that he viewed marriage functionally, as, 'a licence the society gives you as a recognition to live together and have a family'. He then said that providing gay men with relationship equality was the only purpose that made gay marriage worthwhile in his eyes: 'if it is not for equality and it's for something else, I don't really see how it's adding any value'.

Ceremonial

The men in this age bracket held varying views on the matter of weddings and ceremonies for same-sex marriages or unions. They are represented here by accounts of four men, three of whom were in their 40s, the fourth in his early 30s. Two of the men were from London, one was from Hong Kong, and one was from Sydney. One of the four men was strongly in favour of the idea of gay men 'putting on a show' for their marriages, and had done so for his own marriage;[46] one man strongly opposed anything that resembled a wedding;[47] and two men said that they preferred an understated event.[48]

Danny and his partner were married and lived in Hong Kong. They had had two services, one was in Hong Kong and one was in the United States. Danny's thinking on the matter is captured in the following extract:

> Weddings are quite interesting. A gay wedding [is interesting] because its story book is written too and ... as you approach a gay wedding you have to ask, 'What's the formula; are you going to use the religious angle, are you going to have the bride and groom, are you going to follow the straight format for a wedding or are you ... creative again and write your own chapter?' We had a beautiful wedding. ... We held it in a great space ... but we handed all the keys to this wedding to our friends. The decorations were done by certain friends ... someone would get up and sing a song and someone would dance, and we had

no idea what was going on. So we broke the model of what a wedding was because we ... created an experience that we were into and our friends were into instead of having a church, a bride and a groom and ... formality ... and it was beautiful.

At least two points stand out in Danny's extract. Aware of the dominant wedding story and its heteronormative variations, he and his partner decided to create one of their own. The second point of interest is that in order to rewrite the dominant wedding story, Danny and his partner asked their friends to take a major role, if not the major role, in the ceremonies to celebrate their marriage. And, according to Danny's account, their decision to do so meant the event was a surprise for everyone who attended, including the two grooms.

In research conducted in the mid-2000s, Carol Smart identified four different types of same-sex wedding ceremonies: 'regular', 'minimalist', 'religious', and 'demonstrative'. The only one of these categories that described the wedding ceremony of Danny and his partner was 'demonstrative' wedding, the features of which are as follows:

Weddings ... that took an incredible amount of planning, becoming almost military campaigns in some cases. ...Couples in this category often planned to have complementary or matching wardrobes, often had rings especially made, invited large numbers of people and might hire a wedding planner. They set the ceremony or party in a very grand or unusual setting (e.g. a museum), the celebrations might go on for several days, unusual cakes would appear, or the whole affair would simply be tasteful but terribly expensive.[49]

Where Danny and his partner's ceremony differed from Carol Smart's demonstrative type was in their decision to hand responsibility for decorations and entertainment to their friends, which meant therefore that the planning was undertaken in a more democratic or anarchic manner. In other respects, their ceremony fitted her criteria because their wedding was highly organised, held in 'a great space', and 'created an experience that ... [their] friends were into'.

In contrast to Danny's account and experience of a celebratory service were the views of Ethan and Jonathon, both of whom were from London, and Dylan, who was from Sydney. In the earlier section on equal rights, Ethan explained that he preferred marriage over a civil union because of the property rights that the former guaranteed. On the matter of marriage ceremony, however, it was very clear that he opposed anything resembling a marriage service: 'I have not the slightest desire to have or even attend a religious gay marriage. I think it is absolutely ridiculous.' Ethan did not expand on why he thought a religious gay marriage 'absolutely ridiculous', and I forgot to ask him to explain. My impression at the time of interview, however, was that Ethan disliked the idea of a marriage ceremony on the grounds of class and taste, which are intertwined, and that in his view the white wedding, which is reified in women's and men's fashion and gossip magazines, was something he would neither attend as a guest nor celebrate as a man marrying. It was not something someone from his class would do – because in his view it is a clichéd practice, and for this reason kitsch and to be avoided.

While Jonathon from London and Dylan from Sydney did not object to the idea of a ceremony, each said he would prefer something understated. Jonathon said that he and his partner, who had been together for ten years, understood the commitment service to be a private affair:

> We will get married but it's very much about us and the two of us. ... It's not about making a big statement to the world. We have been together for such a long time, everybody knows about it.

At the time of interview, Jonathon and his partner had been cohabiting for 10 years. Their experience is evidence for Lynn Jamieson's argument that couples will now often spend years cohabiting before they marry, and that the numbers of couples doing so has increased as the trend to marry early declined. Their behaviour is similar to what many of their straight counterparts do and have been doing for some time.[50] The views of Jonathon and his partner on ceremony and service were evidence also of Andrew Cherlin's argument that marriage is now 'a status one builds up to' and has become an occasion, which is he says, 'centred on and often controlled by the couple themselves, having less to do with family approval ... than in the past'.[51] Dylan was 32 and single when I interviewed him. He said that if he were to get married, and he hoped he would, he would not try to mimic a heterosexual wedding. 'I would intentionally not want to present it to people that I care about as ... trying to be a straight wedding. I would make sure it was probably less showy, more low key.'

The plan of Jonathon and his partner for an understated and private ceremony, as well as Dylan's wishes for a ceremony that did not mirror heterosexual weddings, are evidence of one of Carol Smart's four categories of wedding ceremony, the 'minimalist' wedding, the characteristics of which are as follows:

> Those who wanted a minimalist wedding tended to be couples who had been together for many years and ... did not want their personal feelings made public ... [or were] worried about recreating a heterosexual practice through ... display.[52]

In summary then, slightly less than three-quarters of men aged 32–51 favoured formal recognition of same-sex relationships – a lower proportion than for the men aged 31 and younger, but a decided majority nonetheless. The men who supported gay marriage drew on two narratives. The first narrative concerned the rights to relationship equality with heterosexuals and to enjoy the same legal and property privileges that attached to heterosexual marriage. The second narrative related to ceremonies appropriate to a same-sex marriage. In contrast to what the men aged 31 and younger wanted, the options the men from this group considered did not include a 'white wedding'. At one end of the spectrum, their alternatives included a ceremony organised by a small group of friends involving participation from friends and family that was a complete surprise for the couple – in the style of Smart's 'demonstrative' wedding – and, at the other end, an intimate ceremony that held a very private meaning for the couple – in the style of Smart's 'minimalist' category.

Men aged 51–87

A total of 41 men, or slightly more than two-fifths of men from the international sample, were aged 51–87.[53] Almost half of the interviewees from this age cohort (*n*=19) said they supported formal recognition of same-sex relationship, but only 12 unequivocally favoured gay marriage, while seven men said they preferred civil union.[54] Of the remaining men, 17 opposed legalising same-sex relationships and five were unsure. In other words, more than 70 per cent of the men from this age group did not support gay marriage. Because many of the men from this cohort came out in the decades prior to gay liberation in the West, their relationship histories were more varied than those from the other age cohorts and included more men who had experienced heterosexual marriages and parenthood.[55]

Of the 12 men from this age cohort who supported gay marriage, four were aged 70 and above, two men were in their 60s, and the remaining six men were in their 50s.[56] Seven men supported gay marriage on principle and without further elaboration. Two men understood gay marriage as an extension of the broader gay liberation movement that began in the 1970s, and the remaining three men referred to property security and the HIV-AIDS experience.

Referring to his involvement in the early gay liberation movement in England, Alfie, a 63-year-old man from Manchester, said, 'It was a statement and we have been involved in gay rights groups since the early '70s. How could we not to do it?' Raymond, an English expatriate who lived in Hong Kong and was 58, used a similar argument to the one that younger men drew on who were in favour of gay marriage, saying, 'we need gay marriage to make us equal. It's a question of ... showing ourselves as being the same and being treated the same.'

One man referred to the question of property, which he said he believed marriage would safeguard. He referred also to many gay men's experience of the HIV-AIDS epidemic when they saw families of dead lovers or friends behaving badly. This man was Cam, aged 56. I interviewed him in Santa Monica in early 2010:

> I don't think people should be allowed to legitimise their relationships and [then] not be allowed to inherit property and insurance policies or be barred from seeing their dying spouses and have their families come in and kick them out of their condo[minimum]s and swoop in and carry all the possessions away and all these other heinous things that happen.

At the beginning of the chapter, I referred to the link a Melbourne man in his 50s made between the HIV-AIDS epidemic and the push for gay marriage. He was one of the few interviewees, from either the international sample or the all-Australian sample, who, like Cam from Los Angeles, saw a link between the way gay men were treated during the HIV-AIDS epidemic and the desire of many from that generation to achieve security for their relationships, a connection that US historian George Chauncey strongly emphasises in his book, *Why Marriage?*:

> Couples whose relationships were fully acknowledged ... by their friends suddenly had to deal with powerful institutions – hospitals, funeral homes, and state agencies – that refused to recognise them at all.[57]

In summary, then, slightly less than 30 per cent of men aged 51 and over were in favour of gay marriage. Those who supported it argued that it was a continuation of their gay liberation commitment, and secured property, and that relationship security was vital after their HIV-AIDS experience. The reasons given by the great majority of men from this age cohort for opposing gay marriage are covered in the next chapter.

Conclusion

The push for gay marriage has had a polarising effect on gay people and, as this chapter has shown, the dividing lines can be strongly generational. I examined the views of the men who supported gay marriage in the context of discussion in an earlier chapter on long-lasting relationships about gay men's capacity to conduct companionate relationships in much the same way as do their heterosexual counterparts, and the tendency for couple relationships nowadays to be more flexible and fragile as a result of increasing individualisation. Notwithstanding the trend to less-permanent couple relationships, a movement for marriage equality began in the West in the decades following the HIV-AIDS epidemic.

As North American historian George Chauncey has argued, one of the important social effects of the epidemic was that it showed gay men that their relationships were not secure and thus provided them with the impetus to demand state recognition of their relationships.[58] During the epidemic, men discovered that their relationships had no standing when families forbade lovers and friends from attending their son's funerals because they did not want to acknowledge the cause of death or hospitals allowed siblings and parents access to dying men but not lovers because they were not kith or kin. The other important effect of the HIV-AIDS epidemic, which I have written about elsewhere, that has bearing on the push for marriage equality, was that it showed that gay men were capable of acting communally and altruistically in the face of a health crisis that threatened lovers, friends, and others like them.[59]

A majority of the younger men from the international sample (aged ≤ 31) supported the push for gay marriage. They argued for it on the grounds of equal legal and property rights, relational equality, the ideal of the wedding day, and marriage linked to social change. Most of the men aged 32–51 were in favour of gay marriage also and, like the younger men, argued for gay marriage on the grounds of equal legal and property rights. Their views on the ideal of the wedding day diverged from those of the younger men. Their options, for example, did not include the 'white wedding' but did include alternatives ranging from 'demonstrative' to 'minimalist' weddings. In contrast to the younger men, very few of the men aged 51 and over supported gay marriage. Of those who supported it, most did so on principle and without further comment. Among the few who gave reasons were men who saw it as an extension of their gay liberation politics, property security, and the HIV-AIDS experience. The views of men who opposed gay marriage are the subject of the next chapter, 'Cohabitation', together with the views of those who favoured civil union but not gay marriage, and those who were unsure.

6
Cohabitation

I think marriage as an institution is passé. And we
are trying to conform too much to a heterosexual
norm. ... My closest friend ... and [I] have made a pact
that, when we reach our diamond age, we both will
start living together as friends. ... For me, sharing my
old age with this friend seems ... a better possibility
than being with a lover.

(Teddy, aged 47, Mumbai)

Introduction

In the previous chapter, I examined the views of 42 men who supported
gay marriage. In this chapter, the focus is on the views of the 23 men
who opposed gay marriage, the 20 men who supported civil union but
not gay marriage, and the views of the 12 men who were unsure what
they thought about it. Analysis showed that men aged 51 or older
were more likely to oppose gay marriage and that the older men who
opposed gay marriage tended to argue that it was a concession to heteronormativity and that gay culture had become too mainstream in a
'family values' way.

Present-day social agitation for gay marriage has overturned understandings of gay relationships that were axiomatic ten or fifteen years
ago.[1] When discussing the features of the lives of people who did not
marry, for example, Martha Fowlkes wrote in 1999 that among all those
whose lives she examined, gay men were the 'marriage nonconformists'.[2]
Since then, things in the West have considerably changed. They have
changed also in cities like Mumbai and Hong Kong, where I found an
understanding among the men interviewed for this book of the signal

if not symbolic importance of gay marriage – even while they acknowledged its eventuality was not likely soon in India or China.

One of the paradoxes of contemporary demands for marriage equality is that they are, as historians John D'Emilio and Estelle Freedman observe, in direct opposition to what gay liberationists campaigned for in the 1970s. Forty years ago, the call was for people to free themselves from the family and to engage in social experiments such as alternative families and urban or rural communes: 'A generation ago, radical gay liberationists presented themselves as exiles from the American family.' This was largely because in the 1960s and 1970s, feminists and social reformers viewed the family with suspicion, regarding it as an institution where women and children were likely to experience physical violence or abuse, which was not part of the life course for most adult gays and lesbians. Non-heterosexuals' desire to have children and seek recognition for their relationships, according to D'Emilio and Freedman, is evidence of the 'trend towards mainstreaming' of gays and lesbians.[3]

Opponents of gay marriage roughly fall into two groups. On the one hand, there are traditionalists and religious conservatives who oppose gay marriage because they believe marriage to be a union between a man and a woman. Catherine Frew explains that in the Australian context opponents of gay marriage used natural law to argue that marriage was a static social institution, 'defined by scriptures, confined by gender differences and, in its traditional form, the building block to a stable society'.[4] Opponents in Australia of gay marriage, such as The Australian Christian Lobby, have used longstanding, anti-homosexual prejudices to support their campaign, arguing that relations between men are 'unnatural' and that therefore marriage could not include such 'unnatural relationships'. Frew says also that opponents of gay marriage made offensive claims:

> In 2009, the Australian Family Association (WA) made the absurd suggestion that the legislation of same-sex marriage could lead to marriage between 'two women and a dog; or a man, a cat and a car'.

In September 2012, Senator Cory Bernardi, a conservative member of the Liberal Party of Australia argued during a debate in the Australian Senate that supporting gay marriage would lead to the legalisation of bestiality:

> There are even some creepy people out there ... [who] say it is OK to have consensual sexual relations between humans and animals. Will

that be a future step? In the future will we say, 'These two creatures love each other and maybe they should be able to be joined in a union'. I think that these things are the next step.

In response to the public furore that followed his speech, Senator Bernardi resigned as an Opposition parliamentary secretary and cancelled an address he was scheduled to make to the European Young Conservative Freedom Summit at Oxford University.[5] At the time of writing, a New Zealand Parliamentary Select Committee had heard evidence from two churchmen who argued against gay marriage because it would encourage incest and lower the prestige of marriage – similar arguments to those Catherine Frew identified about natural law in the Australian context and to those Georg Simmel made about the status of marriage and a relationships hierarchy.[6]

Opposition to gay marriage has come also from non-heterosexuals who have queried the value of marriage, seeing the programme for marriage equality as an impulse towards heteronormalising gay people. In the USA, the fact that Log Cabin Republicans support gay marriage gives credence to gay people's suspicion that it represents another mainstreaming impulse.[7] Some opponents use an argument similar to Simmel's – that marriage as a social institution sets up a hierarchy of relationships with it as the dominant model,[8] which others argue overlooks the dominance of men over women, the dominance of heterosexual over homosexual, as well as the abuse of children and women that can occur in families of married couples.[9] Finally, as my work in this book and other published research shows, gay men who have no wish to marry regard marriage as a patriarchal institution, and, according to Gilbert Herdt, view the movement for marriage equality as a normalising impulse and return to heteronormativity for non-heterosexuals – a view shared by Teddy (aged 47) from Mumbai, who is quoted at the head of the chapter.[10]

In the previous chapter, I divided the international sample into three age cohorts so as to take account of an increasing proportion of men aged 51 and over who opposed gay marriage and an increasing proportion of men aged 31 and younger who favoured it. The first age cohort comprised men aged 18–31; the second cohort comprised men aged 32–51; and the third cohort comprised men aged between 51 and 87. In the sections that follow, the views of these groups are discussed in turn. Some readers might want to skip the introductions to each of the age groups where numbers are recapitulated that were cited in the previous chapter of men for and against gay marriage.

Men aged 31 and younger

Twenty-one men, or slightly more than one fifth of the international sample, were aged 31 and younger at the time of interview.[11] Of these men, two were unsure, one said he opposed gay marriage, and five said they supported civil unions but not gay marriage. As stated in the previous chapter, an overwhelming majority of men from this age group favoured formal recognition of same-sex relationships, and the group of five under study in this section represents less than a quarter of men aged 31 and under. Fifteen men, or more than two-thirds of the age group, were in relationships at the time of interview and seven were single.[12] None was in a civil union or gay marriage, and none was formerly married to a woman or a parent.

Against gay marriage and unsure

Three men did not favour gay marriage or civil union for gay couples and yet were not fiercely opposed to formalising gay relationships. Two of the men were in their 20s, one was in his early 30s, and they came from New Zealand, Britain, and Hong Kong. All men were more focused on marriage in their own lives than in gay marriage as a political issue. Gavin was 31, lived in Auckland, and had been in his relationship for three years when interviewed. He was the only man from the age cohort of young men who was not in favour of gay marriage. The reason he gave was that marriage was unnecessary because his relationship was strong, and he 'could not see the point in it'.

The two men who were not sure if they supported gay marriage gave different reasons. Kenny, aged 24, lived in Hong Kong, and had been in a monogamous relationship for a little under a year when we had our interview. He said that while the laws in China would not quickly change to allow gay marriage, if they did, they were likely to do so first in Hong Kong. He was neither eager to be permitted to marry nor opposed to gay marriage, and was more interested in working toward removal of the discrimination that gay people experienced in Hong Kong. Bailey was 26, a postgraduate student from Britain, and had been in his relationship for almost two years when I interviewed him. He said that he had no intention of marrying but would 'not rule it out as a possibility'.

Civil union but not gay marriage

Although an overwhelming number of interviewees from the cohort of young men supported gay marriage, there were five men who regarded marriage with suspicion and said they would support only civil union. With the exception of a 19-year-old from Melbourne, all these men were in their 20s.[13] Three of the five said that they would support only civil union because they objected to the religious aspects or overtones that were associated with marriage.[14] Two men said that the experience of their parents' separation or divorce had shaken their belief in the institution of marriage.[15]

The views of the men who opposed marriage because they were anti-religious are represented here by an extract from my interview with Eamon, a 28-year-old man living in London. Eamon explained that his recent experience of the dissolution of a long-term relationship had caused him to reflect on and question his beliefs about the permanency of relationships. In the following extract, he reveals the many layers of experience and self-reflection that underlie his views about same-sex marriage.

> Neither of us really believed in marriage as a construct and I think a lot of it was born out of watching my parents' relationship evolve over the years and the fact that both of them had been married previously. People change and marriage is this kind of forever thing, and I think we thought we were both too smart for that. Having said that ... if I end up having kind of a long-term sort of very meaning-ful relationship with somebody, I'd like to draw a line in the sand somehow and say this is it. This is you and me. ... [It will not be] marriage because marriage for me just has too many sort of religious connotations. If the civil benefits were meaningful, then yes [to civil partnership]. But, you know, if there wasn't anything financially to gain or in terms of social services, then I am just as happy having a commitment ceremony or something like that.

This extended extract from Eamon's interview, which took place in a noisy McDonald's café behind Oxford Street in London, strongly indi-cated a thoughtful, considered approach to the matter of the personal life he hoped he would enjoy with another man. It shows as well that the doubts he experienced after the break-up of his relationship added to a scepticism that already existed because of his parents' divorce and one of his parents getting remarried to a divorced person. As well, Eamon revealed a strong preference for cohabitation with perhaps a commitment ceremony only. He could change his mind about this, he said, if the British government legislated to provide appropriate benefits to accompany civil partnerships.

As mentioned, two of the young men who preferred a civil union to gay marriage gave as reasons arguments that did not include anti-religious beliefs or the effect of parents' separation or divorce.[16] At 19, Brody was the second youngest man from the sample. His views on relationships were possibly still forming at the time of our interview and, I sensed, strongly influenced by his six-month relationship with an older man.

> I am like, 'Fine, give it a different name. Like, do not call it marriage but give me the exact same thing in a different name. I will go for that. If that is what you are going to be hung up on, that would be fine.' Right now it is really out of the picture for me.

Unsure whether at 19 he wanted to commit for life, Brody was fairly certain, however, that he would consider partnership of some kind at some stage but only for as long as it was not called marriage.

The other man was Curtis, a 29-year-old from Hong Kong, whose views on relational rights equity were discussed in the previous chapter. He said at the outset that he did not believe in marriage but knew that many other gay people did. In his view, the system in Australian state jurisdictions (discussed above) where de facto gay and straight couples enjoyed the same legal rights as married couples was attractive:

> I like the concept of Australian government about de factos. ... I think it can be worked out in all the developed countries. I'm not sure about China or India or other more conservative countries. I believe the de facto concept works out in those developed countries with marriage law.

> *Author: It guarantees legal rights?*

> Legal rights, yeah. And also the immigration rights. When I told my colleagues ... [at work] about the de facto concept, they quite liked it and we also tried to talk about if it [would] work in Hong Kong.

Immigration rights is an important aspect associated with marriage or partnership rights because it affects the ease with which men who marry or commit to a civil union in one country may return home with their partner and expect to enjoy the same rights and privileges as married people.[17]

While the men who were against or unsure about gay marriage argued on personal grounds – Gavin from Auckland could not see the point of it – those who supported civil union but not gay marriage did so from family experience or anti-religious grounds. Cohabitation suited the men who opposed gay marriage or were unsure, possibly because they had no desire to formalise their relationship or seek any form of external sanction for it. By contrast, the men supporting civil union seemed to be seeking acknowledgement for their relationships, but only as long as it was not in the form of a religious service and was not called marriage.

Men aged 32–51

Thirty four men, or just over a third of the sample, were aged 32–51.[18] Five men from this age group said they opposed gay marriage, five men were unsure, and eight supported civil union but not gay marriage. In other words, slightly more than 50 per cent of the age group opposed gay marriage or were unsure – a larger proportion than for the young age cohort. Half of the men in this age cohort were single ($n = 17$) and half were in relationships ($n = 17$) at the time of interview. By their duration, the men's relationships suggested a strong degree of relative permanency, which is to be expected from people in this age bracket. Of the 17 men in relationships, more than one-third were in either a civil union or gay marriage. In summary, then, half the men aged between 32 and 51 were in relationships and just over half did not support gay marriage.[19] The sections that follow include discussion of the views of the men from each of the categories – those who opposed gay marriage, were unsure, or supported civil union over gay marriage.

Against gay marriage

The five men opposing gay marriage held strong views against marriage in general. When speaking about the matter, they did not discuss and I did not prompt them to discuss civil union as an alternative to gay marriage. Three of the men were in their 40s and two were in their 30s. Two men came from Mumbai and one man came from each of Melbourne, New York, and Sydney.[20] The two men with the strongest views against gay marriage were Teddy (aged 47), who was from Mumbai where he worked in health, and Callum (aged 43), who was from Melbourne and worked in education. Teddy said he believed that marriage in general was obsolete and that it was a backward step to expect same-sex-attracted people to conform to a heterosexual social institution that was languishing. In his view, apart from HIV-AIDS, the more pressing issue was to provide gay people in both developing and developed world with a stronger guarantee of security in old age. Callum worked in education and was acutely critical of what he saw as a vocal minority of privileged gay men in the West advocating for a form of social change that held little value for him and was insignificant alongside previous gay social–political projects, such as 'gay liberation in the '70s and ... the HIV health and political crisis in the '80s':

> I do not know why people want to be the same. I just think what a ... stupid thing to do. If ... marriage is your one special day, I do not want one special day. I want a lot of special days so I do not want to get married, ever.

Callum opposed not only the idea of marriage equality but the growing, powerful narrative of homonormativity or the values of white, middle-class 'good gays' that lie behind it.[21] His arguments were similar to those that English actor Rupert Everett used against gay marriage when he spoke to the *Guardian* in September 2012, an excerpt from which follows;

> Why do queens want to go and get married in churches? Obviously this crusty old pathetic, Anglican church – the most joke-ish church of all jokey churches – of course they don't want to have queens getting married. It's kind of understandable that they don't; they're crusty old calcified freaks. But why do we want to get married in churches? I don't understand that, myself, personally. I loathe heterosexual weddings; I would never go to a wedding in my life. I loathe the flowers, I loathe the fucking wedding dress, the little bridal tiara. It's grotesque. It's just hideous. The wedding cake, the party, the champagne, the inevitable divorce two years later. It's just a waste of time in the heterosexual world, and in the homosexual world I find it personally beyond tragic that we want to ape this institution that is so clearly a disaster.[22]

The remaining three men who opposed gay marriage were from Mumbai, New York, and Sydney. Edmund, who was 44 and owned a large holding of agricultural land in India, had formerly been married to a woman. He doubted marriage would guarantee happiness and he and his male partner had settled for cohabitation: 'We believe in being together, living in a relationship and I don't think we would like to get married in the future.' Liam, who was 37 and lived in Sydney, said he had no wish to be married, partly because of his Catholic upbringing:

> I do not understand marriage as a concept and maybe this goes back to the whole Catholic Church thing. I identify marriage as being ... based in that world and I do not have any desire for that kind of validation and or that kind of structure to the relationship. ... We have made a commitment to each other and ... if it keeps being as good as it is now, great. If it does not that [would be] sad but that sort of thing happens. I don't have any desire to make a commitment ... before any kind of institution.

Liam was satisfied with the personal commitment he and his partner of eight years had made to each other. He opposed marriage because of its association with the Catholic Church, had no wish for that church or any similar religious institution to validate his relationship.

Finally, there is Findlay, who was a 33-year-old African-American I interviewed in New York. At the time of our interview, he was in the early stages of a new relationship with a 41-year-old man. Like the men before him in this section, Findlay seriously doubted marriage's worth, his concerns relating to some questionable practices he had observed in heterosexual couples;

> The institution of marriage is false ... and it holds no weight. It is a money-making institution. I will marry you. I will stick with you for four or five years. I will say you cheated on me and file for irreconcilable differences and I will take half when I leave. I do not see any truth in it and maybe it is because of what I have seen marriage do to my mother and father and other members of my family. I just don't see any truth in it.

Findlay was aware, however, that gay marriage would bring with it improved social security arrangements for gay couples. As he explained in the following extract from his interview, because of the way health-care operates in the United States, these could be life-and-death considerations for many men in his situation:

> I advocate us as a community receiving each other's benefits. Say ... I need to go to the dentist. I know that my boyfriend's dental care is going to cover me as well. That is something I understand because a lot of people cannot afford insurance. It is what it is. ... [If] my insurance

is better than his, will my partner be able to get the med[ication]s that he needs? The person I am seeing is HIV positive.

The men from this mainly middle-age group who opposed gay marriage did so for a number of reasons. All seriously doubted the value if not the validity of marriage as a social institution, and as such were the first group of gay marriage opponents to involve the idea of marriage as a bad institution. For at least one, his experience of Catholicism soured his regard for marriage, while at least two men strongly resented the heteronormalising of gay relationships, which they saw as the inevitable consequence of marriage equality.

Unsure

The five men who were unsure what they thought about gay marriage were three men in their 30s, one man in his early 40s, and one man in his early 50s. Two of the men were from London and there was one man from each of Hong Kong, Melbourne, and New York.[23] The man in his early 50s was Calvin, who lived in Melbourne and worked for a large corporation. Single at the time of interview, Calvin had previously had two long-term relationships. Like a number of men whose views were discussed in the previous part of this section, Calvin objected to the heteronormative impulse behind gay marriage activism and said that it was not necessary, 'to mimic the marriage situation for heterosexuals ... in order to recognise the committed gay relationship'.

Charlie was 40 and lived in Hong Kong. Also single at the time of interview, his confusion about gay marriage was more pronounced than Calvin's. On the one hand, he believed marriage unnecessary, 'just a piece of paper', because 'if you get along well, are going to be together, you will do it anyway, without getting married'. And yet, on the other hand, Charlie said, laughing, 'but I would not mind if someone proposed to me and I would not say no'.

I interviewed two men who lived in London, both in their mid 30s. Aiden, who was 33, said he was not sure at the moment and had other bigger things on his mind, such as resolving problems he and his partner were having with their sex life. Anton was 35 and knew a little about marriage from the sort of work he did in the City. He argued that marriage could be tax efficient, in terms of reducing the tax on inheritance, but that if he had his way he would abolish marriage altogether and introduce something far more radical:

> I would ... just have civil partnership ... divorced from any religious connotations and I would probably extend it ... so that a couple of

old, non-married spinsters or sisters could award each other the right to responsibilities in a civil partnership and then if people want to get married in a church and have the whole blessing thing, then they can do it themselves.

What Anton described is similar to what the French Government introduced when it passed its *pacte civil de solidarité* or civil solidarity pact, which provides benefits for varying households, including two siblings who live together.[24] Underlying the French civil solidarity pact is an egalitarian understanding of the various forms of relationships people have created to satisfy their intimacy needs, and more fully represents the different types of households that exist in large cities in the West, with echoes in privileged circles in the large, westernised cities of the developing world.

Jackson was the last of the five men aged between 32 and 51 who said he was unsure what he thought about gay marriage. Born in the Caribbean, Jackson was 32 when I interviewed him, and in a relationship of four years. From his experience, he said he believed his relationship with his partner was, 'a lot like what people who married do'. His uncertainty about marriage dated back to his childhood: 'I did not grow up with my parents being married, so I don't think it is something I have considered very important in my life.'

In contrast to the younger men who were unsure about gay marriage, these men who were mainly in middle age were more politically aware about the programme in favour of marriage equality and its likely consequences for gay men and their relationships. The younger men drew on their personal situation, family experience, or anti-religious views, whereas the men from the middle cohort questioned the value of marriage, its usefulness for gay men, and whether better relationship models were available such as the French civil solidarity pact, which could suit the needs of a variety of couple types.

Civil union but not gay marriage

Eight men said that they were in favour of a civil union but not gay marriage. All were older than 40.[25] A number of these men opposed marriage but favoured civil union because of their Catholic backgrounds. The reasons the men gave for opposing gay marriage but not a civil union fell into two broad categories. First, they rejected marriage as a social institution in its entirety; second, they were anti-religious. The views of the eight men are represented here by those of three men – Nathan from Auckland, Jacob from Melbourne, and Connor from London.

Nathan was 50, worked as a small businessman, and was in a relationship of six years. He said he would follow the example of some of his friends who had civil unions:

> I know 'civil union' sounds rather clinical but it is better than marriage. ... I am against the whole marriage thing ... because the marriage institution is something that has ... kept gay men squashed. ... It has controlled a lot of people's lives ... especially the religious aspect.

Later in his interview, Nathan explained that while he had been willing to take his partner to his sister's wedding in the South Island of New Zealand, he was aware that his gay and lesbian cousins did not take their same-sex partners to family gatherings. He understood their decision as a reaction to homophobia in his wider family, as a result of which they hid their sexuality. While Nathan said that he was anti-marriage and anti-religion, I sensed his dislike of religion was stronger and was the chief reason why he opposed gay marriage and would prefer a civil union. He seemed to distrust marriage because of its religious connotations, and his dislike of religion stemmed from a belief that it gave rise to homophobia. In his view, religion was therefore the cause of the sort of dishonest behaviour he had seen gay men and lesbians adopt in the face of the homophobia that is common in isolated, rural communities. And for this reason he would prefer a civil service if and when he wanted to formalise his relationship.

Jacob (aged 42) worked in social research in Melbourne. He and his partner had been together for more than 10 years and were happy living together with the recognition their relationship received from family and friends. Jacob said he was surprised that gay people were interested in marriage at all:

> I am sometimes horrified that some ... gay people want to go down that avenue. My attitude is, 'Why should we be as unhappy as the rest of them?'

Although dubious of marriage's benefits, Jacob favoured relationship equality, citing relationship legislation that existed in Victoria and other Australian states providing gay couples with the similar status and rights that heterosexuals enjoyed in de facto (that is, cohabiting) relationships.

Like Nathan and Jacob, Connor, who was 41 and lived in London, did not believe in marriage:

> I don't believe in gay marriage. I certainly believe in equal civil part-nerships and a civil union in secular law. ... I don't know whether this is from a Catholic upbringing ... but I am vehemently atheist and vehemently anti-religion. ... I certainly wouldn't want to ape marriage ... but if the situation were right, I would consider a civil union, or partnership, yes.

Connor's reasons were both similar to and different from those that Nathan and Jacob gave, raising as they did the matter of religion. Connor was not the first man from this international sample to raise the matter of his past (unhappy) religious experience as a Catholic, and as a result his antipathy to anything religious in nature.

Among those who did not want gay marriage, opinions varied as did reasons for the opinions. To some extent, the opinions of the young-est cohort were more personal and the opinions of the middle cohort more political. One explanation for this could lie in the men's dates of birth. The men from the middle cohort grew up and came to maturity at a time when homosexuality was forbidden or at the least not easily tolerated. As a result of the influence of the women's liberation and gay liberation movements they had come to understand their sexuality as political, and that political action was needed to bring about social change and greater relational and sexual freedom. As well, these men will have had longer experience of cohabitation, perhaps have even grown used to the idea that cohabitation was the only relationship option available to non-heterosexuals. As ordinary as cohabitation has come to be seen in the last 20 years, at one point in the final quarter of the twentieth century it represented a simple means of defying mar-riage's hegemony. I suspect that among some of the men from the mid-dle cohort cohabitation still retained its anti-establishment, alternative meaning and significance.

By contrast, the men from the youngest group grew up and came to maturity at a different time, when greater social tolerance prevailed and homosexuality was not frowned upon or scorned. For many of these men, being gay was something they anticipated from an early age, and the idea of a same-sex relationship was not regarded as something to be conducted in secret or avoided. In the next section, the opinions of the oldest group are considered, the age cohort where men who opposed gay marriage were in greatest number.

Men aged 51–87

Forty-one men, or slightly more than 40 per cent of the sample, were aged 51–87, with many of them in their 50s.[26] Seventeen men from this age group said they did not support gay marriage, five men were unsure, and seven preferred civil union. As explained in the previous chapter, 70 per cent of the men from this age cohort opposed gay marriage, which was considerably more than those from the younger cohorts who opposed it. In terms of relationship experience and status, the majority of the oldest men were in relationships.[27] As I argued in Chapter 3 on long-lasting relationships, it is remarkable that so many men showed evidence of a capacity to conduct long-term, couple relationships.[28] Because many men from this group came out in the decades prior to gay liberation in the West, their relationship histories were more varied than those of the men from the other age cohorts, and included more men than who were formerly married, still married or in relationships with women, as well as more men with children from previous hetero-sexual relationships, and more men in civil unions.[29]

I would argue that these men's relationship histories help to explain why gay marriage had less to offer them and other men like them in this age cohort, and why a majority opposed it. A great many of them were in settled, long-lasting relationships. Both this and the fact that more of them were in civil unions than the younger men suggest that cohabitation had worked for them and they were happy with it. As well, it makes sense that, at their stage of life, they would possibly have less interest in getting married in order to mark the status of their relationship or relational achievement. It makes sense also that gay marriage would be of more interest to young men in their 20s or 30s embarking on relationships.

Against gay marriage

The 17 men who opposed gay marriage used two narratives to explain their opposition. First, they argued that marriage was unnecessary because cohabitation was satisfactory and met their relational needs. Second, they made a political argument similar to what some of the men from the middle cohort argued, which was that they opposed gay marriage because marriage was a failed social institution.

Eight men drew on the first narrative. They comprised a man in his 80s, four in their 70s, two in their 60s, and a man in his 50s.[30] These men were content with their cohabitation arrangements and said gay marriage was unnecessary because of the legal implications of marriage or because marrying would jeopardise their existing relationship.

Three men spoke about the legal implications of marriage and why it turned them against gay marriage. The first was Randall, an 87-year-old man who lived in Melbourne and had been in a same-sex relationship for 37 years. In answer to the question about gay marriage, Randall said that he would not want to confuse marriage and a gay relationship, that he was 'happy to live beyond the law if ... [he] was satisfied that what ... [he] was doing was right'. Randall had begun and maintained his same-sex relationship through periods of social hostility, when being gay was a criminal offence, but because his conscience told him that what he was doing was not wrong, he had come to believe that it was all right to live 'beyond the law'. For this reason, and I suspect because he had been formerly married and a husband and was a father, gay marriage held no appeal to him or his partner.

Two other men used quasi-legal reasons for opposing gay marriage. They were Hugh (aged 62) from Melbourne and Hilton (aged 53) from New York. Hugh said that the relationship that he and his partner had was sufficient and they did not need 'legal documents to say that ... [they were] committed to each other'. Hilton's situation was somewhat different from the other men because he had been married to a woman and was divorced. He objected to the idea of gay marriage because of the 'legal and civil connotations' as well as the notion of monogamy, against which he said he would struggle because he still enjoyed having adventurous sex.

Because they were happy with their existing relationships, five of these older men said they found it difficult to consider the idea of getting married. Their views are represented here by two men in their 70s, Drake and Christian. Drake was 77, and lived in Melbourne with his 56-year-old partner. They had been together for 31 years. In the following extract from his interview, Drake explains why same-sex-attracted men can find themselves struggling with heteronormative institutions like marriage and heteronormatively framed romance:

> When [my partner] and I first fell in love ... I would have done it ... I would have done anything to be able to walk down the street holding his hand, to walk along with my arm around his waist, not the whole time but because the gesture felt right. ... I could become angry at the pressures not to do that or to do it ... [so that] it becomes a pretentious act, whereas everybody else is doing it and it is natural. Had it been [available] back then, I probably would have wanted to rush into marriage. ... Now I don't think we'd bother to get married. We do not know what it would mean. I think we are both a bit proud

> of the fact that ... [we have] something that has lasted so long. We wonder if we got married if we would break up [*laughs*]. Why that would happen I don't know.

This account of aspects of the romantic and intimate history of two men is significant for what it says about the compromises gay men have had to make and continue to make because of heteronormative assumptions that influence couple relationships and intimacy in western countries like Australia. When Drake and his partner met, which was in the early 1980s, neither gay marriage nor open demonstrations of affection between gay men were possible. Afraid of arousing homophobic abuse or appearing forced or phoney, Drake found it impossible to publicly express his natural feelings for his partner – by, for example, holding his hand – and, as he said, this made him angry. By the 2010s, both Drake and his partner were proud of what they had achieved and sceptical that marriage would bring any benefit to their relationship.

On this last point, their view of gay marriage and its effect on their relationship coincided with the views of Christian and his partner, two men in their early 70s who lived in Sydney. In the following extract, Christian explained why he and his partner would not marry even if the option were available to them:

> We are perfectly happy as we are and have been for such a very long time up till now. We have even talked about the danger that getting married at such a late stage would be changing the dynamic. Therefore neither of us wants to do that. We are very happy with things as they are.

When Drake said that he and his partner feared marriage might cause their relationship to break up and when Christian said it would change 'the dynamic', I assume that they and their partners feared that the formality or arrangements that accompany any act of marrying, even in a park or town hall, would upset the balance they had achieved in their relational and intimate practices over the years. The four men who comprised these two couple relationships had been together for 30 years and more.

The second, more political narrative that the older men used against gay marriage was that marriage itself was a flawed social institution. This group of five comprised two men in their 60s and three men in their 50s.[31] All the men used relatively passionate language when explaining why they rejected what they variously described as a 'failed' system or institution.

Zachary, who was 52 and an expatriate living in Hong Kong, said that he and his partner were not in favour of marriage because they came, 'from families where the marriages broke up':

> At one point when I was at high school, I remember stopping to think and ... only one out of my group of friends had their original set of parents and may be it was our generation ... but ... marriage is not a flawless institution. It was never anything that held much esteem for us.

When the interviewees answered the questions on gay marriage,[32] I did not explore any connection between the marital status of their parents and their views on gay marriage. In the case of Zachary and his partner, however, and at least one other man, Jackson, aged 32, from New York (see above) the marriage history of their parents strongly influenced the negative views they held and related about gay marriage. The remaining men argued against gay marriage on similar grounds to Zachary, that it was not 'flawless'.

Sean (aged 67) from Auckland was not in favour of civil unions and said he did not respect heterosexual marriage, and by association, gay marriage, because the institution was, 'ephemeral and value-laden in negative terms'. As well, he said: 'I don't ... need the ceremony or the thing to validate the relationship that I have.'

Marvin, who was 59 and lived in Los Angeles, argued in a similar vein, making one of the more cogent, impassioned cases against gay marriage and in favour of the cohabitational relationships with which gay people have been experimenting for at least the last 180 years.[33] In making his argument, Marvin drew on the experience of a relatively long-term relationship he had with a former partner who died more than 15 years earlier;

> I also don't for the life of me understand why the gay community has decided to emulate an institution that doesn't work for even straight people. ... My relationship with [my partner] did not have that kind of global definition. We operated really fine. We had to take care of ourselves legally ... so that, if anything happened between either one of us, the other person was taken care of. ... I love the idea of two people professing their love for one another but emulating that model to me is just another way of whittling away that thing that made us unique in the first place.

Like many men his age, Marvin was proud of his 'outsider' status and the relationships that he and other men were forced to create when they lived at some emotional and cultural distance from the heterosexual mainstream. This was particularly the case in the decades of the HIV-AIDS epidemic when in the USA few politicians or social commentators embraced any aspect of the gay lifestyle. He explains in the extract above that he and his former partner were able more than 15 years before to set their relationship on the right legal footing so that, in the event of one of them dying, the other would be looked after, which, Marvin said, did happen when his former partner died. Again, like other men his age, Marvin resists moves to draw gay men's lives into the mainstream, the effect of which he said was 'of whittling away the thing that made us unique', which resonated with what Timothy from New York (aged 46) said in relation to gay marriage: 'I am old enough to remember the idea that being gay was an alternative, a different kind of life,' Later in his interview, Marvin admitted that few of his friends shared his view of gay marriage:

> I do not get it ... [or] get fired up about it the way a lot of my friends do. I have not had arguments with my friends about it but certainly discussions when they don't understand where I'm coming from ... [and] I don't get why they are asking for that [gay marriage].

Like earlier political movements such as gay liberation in the 1970s and ACT-UP in the late 1980s,[34] the push for gay marriage has had a polarising effect on gay people, and, as this and the previous chapter have shown, generation may be one dividing line. One effect of the polarising influence of the political debate can be that each side is left feeling incredulous about the views of the other, which was certainly the experience of the men who made articulate arguments against the push for gay marriage.

The last man in this group of five was Arthur, a 62-year-old man who lived in London. Arthur said that he was satisfied with the level of social acceptance that gay people had already achieved in the West, and that he believed the divorce rate for gay men who were gay married was higher than the divorce rate for straight men. He reiterated the premise, which the other men in this group used to underpin their argument against gay marriage, that 'the marriage ... they are fighting for ... is unnecessary. We are mimicking a failed system.'

One final point regarding opposition to gay marriage is the arguments that four men made, which fell into neither of the principal narratives.

Two men, who were separated by 20 years in age, said that, as it was too late for them to worry about marriage, they were not in favour of it.[35] A third man said he opposed it because he was anti-religious: 'I do not think there would be any need for a ceremony for us. I am a lapsed Catholic and I do not believe in church.'[36] And the fourth man said he would not support gay marriage because, as a man with property, he feared the financial losses a divorce might cause him: 'If we broke up, I have no means of replacing anything in my time of life, so I would lose big time.'[37]

Unsure

Five men from the oldest cohort were unsure what they thought about gay marriage. They comprised three men in their 50s, one man in his 60s, and one man in his 70s. Two of the men were from Melbourne, two were from New York, and one man was from London.[38] Two of the men were unsure what they thought about gay marriage because of complications in their personal life; the three remaining men had individual reasons for being uncertain about it. All are discussed below.

The two men with complications in their personal life were Parry, a 63-year-old New Yorker, and Arran, a 70-year-old man from Melbourne. Readers will be familiar with Parry because the story of his long-term relationships was discussed in some depth in the chapter on long-lasting relationships. When asked about his views on gay marriage, Parry said that he and one of his partners wear rings on their non-marriage hands, 'as part of a protest that we're not legally married'.

Unfortunately, I did not ask Parry to explain which partner's ring he wore, but assumed because of how he spoke about the special status of their relationship that his first partner had given it to him. I did not investigate this detail at the time of interview because I was having difficulty hearing Parry and struggling to make sense of the story of his relationships. It was only after his interview was transcribed that I began to make sense of what he had told me. Because I had not heard a similar story before and wanted to make sure I understood what he said, I often had to return to the recording to confirm the meaning of what Parry told me.

Readers will recall that, in Chapter 3, I described the details of Parry's intimate life and that he was conducting what he understood to be separate, monogamous relationships with two different men. Parry explained that the decision not to marry was his partner's choice, and that he was 'still betwixt and between about marriage' even though he had 'no problem with being committed'. When I pressed him, saying

140 *Gay Men's Relationships Across the Life Course*

that marriage would preclude his second relationships, he replied as follows:

> It would just be adulterous. ... In some ways I guess [my second partner] is my mistress and I don't see anything wrong with that. I don't see any problem with being loved by many people.

The second man whose personal life made a gay marriage or civil union impossible was Arran, who lived in Melbourne, and was in a relationship of 25 years with a man who was 11 years his senior. According to Arran, the fact that his partner was still married to a woman he married meant that gay marriage or civil union was out of the question. The complications of life for these two men in their eighth and ninth decades is clear from the following:

> We do have a wife and she has this huge apartment which is filled with furniture and ... she thinks that the three of us could live together and rent a house. She imagines that we will be able to rent a house somewhere nice and big enough to live independent lives, you know. I am not easy about that. I do not like ... renting particularly.

The three men with their own individual reasons for feeling uncertain about gay marriage were Isaac, a 56-year-old from Melbourne, Tate, a 51-year-old from London, and Earl, a 51-year-old from New York.

Isaac was unsure if he supported marriage reform because while he believed gay people should argue in favour of marriage equality – to ensure that what he observed during the HIV-AIDS epidemic never recurred – he and his partner of 31 years were satisfied with the privileges and benefits they already received from the state. To underline the last point, Isaac said that Centrelink, the Australian government's social security system, recognised their relationship and that when he was recently in hospital, 'there was never the slightest ... problem that our relationship would be recognised'. His personal experience meant that he and his partner had no need of gay marriage.

Tate, who was an expatriate living in London, was not sure what gay marriage meant or what use it would be to him. A rich man who grew up and was educated on the East Coast of North America, at the time of our interview, Tate had recently begun a relationship with a man 25 years his junior. Like other men his age, his views on gay marriage were split between the personal and the political or the public, and in the following extract from his interview, Tate revealed his political belief in the desirability of marriage equality and his relative uninterest on the personal level:

> I think there is no question that gay couples should have all the access to the same sort of legal rights that straights have. I have never been particularly concerned about whether it is actually called marriage or not but ... the real question you are asking is whether I personally would [get married]. ... I would not rule it out but it is something that never in my life have I really thought about ... so clearly it is not terribly important.

The third man was Earl, who lived in New York. When his partner of 22 years was alive, the two of them were regarded as a couple in their friendship circle as the following extract from his interview shows:

> [W]e eventually moved in, travelled together, went to Europe. It was not the most sexual relationship ... but a very loving, platonic relationship. I was never really drawn to him sexually but we became a couple and were known as a couple at the Temple and were asked to things. We were invited everywhere that people knew us. ... We never filed the domestic partnership agreement. ... We had it all completed but we never got it down so I got bought out of the apartment.

From the little that Earl revealed in his interview – and the extract from his interview cited above is all that he said about his previous relationship – it would seem that the absence of sex from their relationship – and a 19-year age difference – might explain why Earl did not take the next step and have their relationship officially registered. The fact that they had completed a domestic partnership agreement but omitted to file it suggests uncertainty on the part of at least one of the men. As Earl was the younger man and as he had more to gain from a registered partnership, which his comment about losing the apartment suggests, I wonder if the absence of something stronger than their friends' approbation explains his uncertainty and his unwillingness or inability to formalise their relationship.

Civil union but not gay marriage

Seven men from the oldest cohort said they would support civil union but not gay marriage.[39] Of these, three said without going into more detail that they thought the idea of marriage 'strange' or unattractive; they said also and without elaboration that the idea of civil union

142 Gay Men's Relationships Across the Life Course

appealed to them more than did marriage. As I explained when previously describing responses such as these, I did not always test the men's views at the time or ask them to elaborate, the responsibility for their brief answers being therefore more mine than theirs. The remaining four men drew on two familiar stories when explaining why they preferred civil union to gay marriage. The first narrative was that a civil union ensured that a couple's property rights were protected; the second narrative was that the general public was not yet ready for gay marriage.

Property rights and the desire to protect them have recurred in this and the previous chapter as an important reason for supporting gay marriage or civil union. In the case of the three men from this age cohort, their explanations were both similar and different from those already considered. The most colourful explanation came from 72-year-old Jeffrey, who lived in Auckland and was a retired railway worker. He argued that a civil union most likely provided protection in law: 'There should be a way of protecting yourself from nasty families.'

Bryce from Manchester was nine years Jeffrey's junior, and already securely settled in a civil partnership with his partner of 39 years. From his point of view, the civil contract, which they had, protected their inheritance and other matters concerning, 'the next of kin and ... pension considerations'. The third man, Bernard, was a 59-year-old from Hong Kong. His views about civil union were that it provided the same rights as marriage but without the connotations that accompanied marriage;

> Marriage seems a bit strange for me, I do not reject the idea. I understand that some people can marry but there is something strange. I prefer the idea of a civil union, which gives you the same rights without the official aspect.

The second narrative the men drew on who favoured civil union concerned public opinion, and was the expressed view of 81-year-old Clancy from Melbourne. He said he believed that a contract was a good idea but that gay marriage was too radical an idea for citizens of Australia:

> I do not think the population is ready for it. ... We are a middle-class country and ... I am afraid the middle-class government is not going to be too radical. ... Hopefully gay marriage will come in but I do not particularly agree with marriage whether it is a heterosexual one or a gay one. ... I think a contract is the way to go. If the world wants to be married, it is okay by me.

Clancy's views mirror many of those of the younger men from this international sample of 97 men. He argued that gay marriage might be too radical for mainstream, western society. And while acknowledging that marriage itself has its shortcomings, it is clear that he was willing to support the push for gay marriage, saying that, 'if the world wants to be married, it is okay by me'. He is more sceptical about the institution than the pro-marriage youth (whose views were discussed in Chapter 5), but shares the idea of individual choice that is so important to them.

The group of seven men from this cohort who said they would support civil union but not marriage used three arguments to explain their views. The first was that marriage was 'strange'; the second was that same-sex couples needed binding agreements to secure their common property; and the third that the general public would accept civil union, but was not yet ready for gay marriage.

Conclusion

As shown in the previous chapter and here, very few young men opposed gay marriage. A small number said that they preferred civil union, citing anti-religious sentiments or personal experience as reasons. Some middle-aged men used anti-religious sentiments also as a reason for opposing gay marriage, while another group said they would not support it on the grounds that legalising gay marriage would result in heteronormative values being imposed on gay men and their relationships. Making a more political argument, other men from the middle cohort said that gay marriage would be a foolish experiment since marriage was a failed institution. At least one of the men who opposed gay marriage for these reasons said that he preferred the varying relational possibilities that sexual libertarianism allowed and which had been a feature of western gay life since at least the late nineteenth century. He enjoyed his outsider status and vehemently opposed what he regarded as the *embourgeoisement* of gay life, mocking, like Rupert Everett, the idea of church or white weddings. Among the men from the middle cohort who were unsure about gay marriage were some who queried the purpose of marriage if cohabitation arrangements were satisfactory. Less revolutionary than the libertarian who could not understand why some gay men wanted to get married, these men shared a view similar to his – that gay marriage would restrict the relational possibilities that were open to gay men, have a limiting effect. As mentioned in this chapter and the previous one, the older men opposed gay marriage in greater numbers than the younger men, giving reasons that were also personal and political.

The personal reasons that the older men gave were that cohabitation arrangements were satisfactory and suited them, and that they saw no need to change. I argued that their view of gay marriage most likely formed during the mid twentieth century, when in the faces of varying degrees of homophobia they had to make strategic decisions about what sort of relationships to experiment with and how to conduct them. In line with the work of scholars such as John Boswell and George Chauncey, I argued that gay men often had to lead clandestine lives or marry and live double lives in order to survive during in times of hostility or repression. I suspect also that many of these older men were already set in their ways when the level of social tolerance began to increase, as it did in the 1970s in the West, when men like them were able to experiment with living more openly as gay men and in gay couple relationships.

The political reasons the older men used to explain their opposition to gay marriage mostly concerned their negative view of marriage. Some of the men explained that they would not support the move toward gay marriage because of marriage's legal standing or legalities associated with it; others argued that they thought it bizarre that gay men would want to copy 'a failed system', to use the words of Arthur (aged 62) from London. Like the libertarian from the middle cohort, at least one of the older men strongly opposed what he regarded as the 'mainstreaming' of gay life, believing that it would erase what was unique about gay men. In general, older men who were unsure where they stood in relation to gay marriage said that they were content with their cohabitation arrangements. I suspect that a common thread uniting these men's lack of interest in marriage generally can be found in the women's liberation rhetoric of the 1970s. Many of these men, having formed views about marriage when they were in their 20s, saw no reason to change them or to embrace an institution that in their view had lost its value or held no value for them.

7
Living in the Midst of HIV-AIDS

I think it is probably one of those things that kind of made it a fraction harder to be homosexual. I have never felt really at risk of contracting the virus, so it has always been ... something that has happened outside my life. Although of course like every homosexual in the early days I had a test, I worried, and then we were not sure how easy it was to contract and so there was that anxiety that went on for a long while about it.

(Michael, aged 52, Melbourne)

I have a rule about safe sex, and generally I have kept that rule fairly strictly, *but* in some ways it is a very scary proposition as well. I have never been tested [for HIV] and that has been a cause of concern among my friends ... who have said that I am basically an idiot. I have been making commitments for over a year to do it. I do not think that I have put myself or anyone else ... [at] risk of anything ... to the extent that I know that I am not HIV positive but it is a big psychological thing.

(Jack, aged 22, Sydney)

Introduction

For most of the final decades of the twentieth century – and until HIV infection rates began to increase in 1999[1] – the focus of HIV-AIDS policy and debate in countries like Australia was on the sexual health, practices, and wellbeing of the initial age cohort of gay men who were affected by it, the so-called 'baby-boomer' generation.[2] These men were

145

born in the late 1940s and 1950s and grew to social maturity in the mid to late 1960s and early 1970s. They either participated in or were strongly influenced by the social movements of the time, such as the anti-war movement and the women's and gay liberation movements. By a cruel irony, just as many were enjoying the freedom of expression that accompanied a growing tolerance towards non-heterosexuals, the HIV-AIDS epidemic began.

In Australia and similar western countries, gay men and intravenous drug users appeared particularly vulnerable in the early years of the epidemic. And while medical and scientific establishments struggled to understand its mode of transmission and moral conservatives condemned sexual nonconformity as the cause of the disease, gay men in their hundreds were succumbing and dying. In the midst of the crisis, Dennis Altman argued that while AIDS affected gay sex, it would not alter the 'fundamental reality of homosexuality'. On the whole, he was proved right for many gay men chose celibacy, monogamy or 'safe sex' to 'protect' themselves from the virus,[3] and, even if their response to AIDS was to be celibate, as it was for some, their identity was still gay:

> any sense of gay identity [is] quite meaningless if we try to deny it is an identity clearly based upon sexual preference, even if this preference is not always acted upon.[4]

Most commentators agree that a notable, positive effect of AIDS was to revitalise gay communities in western countries. Groups of gay men drew on their own labour, time, and communal leadership and then, in the case of countries such as Australia and New Zealand, worked with governments to formulate health policy, notably to insist that education was most likely to effect the kind of change required in gay men's sexual practices.[5] A first age cohort of gay men experienced the onset of the HIV-AIDS epidemic in Australia as both a time of extreme fear, loss, and recrimination and a time of a notable communal response in the gay world.

More recently, however, a second age cohort of gay men has shown signs of being affected by the disease just as the first age cohort was in the early 1990s.[6] Men from the second age cohort were born into a world where HIV-AIDS already existed and its mode of transmission was public knowledge. They were the beneficiaries of sustained, publicly funded health messages emphasising the importance of safe sex in any sexual encounter outside a monogamous relationship. This chapter compares the generation of gay men who experienced HIV-AIDS as a *new* fact of life to the generation who grew up with it.

The first generation whose experiences of HIV-AIDS are discussed in this chapter comprises men who were young and in their 20s and 30s when AIDS was first made public, in the early 1980s. The second generation are young men now. They were in their 20s and 30s when interviewed, and grew up and came out with some knowledge of the virus and its implications for the sexual health of sexually active, young people. The central questions at the heart of this chapter are how a second generation of gay men understood the threat of HIV-AIDS and whether their understanding differed from or was similar to the first generation's experience and understanding of the disease. The 58 men whose stories form the basis of this chapter were, with the exception of three interviewees, HIV negative at the time of interview.[7] The purpose of the chapter is not to explain how HIV-positive men have been affected by the virus but to return to an old story, rarely told nowadays, which is how the presence of the threat of HIV affects the identity or sense of self of gay men who are HIV negative.

These 58 men came from the all-Australian sample and were divided into two age groups.[8] The first age group I called the 'pre-HIV' generation, and it comprised 30 men aged 40 to 59, half of whom were in their 40s. and half were in their 50s[9] The majority of these men were, in other words, mature adults and likely to have been sexually active at the time of the onset of the HIV-AIDS epidemic in Australia, and in the 1980s would have seen more people dying fast of AIDS.[10] The second, or 'post-HIV' generation comprised 28 men aged 22–39, 10 of whom were in their 20s and 18 in their 30s.[11] In November 1982, the great majority of these men were aged 16 or less. Nearly all of them were therefore young teenagers or children at the onset of the HIV-AIDS epidemic in Australia.[12] They would have seen the Grim Reaper advertisements on television as they were forming views about their sexual identity or coming out.[13] By comparison with the experience of the older cohort of men, the post-HIV men would have seen people living with HIV, not dying of AIDS so often.

My rationale for focusing on a mono-culture to discuss the effects of HIV-AIDS on two age generations of gay men was twofold. First, the varying cultural understandings of HIV-AIDS in the developing world and the developed world were beyond the scope of this book, and beyond the purpose of the interviews I held with men from the international sample in 2009–11. Second, I had a strong sense that the recent focus on HIV-AIDS prevention that has taken place Australia deserved more attention for what it showed about memory and understanding in a sub-culture at risk, which is the underlying theme in this chapter.

Three principal narratives

When interviewed, the men from both generations seemed to shrug off or dismiss the seriousness HIV-AIDS represented. Most accepted without alarm the threat HIV-AIDS posed to their lives and/or the lives of their friends, partners, and acquaintances. For example, one of the interviewees, Patrick, who was in his early 50s, said the following when explaining whether or not HIV-AIDS had affected his sense of self:

> Well, none except that my partner is HIV positive and so it's had a big effect on my sense of security, ... It's like the calm before the storm. I look around myself now and think, 'everything in my life is so good, when is it all going to come crashing down?'

Patrick's immediate response was to say that HIV-AIDS had no effect on his sense of self. Then, without pausing, adds that his partner is HIV positive. How does one understand such a response? One possible explanation lies in the last sentence of this excerpt from Patrick's transcript. Perhaps a greater fear existed that prevented him from dwelling too closely on his partner's present circumstances, which is that at some point in the future the disease will kill him and then their life together will 'come crashing down'.

Patrick was not the only interviewee who responded this way to the presence of the disease. When asked about the effect of HIV-AIDS on his sense of self, another man, Bill, who was also in his early 50s, answered: 'Very little ... a lot of the people that I know died. The gay group I knew from the early '70s was just decimated.' And then a man in his late 50s, with a long history of caring for people living with HIV-AIDS (PLWHA), said in regard to its effect on his sense of self:

> Most of the guys I knew in my 20s and early 30s died of AIDS; very few of them are left. It doesn't have a lot to do with my identity. I have just lost a lot of friends through it. (Samuel, aged 56)

To some readers it might seem strange that some gay men can accept such personal losses so calmly. There are, however, many reasons for their doing so. For instance, as a number of interviewees testified, messages about HIV-AIDS have been heavily and regularly disseminated in the gay world for more almost three decades; also, in the face of large-scale tragedy, one typical human response is to play down the enormity of traumatic events. Alternatively, the men's calm response to the threat the disease poses might be evidence of gay men's refusal to admit to any conflation of gay identity with HIV-AIDS; or, as almost all the men interviewed for this chapter were HIV negative when interviewed, their automatic response might have been to distance themselves from the virus, despite what friends, partners, or lovers might have experienced or be experiencing.[14]

The question the interviewees answered was 'What effect has HIV-AIDS had on your sense of self?' In reply, the 58 men drew on three principal narratives. I called the first narrative 'fear, vulnerability, and stigma', the second narrative 'changed sexual practices', and the third narrative 'loss and solidarity'. Almost two-thirds of interviewees (or 36 men) used the first narrative – fear, vulnerability, and stigma – to explain the effect HIV-AIDS had on their sense of self. Half the interviewees (or 29 men) used the second narrative – changed sexual practices. And slightly more than 40 per cent of interviewees (or 24 men) drew on the third narrative – loss and solidarity – to explain the effect of the disease. My analysis showed broad similarity but differences of nuance between the two generations' understanding of the disease's effect on their identity. The three narratives are discussed in turn.

Fear, vulnerability, and stigma

The first narrative concerned the interviewees' emotional responses to the threat of the virus. In all, 36 men (or 62 per cent of the sample) said they were frightened, felt vulnerable and/or experienced greater stigma once they learned of HIV-AIDS and its mode of transmission.[15] This was so both for men from the pre-HIV generation who were in their late 20s when HIV became public knowledge in the West, and the men from the post-HIV generation who grew up in its midst from when they were children or teenagers.

Feeling frightened or vulnerable are fairly natural, human responses to news that one could run the risk of being infected with a life-threatening illness. A diseased body, however, is not always a stigmatised body and, with the exception of two men in their 30s and one man in his late 40s, the overwhelming majority of men interviewed for this chapter were not responding to personal experiences of HIV infection. They were speaking about how the virus affected their identity, their sense of self as gay men, and how they understood living in the midst of an epidemic where men like them were ill or dying from the disease.

As Susan Sontag and others have shown, HIV-AIDS is a disease with a marked capacity to stigmatise its sufferers and people who ran the risk of contracting it or coming into contact with it.[16] In relation to HIV-AIDS, gay men have always faced a particularly acute stigma because of prejudice against the type of sex some have and transmission of the disease, that is, the contact that can occur between semen and blood when men have unprotected anal sex.

Middle generation

Twenty-one men, or more than two-thirds of those from the pre-HIV generation, reported feeling afraid, vulnerable, or stigmatised because of HIV-AIDS.[17] This was the principal narrative. Of these, slightly more than half (12 men) mentioned its stigmatic effect.[18]

The men from the middle generation gave two reasons for why they felt frightened or vulnerable in the face of HIV-AIDS, and both concerned transmission. Many recalled how, as younger men in the early 1980s, they were afraid because neither government health authorities nor scientists were sure of the virus's origin or means of transmission, and gay men and intravenous drug users seemed especially vulnerable.[19] These uncertainties understandably caused the men some anxiety, an example of which is represented here by the account from a man aged 45, who was 29 in 1985. Scott said that news of HIV-AIDS and its mode of transmission 'cast a shadow' over his life and that then, 'people talked about five or ten years being the period when you judge whether you are going to be [HIV] positive or not, whether you are going to come down with it'.[20]

Another man from the pre-HIV generation, Lionel (aged 59) said that news of the disease made him feel vulnerable – because of the risk of infection associated with sexual encounters and the conflation of homosexuality and the virus in the media and more generally:

> It scared me shitless when it happened. It ... changed the way I felt about sexual encounters. ... [But] I do not know that it has changed my sense of self, except that you feel vulnerable ... suddenly you are vulnerable. I guess the other thing that happened is that it brought up a whole lot of anti-gay sentiment in certain sections of the community and the media.

The other reason men from the middle generation gave for feeling frightened and vulnerable was a retrospective fear of infection. From their accounts it is clear that in the time between when (a) news of the disease was made public and (b) its mode of transmission was known and the test for antibodies became available, many of these men were afraid because they had no way of knowing if they were already infected as a result of previous sexual encounters. Their sentiments are represented here by an extract from the account of Neil (aged 46), who recalled that learning of the disease, in his own words, 'frightened the shit out' of him;

> It was not that the sort of sex I had done was risky but it did not take much. When it first came out in 1983 and the news became more widespread about how it spread, there was a possibility that because of the few occasions of risky sex in the past I was walking around with it. But once I was over that hurdle, it certainly changed forever my sexual habits.

It is instructive that Neil first said he was not in the habit of having risky sex. As he continued to recall his sex life 20 years before, he admitted feeling frightened at the time because of previous sexual encounters when he had had 'risky sex' with men. Once he was certain that his prior sexual practices had not put him at risk of sero-converting, he stopped having risky sex – unprotected anal intercourse, for example.

Twelve men from this generation referred also to the stigmatic effect of HIV-AIDS. Among the stories they recounted were the following. Two men in their late 50s said the response to HIV-AIDS caused many gay men they knew to return to the closet. One of these men, Roy (aged 58), described the public then private effects of the stigmatising that occurred when he was younger;

> I was 40, fully out and ready to be a very active gay man only to find that everyone had gone back into the closet. I felt as though I had been cast aside. ... To top it off, I went through a period of depression and I felt as though I had the symptoms of HIV. I started to get the night sweats and ... made up my mind that I was HIV positive. I saw a doctor and he tested me for a number of different things. ... [Waiting for the results] were the worst three or four days I have ever had. ... When he told me I was clear ... I realised that HIV had triggered a psychosomatic exercise with me.

Another man in his late 50s described the early 1980s as a period when feelings of, 'threat, menace and contagion ... were very strong'.

Finally, three men understood the stigma they experienced as arising from a conflation of HIV-AIDS and homosexuality. Their views are represented here by Kevin, a man in his early 50s:

> I have had ... that feeling of belonging to a minority group since HIV-AIDS first was talked about 15 years ago ... and the publicity ... reminded you that you are in that group ... that little box over there

of how all people regard gay people as being involved in that activity, and therefore you must be part of that.

In summary, what can be said about the effect of HIV-AIDS on the men from the pre-HIV generation? Unlike the young cohort, who were only children or teenagers in the 1980s, the men from the older cohort could draw on their lived experience to explain how the disease affected them when they were in their 20s. Feelings of fear or vulnerability that they recalled were the result of (a) medical and scientific communities then being unsure of the disease's mode of transmission, (b) reports that gay men were particularly at risk of infection, and (c) not knowing if their prior sexual history put them at risk.

Young generation

Fifteen men, or 54 per cent of those from the young generation, spoke of feeling frightened, vulnerable, or being aware of increased stigma because of HIV-AIDS. Those who reported such feelings were mostly in their 30s and, as in the case of the men from the middle-aged generation, fear or vulnerability struck a stronger chord with them than did stigma. Of these 15 men, 12 described feeling frightened or vulnerable, and six spoke of the stigmatising effect HIV-AIDS had on them, three of whom did not refer to feeling afraid or vulnerable.[21] In the following section, the discussion concerns first, the men who spoke of feeling frightened or vulnerable in face of the disease, and then those who referred to its stigmatising effect.

The 11 men who said that HIV-AIDS affected their sense of self because it frightened them or made them feel vulnerable fell into two categories. The first group, which is relatively small, comprised three interviewees who described the fear they associated with HIV-AIDS in general terms – as frightening simply because the idea of such a disease was terrifying. For two of the men, both in their 20s, their fear was linked to the image of the Grim Reaper, which, as mentioned in an earlier footnote, was shown on Australian television in 1987 as part of a campaign to alert people to the disease's presence.[22] As Ian (28) recalled:

> When I was in high school, the big advertising campaigns scared me to death. I was so scared that I tried not to be gay because I did not want to die.[23]

The second group, which comprised eight men, described feeling frightened or vulnerable because of how the disease affected them personally. For example, one man in his early 20s was too afraid to be tested for the HIV antibodies; another, in his 30s, had been too frightened to visit a friend in hospital as he died from AIDS; and a third, also in his 30s, delayed coming out because of his fear of HIV-AIDS. For others from this group, it was the immediate proximity of the disease that frightened them, especially those men who were HIV positive.

Jason was in his mid-30s, and is one of the three men in the sample who was HIV positive. When he spoke of the effect the disease has had on him, he recalled the late 1980s when he was in his early 20s: 'It was just routine testing. I did not suspect that I was positive and the results ripped me apart.' With the help of his parents, he regained his emotional footing, enrolled in a university course, and began to feel more in charge of his life. While the threat of death is more distant now, and his viral load is under control, Jason said that HIV-AIDS continued to have 'a dramatic effect on my life to this day'.

HIV-AIDS has a pronounced capacity to mark with stigma people it infects or who are at risk of infection. Most of the men from the young generation who experienced HIV-AIDS as stigmatising, spoke of its conflation with the gay identity, that is, as one man in his mid-20s said, 'the stereotype is that all gay people must have AIDS or carry the virus'. All the men who held this view were in their 20s. Angus, who was 23, said that when he came out, which was in 1997,

there was already a perception in the community that gay equals HIV. It would have been worse if I had come out five years earlier, because then not only was there a perception in the community but people were talking about it. I remember in Year 10 Science we had sex education, and the one time HIV was brought up was in respect to gay sex, otherwise it wasn't talked about at all. The one time I get to be talked about as a gay man at school, it's to do with HIV. The only picture I ever got in the country of the gay man was to do with the virus.

Angus's recollection is instructive for what it says about the homophobic nature of sex education provided in Australian schools and the negative effect this can have on non-heterosexual students.[24] It was also mirrored in the experience of another man in his 20s who, until he did his own research, said that the message he drew from advertising and educational campaigns was that all gay people would get HIV-AIDS and die.

An unintended consequence of these campaigns, therefore, might have been to stigmatise gay men, and possibly lesbians too, at least in the early days. Importantly, however, for managers and workers in GLBTI[25] community organisations and sexual health centres, all those men in their 20s who noted the stigmatising effect of HIV-AIDS also said that it was through contact with local gay communities or sexual health services that they learned the truth of the virus and how to minimise or eliminate risk of infection through 'safe sex' practices.

Changed/changing sexual practices

As a response to the fear, vulnerability, and stigma they felt in the face of the virus, many of the men interviewed for this chapter then spoke about how they changed or adapted their sexual practices as a precaution against contracting it. Twenty-nine of the 58 men (or 50 per cent of the sample) referred to these changes.[26] As many commentators have shown, not only did AIDS cause gay men to reassess their sexual relations, it also made many of them review the nature of their affective relations and engage in a broader range of relationships. For some, monogamy became more attractive, as historian Angus McLaren has observed, while for others, as activist Simon Watney noted, 'safe sex' was only one adaptation that enabled gay men to continue sexually adventurous lives[27]:

> [S]afer sex ... [was] a way of sustaining their commitment to erotic pleasure and freedom of choice. The widespread formal and informal institution of 'jack-off' groups and parties ... evidently sustains a cultural identity that confidently refuses the crude anti-sex messages that make up so much official government-sponsored AIDS 'education'.[28]

The second narrative that the men drew on concerned their sexual practices and how, in response to learning about HIV transmission, they tried to minimise their chances of contracting the virus by a number of means including monogamy, celibacy, risk avoidance, and selective participation in casual sex encounters. In the discussion that follows, consideration is given first, to the accounts of the men from the middle generation and second, to those from the young generation.

Middle generation

Fifteen interviewees, or half those from the pre-HIV generation, referred to their sexual practices when explaining how HIV-AIDS had affected their sense of self. All who did so, explained that the threat of HIV had the effect of convincing them to change their previous sexual behaviour in order to minimise any risk of infection. These men's preferred strategy of choice was to practise safe sex with strangers or safe sex in the context of monogamous relationships.[29] In the following section, these two sets of accounts are considered in turn.

In the accounts of the men from the middle cohort, there is evidence of gay men's ability to change their sexual behaviour in face of the threat that HIV-AIDS posed in the 1980s. For example, Lionel, aged 59, said that before AIDS, his overseas holidays, especially to the USA, had been 'big sexual adventures'. By the 1980s all that changed, and instead he found himself 'taking more interest in museums and going to bed early'. Another man in his 50s said AIDS brought to an end the 'sexual play' that had been such a part of the 1970s. Among 40-year-olds who described the effect of HIV-AIDS on their sexual practices, Trevor, aged 49, said it was no longer 'worth going out and getting a one-night stand and fucking your brains out'. Glen, aged 49, said he always had safe sex and Ivan, aged 40, reflected, 'it probably prevented me from dipping my toe too deeply.'

Four men from this generation said they, or friends they observed, had retreated from their previous sexual adventurism and now relied on their monogamous relationships to protect themselves from risk of the virus. Their views are represented here by the accounts of Richard (aged 58) and Bill (aged 52).

Richard explained that a chance decision to embark on a 'fairly monogamous' relationship saved him from the high-risk life that he had led in the 1970s involving adventurous sex and intravenous drug use:

> It has not had much effect on me because I am not HIV and there was little likelihood that I would ever be HIV especially since I met [my partner] because it has been a fairly monogamous relationship. But had he not come along, I could easily be HIV ... and I think that I am very lucky that I don't have it. ... I [had been] quite promiscuous [in the 1970s] and was shooting up drugs too, which is another thing. I was very fortunate that it did not happen later. Because ... [I] could easily have ... carried on as usual.

Bill was coy about its effect on his own sexual practices, but had observed the effect that the presence of HIV had had on men in his friendship circle. Like others in the pre-HIV generation, they had enjoyed relatively unrestrained sex lives in the 1970s, all of which changed with the arrival of the disease:

> One thing that became fairly evident was that many of the people that I had known who had been fairly free spirits tended to couple up very quickly and they became pairs of people as a security blanket as much as anything.

Young generation

Fourteen men, or half the interviewees from the post-HIV generation, raised the matter of sexual practices when explaining how HIV-AIDS had affected their sense of self. According to the testimonies of those interviewees who referred to sexual practices, they understood the effect of HIV-AIDS as underlining the importance of (a) safe sex, (b) monogamous relationships, or (c) sexual relations with men who were not HIV positive. In other words, the interviewees either withdrew from sexually adventurous encounters altogether or continued to have them. If they continued to have them, they did so either according to safe-sex principles or by participating selectively. Interestingly, none mentioned celibacy.[30] In the following section, these three sets of accounts are examined in order.

Of the 10 men who spoke of practising safe sex, only one man, Drew, aged 39, had been sexually active in the time before HIV-AIDS was detected in Australia (early 1980s). 'I remember pre-AIDS,' he said, 'and things were so much easier. You did not have to take precautions. It did not matter what you did.' Drew's reminiscences contrast an imaginary, halcyon time of seemingly 'easy sex' with the serious-minded approach now required in order to avoid contracting the disease;

> In those days, nothing like ... [safe sex] mattered. There was a group of maybe 30 that used to hang out in the gardens at night. Everyone was sleeping with everyone and it was not a huge issue then, but now you just cannot do that anymore. It is not worth the risk. It has impacted a lot but it is easy to take precautions to make sure that it is not going to affect you.

Drew's account is notable for two other reasons. It demonstrated first, his ability to adapt to changing sexual mores and practices, and second, his responsiveness to state-funded sexual health campaigns.

One of the three Aboriginal interviewees in this sample, Vincent, aged 30, spoke of practising safe sex so as to take control of his sexual identity and sex life:

> [W]hen I started having sex in 1994–5, you were told, 'condoms, condoms, condoms'. There was a bit of fear about it, but I made a conscious choice that I was not going to let that fear control my sexuality but that I would always have safe sex.

The remaining eight men variously referred, like Vincent, to having no sense of things being different, that is, that safe sex was *de rigueur* from the moment they became sexually mature, and being, in the words of one of them, 'bombarded when I first came out with information about safe sex' (Harry, aged 28).

Two men said that they withdrew from sexually adventurous encounters because of the threat of HIV-AIDS.[31] Mick (aged 33) was one of the men who said he found the disease frightening. He was in a stable relationship now, which he said was preferable to his previous relationship, where his partner did not want to 'settle down':

> He wanted to play up outside but then come home to a relationship.[32] To me that was very frightening because I … [did] not know who he was mucking around with and what they could have passed on to me.

Travis (aged 38) was the other person whom it could be said had withdrawn from sexual adventurism in the face of the threat HIV-AIDS posed. In his view, HIV-AIDS had not affected his sense of self because his partner was the only man with whom he had had a relationship and, in his words, 'because we have a monogamous relationship, it has not affected us in any way'. In Travis's mind, HIV could only affect a person's identity if s/he were infected by it.

As mentioned, when describing how HIV-AIDS affected their identify, two groups of younger men said that they continued to engage in sexually adventurous encounters. The first group, comprising 10 men, did so by following safe-sex principles. The second group, consisting of two men, spoke of avoiding sex with men who were HIV positive, a strategy that many health officials understand but none recommends. This is also known as 'negotiated safety', and is an arrangement that allows gay men to have sex without what some regard as the limitations of safe sex. When two men have what is called 'negotiated safe sex', they arrange or decide to have unprotected anal intercourse on the understanding that each is HIV negative. Such an arrangement is not as foolproof as protected anal intercourse because its 'safety' rests on two important assumptions: that each man knows that he is HIV negative and is telling the truth about what he knows. As well, such arrangements are not always made in advance after an exchange of views but in the heat of the sexual moment or on the basis of the other's features, 'how he looked' across a crowded bar or in a sex club. Negotiated safety and other strategies more common in groups or communities of HIV-positive men, such as 'sero-sorting' and 'strategic positioning', are regularly discussed in publications of the Australian Federation of AIDS Organisations (AFAO) and the National Association of People Living with HIV-AIDS (NAPWA).[33]

The two men who said that their response to HIV-AIDS was to avoid sex with men who were HIV positive were aged 36 and 24 respectively at the time of interview. The account of the first man, Jeremy, was fairly straightforward, and concerned only one, albeit significant, experience where he terminated a budding relationship when a man in whom he was interested disclosed that he was HIV positive. 'It was a real head spin,' said Jeremy. 'I was scared for him. I was scared for me. "What have I done? Have I contracted it?" I asked myself.' Very quickly, Jeremy's fears overwhelmed him, prevented him from considering safe sex as a means of continuing sexual (and/or affective) relations with his putative partner, and they parted as friends.

The account of the second man, Troy, was less straightforward because it revealed a more confused understanding of the virus and its threat to an individual's health. In the first part of his narrative, Troy admitted to having had unprotected (anal) sex, which he said occurred in 'the heat of passion'. Nowhere in his interview did he indicate whether he was penetrated, penetrating, or a combination of both in his sexual practice. The second part of his narrative concerned his friends' response on learning that he had unprotected (also known as 'unsafe') sex: 'my friends smack[ed] me in the head for doing that'. Troy did not seem seriously concerned, however, for in the third part of his narrative he said that 'scare campaigns' [that is, sexual health campaigns] caused 'the fear factor about AIDS'. In the final, increasingly contradictory, part of his narrative, he said that he would avoid having sex with someone who was HIV positive, admitted that this was 'a bad prejudice on my part', and then acknowledged that 'you can still enjoy someone [who is HIV positive] and not be exposed to it' – presumably by practising safe sex. The final part of his narrative was contradictory because elsewhere in his interview Troy explained that a former partner was HIV positive.

Troy was 24 when interviewed. He appeared to be a confident, self-assured man. During his interview, he said that his sex life began as a young teenager. His narrative on safe sex was inconsistent because it contained elements that jostled with one another: sex in the heat of the moment, which he later regretted and for which friends reprimanded him. Possibly too frightened to accept personal responsibility for his actions, he blamed the education campaigns for spreading fear. The least consistent aspect of his narrative concerned his sexual relations with an HIV-positive man, a former partner. Here Troy advised against so doing, then almost immediately contradicted himself, insisting it was possible to enjoy oneself and not be exposed to the virus.

There are a number of possible reasons for Troy's inconsistent narrative. For instance, it was heavily influenced by the views of his friends, sexual and affective partners, and perhaps also by his desire to please in the interview. I had the distinct impression also that as well as wishing to please in his interview, Troy wanted to show me that he was aware of the practices and principles of safe sex, which he might have assumed were expected of him as a young, sexually adventurous, gay man.

From among the young generation who said that the virus's effect was to cause them to practise safe sex, only one (of 14 men) reported any experience of loss.[34] This suggests that their willingness to adopt safe-sex practices was more a consequence of the public education campaign that began when they were children or teenagers, and continues to be disseminated now that they are adults. In other words, unlike the men from the middle generation, who witnessed the death of friends at time when being HIV positive frequently meant contracting AIDS and then dying, the young men in this sample were not practising safe sex in reaction to the seen, visceral consequences of becoming HIV positive but as learned experience.

Loss and solidarity

The third narrative concerned the men's witnessing friends or lovers' illnesses or death, and/or caring for them while ill or dying. Twenty-four interviewees (about 40 per cent of the sample) said they gained a greater sense of connection with other gay men as a result of these experiences and, in so doing, could see that this might have contributed to the growth of a stronger 'gay community'.[35]

Scholars are generally agreed that one of the more remarkable effects of AIDS was to invigorate gay communities in western countries in the mid to late 1990s. In the first place, groups of gay men used their own resources in the form of their labour, time, and community leadership to organise, lobby, and care for people living with the virus. Then, in the case of some countries – for example, Australia and New Zealand – they were able to work co-operatively with governments in shaping health policy.[36] Networks of gay men, whose engagement with gay culture before the advent of AIDS had mainly focused on hedonistic pursuits, such as dancing and having sex, showed themselves able to respond altruistically and communally:

> AIDS provided a powerful and renewed source of strength to gay identity and gay institutions because, at least temporarily, it made any divisions in the community relatively less important, since the common life-and-death struggle took precedence over almost all differences; it formed a set of issues around which all parts of the community, including those excluded by male sexual practice, could work together; and it created a sense of crisis that moved even the most nonpolitical homosexuals and those whose participation in the community had hitherto been marginal to provide their money, labor [*sic*], and talent for the struggle.[37]

Gay community networks in Australia and similar western countries became stronger as a result and began to transform into more diverse, inclusive social structures. Ken Plummer has argued that by the final decade of the twentieth century, the growing acceptance of gay men could be measured by the expanding volume of stories they were telling about their lives.[38] Despite the growth in homophobia that some western countries experienced in the 1990s and 2000s, stories such as those that Plummer identifies continue to be told and add to a greater, more positive gay presence.[39] One of the important social effects of the epidemic was that it showed gay men that their relationships were not secure and provided them with a very strong reason to demand state recognition for their relationships. During the epidemic, men discovered that their de facto relationships had no standing when families forbade lovers and friends from attending their son's funerals because they did not want to acknowledge the cause of death, or when hospitals allowed siblings and parents access to dying men but not lovers because they were not kith or kin. As discussed in Chapter 5, experiences such as these underpinned gay men's energetic involvement in the gay marriage campaign in, for example, Europe and the USA.

The third narrative might appear paradoxical, combining, as it does, the loss many men experienced, especially those from the middle generation, when friends diagnosed with AIDS died in the 1980s and 1990s, and the solidarity they experienced as they and others worked together to care for ill and dying friends and strangers, to raise money, to lobby governments, to organise themselves, and raise the consciousness of other gay men and heterosexual citizens. This is best expressed in an extract from the transcript of interview from a 50-year-old man, Des, who worked in health:

> It really has not had a lot of effect on me personally except the ... loss of close friends who ... died ... of HIV, and the violent reaction that the community had against gay men [in the early years]. But then politically ... it was [possibly] the best thing to happen. Sometimes when something drastic happens, it is like opening a wound. ... [T]he ... gay community united ... stood up and said, 'We are not the devil. We are not what you perceive us to be. We are a loving, caring, and giving community like everyone else; and we demand respect.'

Middle generation

When recounting the sense of loss they experienced as a result of HIV-AIDS in Australia, almost all this group of 16 men from the middle generation recalled deaths of friends, partners, or acquaintances. Interestingly, given what many scholars have observed about their generation's involvement in building a stronger gay community both during and after the worst of the epidemic, only four men referred to it in their interviews.

It is clear from the accounts of the men who recalled the deaths of friends and partners that the experiences profoundly affected them at the time. Samuel (aged 57) recalled many funerals he attended; the one man in this generation who was living with HIV-AIDS, Stuart (aged 49), said that his friends were dying all around him as he 'became sick'; Jerome (aged 49), remembered visiting hospital 'three of four times a week every week for long periods'; and Scott (aged 45), who was travelling in Europe and the USA when the epidemic began, recalled, 'when I came back from overseas ... so many people I had known ... were no longer there'.

As mentioned, four men from this group referred to gay solidarity along with loss. Two of these men did so when describing the effect of the disease on gay men in general. The first, Noel, aged 58, observed that the disease 'had a positive impact on the gay rights movement'; and the second, Des, aged 50, noted 'the gay community united in solidarity'. The other two men demonstrated their involvement in gay politics and community-building in the accounts they gave of care work they did, and in the case of one still do for PLWHA. Trevor, aged 49, said that he and his partner

> looked after people who have been dying with AIDS. ... We've gone to fundraisers. ... The last few years, we've been making up hampers to help people with AIDS. We buy socks and tee shirts and food for them at Christmas time. It's usually 20 people that we contribute towards making up hampers [for]. We spend ... close to a thousand dollars on these hampers. ... It's the only way we can really help in the gay community.

Finally, Samuel, aged 57, who still works with PLWHA, said that when the epidemic was at its fiercest, he 'worked with people with HIV-AIDS and have quite a lot of clients who have died of AIDS'.

Young generation

Three men interviewed for this chapter were HIV positive at the time of interview, two of whom were from the young generation. Included in these two men's interviews were frank, poignant stories of how, on learning that they were HIV positive, they adjusted to the loss of who they might have been and become. Julius, aged 34, said 'I found myself somewhere I never thought I would be.' Unwilling to expand on this statement, he limited himself to saying that he had learned to love himself more, to enjoy life more, and, in his words, 'to set myself goals, which I never did before. I have begun to live day by day.'

The other HIV-positive man from the young generation was Jason, who was aged 35 at the time of interview. He provided a fuller account of how he learned to adjust to the loss of who he might have been. It took him five years, he said, 'to pull [him]self back together mentally'. When he was diagnosed, he was 22, when many of the HIV treatments were still in an experimental phase, and Jason was terrified.

The remaining six men from the young generation who drew on the third narrative to explain the effect of HIV-AIDS on their sense of self spoke of loss in isolation did not refer to any experience of gay community solidarity. All of them had stories of losing friends, partners or, in the case of one interviewee who was a health worker, clients as well:

> When friends have died or been really ill and I have been dealing with that in my personal life, and with HIV prevention as work, I have almost felt that my life was defined by the virus, that it was part of who I was, even though I am not [an HIV-] positive person. (Joseph, aged 35)

Another man in his 30s was so affected by the thought of the disease that he was unable to visit a friend in hospital who was dying from it: 'he was demented and I did not have the courage to do it'. Despite this, and despite being exposed to the disease in the 12 months before his interview and undertaking the post-exposure prophylaxis treatment and speaking to counsellors at the time Robert, aged 38, still began his narrative account of the effect of HIV-AIDS on his sense of self with the sentence 'In some ways, I have not really confronted the question of HIV-AIDS.' Paradoxical as this might seem, what Robert might have been saying is that he had not yet found a way to deal with the terror it aroused in him, that, in a sense, he was still in its thrall – so much so, that at the conclusion of his answer, he rationalised his fear thus: 'it is a fact of life, like a lot of other risks we take. People drive cars and a lot of people die from car accidents.'

Intuitively, and on the basis of what is known about the period from other research, it makes sense that more men from the middle generation than from the young generation (twice as many) spoke of loss and solidarity, for theirs was the generation most immediately affected by the epidemic and from whom the largest number of volunteers and workers came who devoted themselves to the work of recovery.[40]

Conclusion

On comparing the two generations of men interviewed for this chapter, only minor variations would appear to exist between how they drew on the three principal narratives to explain the effect of HIV-AIDS on their sense of self.

In regard to the first narrative – fear, vulnerability, and stigma – while the men from the pre-HIV generation recalled the rise in stigma that occurred in the early years of the epidemic, their chief fear centred on the disease's mode of transmission, that is, specifically which sexual practices involved risk and which did not, and whether in the years before modes of transmission were known or the test was available their sexual history meant that they had contracted the virus. Any fear or sense of vulnerability the men from the post-HIV generation experienced mostly concerned their present-day sexual practices, and in general terms whether there was any possibility they had 'slipped up' or would 'slip up', in other words would engage in unsafe (unprotected anal) sex, in the words of an interviewee in his 20s, 'in the heat of the moment'. What experience the young men had of stigma seemed to be a carryover from the initial outburst of homophobia that accompanied the onset of HIV-AIDS in Australia in the mid to late 1980s. These men grew up in a time when knowledge of HIV-AIDS was widely known, and yet as Angus (aged 23) explained (above), sex education classes in secondary school could be occasions for public outburst of homophobia that conflated homosexuality and HIV-AIDS.[41]

The second principal narrative – changed sexual practice – was used similarly by both age cohorts. The men generally spoke of the importance that they placed on their knowledge of safe-sex practices, while a small number from both age cohorts explained how they understood and practised monogamy as the best defence against the threat of the disease. The exception to these two trends was a minor narrative that two men from the post-HIV cohort used to explain how they employed a strategy of selectively engaging in sexual encounters with men whom they judged not to be HIV positive.

The third principal narrative – loss and gay solidarity – showed only one difference between the two cohorts. This was that almost all the men from the pre-HIV cohort who made use of the narrative had experienced deaths of friends or partners, whereas only a handful of men from the post-HIV cohort had similar experiences. Their relatively limited experience of death from AIDS might help to explain why the disease held more terror for the men from the post-HIV generation than for those from the older generation. Expression of gay community solidarity was fairly evenly represented by generation, with the men from the middle generation showing a slightly more practical engagement.

A clear, although not especially significant, generation difference existed in relation to the third principal narrative, loss and solidarity. The men from the pre-HIV generation reported experiencing both loss and solidarity, often describing a causal connection between the two, while those from the post-HIV generation experienced only loss in response to witnessing the deaths of friends or lovers. This makes sense historically because, as discussed, most published research identified the community-building that took place in the midst of the epidemic as a marked, positive response to the disease. This community-building occurred in the 1990s, when the older men were able to take part in the rebuilding or witnessed it or its benefits, but when the men from the post-HIV generation were still children or teenagers and only beginning to become aware of the disease. What differences in attitude that exist between the two generations of men were results of the men's birth years and the social/medical context prevailing as they grew to adulthood.

Conclusion

> The important thing is that we need to have a much
> deeper understanding of these ... gay ... communities.
> They are not one single community. We tend to gen-
> eralise hugely, and so the more research that is carried
> on, the more oral histories, the more intelligence-
> seeking information about patterns of life, the better
> the future will be for people like us.
>
> (Amery, aged 82, Sydney)

Two underlying ideas connect the stories that my interviewees told me
and the larger stories that I have told in the foregoing chapters. They
are first, a propensity for gay men to conform to existing, mostly heterosexual patterns of relationships, and second, to create relationships
that more closely suit their circumstances and needs. These impulses
to conform to heterosexual norms or to create new patterns of relations and behaviour mean that the relational lives of gay men are both
similar to and different from those of the heterosexual majority. Gay
relationships that are similar makes them easy for outsiders to identify
and understand; those that are different require outsiders to take more
time to understand them. I hope this book goes some way to help gay
men understand the variety of relationship types available to them and
where those came from that are different from the relationships their
straight friends enjoy and why they were fashioned the way they are.
I hope also it goes some way to help straight readers understand the
reasons for gay relationships being as they are and why they were created both in the shape of heterosexual relationships and differently in
order to suit gay men's social and sexual needs.

In the paragraphs that follow, I summarise some of the more important findings from the preceding chapters, beginning with Chapter 1,
where I explained when and how I recruited the 97 men for the international sample and the 80 men for the all-Australian sample. The stories
the single men told were considered in the context of increasing numbers of people in their 20s and 30s living single lives (Chapter 2), and
two myths about friendship and loneliness. My analysis of the stories
the single men told showed that almost half them (n = 41) led full and
active social lives. I found also that age was not a crucial factor in men's
experience of being single, and also strong evidence of their capacity
to practise friendship well. This last finding was significant because it
helps explain why, contrary to negatives myths, a single life is not a
lonely life and that, again, contrary to negative myths, gay men can
maintain strong, mutually beneficial friendships.

Examination of the stories the men told about their intimate lives
(Chapter 3) showed that gay men's long-lasting relationships most
strongly resembled the companionate marriage in quality and nature and
were not overly sexualised, except in the first, early blush of romance, or
if the men conducted open relationships. In support of this argument, I
found evidence in the men's relationship stories of three companionate
traits, which I identified as a cosy togetherness, companionship, and
partnership. Evidence for cosy togetherness came in men's accounts
of the physical intimacy of sharing a bed to 'snuggle up' and caring
for one another's wellbeing. Companionship is more complex, and
evidence for it was found in men's accounts of the emotional support
their partner provided. The relative insignificance of sexual relations
in the stories the men told of their relationships was notable because
first, it is often assumed that sex plays the most prominent role in gay
men's relationships, and that gay men are highly sexed and sexualised;
and second, because of how similar these long-lasting relationships are
to the image of long-term heterosexual couple relations. Two groups of
men spoke of the sex in their relationships. The first group did so when
referring to an early period in their relationship when they had a lot of
sex, or to the fact that their relationship was now less sexualised or had
transformed so that sex was only one means of expressing their affective
bond. The second group of men referred to sex in the context of their
relationship as an open relationship. Finally, I found a minor narrative
as well in the men's stories about love, how they understood it, and
how they expressed it. Generally speaking, I inferred love's presence in
the men's relationships when they used companionship or partnership
narratives, which was the case for a small handful of men from cities

including Manchester, Melbourne, Sydney, and New York. Like many of their straight male counterparts, the men interviewed for this book showed a strong reluctance to use the word 'love' when speaking about the qualities of their couple relationships.

Fourteen Australian men and eight men from the international sample had stories to tell of fatherhood (Chapter 4). These men came to be fathers as the result of former relationships with women or 'everyday experiments' (for example, with a lesbian couple or surrogacy). Heterosexual fatherhood represented the experience of the large majority of gay men interviewed for this chapter. Non-heterosexual fatherhood represented the experience of five men from this sample, three of whom were in their 30s. The fatherhood stories the men interviewed for this chapter related ranged from accounts of intense, involved fathering – including those from four of the five non-heterosexual fathers, as well as men in their 50s and one in his 60s – to relationships that were regular and close, to more distant relationships, and no relationship at all. The accounts of intense, involved fathering reflected an explicit dedication and willingness to commit to fathering, which is in contrast to prevailing stereotypes of (a) men's general unwillingness to devote time to caring for their children unless asked to so by their wife or female partner, and (b) gay men's self-centredness.

The focus of Chapters 5 and 6 was on why a majority of younger men favoured gay marriage and why a majority of the men aged 51 and older did not. My analysis showed that more than 40 per cent of the international sample favoured gay marriage, and that another 20 per cent favoured civil union, but not gay marriage. Therefore, more than 60 per cent of the men interviewed for this book were in favour of legalising same-sex relationships. I found a number of themes when I looked at the men's arguments about legalising same-sex relationships. The younger men (aged 51 and under) mainly argued in favour of legal/property equality, relational equality, and recognition of relationship success through marriage. In doing so, they were using arguments similar to those that have been in circulation in the West since the push for marriage equality began in the 1990s. The close correlation between the men's arguments favouring gay marriage and arguments in the literature on same-sex marriage suggested strong cross-germination of ideas between scholars in gay and lesbian studies and GLBT activists in the West. While the older men (51 and over) drew on similar narratives about legal/property equality and relational equality, some of them saw support for gay marriage as a continuation of their earlier involvement in social activism, beginning in the days of gay liberation. Others among them drew on practical arguments about the suitability of tried and true cohabitation arrangements. These men said that if their relationships were serial, stable, and monogamous, they were married in all but name and that therefore gay marriage was unnecessary. More than 20 per cent of the sample opposed gay marriage. Here, the men's principal arguments were that many gay men had no wish to marry, that marriage was a patriarchal institution, and that gay marriage would represent a return to heteronormativity for gays and lesbians.

Different generations of gay men – men who were sexually active when HIV-AIDS was first diagnosed in the West (the early 1980s) and men in their 20s and 30s and sexually active in the early 2000s – mostly regarded the threat of the disease similarly. My analysis of the men's stories in Chapter 7 showed strong evidence for the effectiveness of the safe-sex message. I found also evidence of greater willingness among men in their 20s to take 'strategic risks', which is in line with other published research. By contrast, I found no evidence of willingness to take such risks from the men who belonged to the pre-HIV generation, who were sexually active when the disease was first diagnosed in Australia and other western countries, who had first-hand experiences of the havoc it caused gay men's friendship networks and communities in the 1980s and 1990s. What I did find from these men, however, were recollections of risky sexual behaviour in the years before the onset of HIV-AIDS and memories of the fear these caused them when news of the mode of transmission became public. Unlike a small group of men from the post-HIV generation who were willing to engage in risky sex, the older men showed strong signs of having absorbed public health messages about safe sex and duly adjusted their sexual practices.

Unlike positivist scholars, I did not include a control group of heterosexuals, against whose relationship stories I could compare those of the gay men interviewed for the book. Instead, I relied on the work of other scholars such as Zygmunt Bauman, Ulrich Beck, Elizabeth Beck-Gernsheim, Lynn Jamieson, Martha Nussbaum, and Nancy Polikoff, among others, to provide insight into the state and status of heterosexual relationships in the late twentieth and early twenty-first century in the West. I used their accounts of changing or persisting patterns of behaviour as a basis for comparing the stories my interviewees told me about their lives as single men, their experiences of long-lasting relationships and fatherhood, their views on gay marriage, for and against, and their experiences of living in the midst of HIV-AIDS.

The book continues to challenge myths about gay men and their relationships, namely, that they are sex-obsessed, incapable of sustained, long-lasting relationships, and live lonely lives if single. Like Dennis Altman writing in the 1970s,[1] I hope to live long enough to see the end of the sexual apartheid that has beset the West since the late nineteenth century when doctors and lawyers began distinguishing between and moralising about human sexual behaviour on the basis of individuals' erotic desire. And, like many other researchers in this field, I see a close connection between sexual freedom and human rights. To me, it seems very strange, as John Boswell pointed out in the 1990s before his death from HIV, that it is easier for some people to speak about individuals who commit murder or genocide than to mention men who sleep with men.[2]

At the very least, what I think this book has shown is how alike gay men are to the rest of the population – how alike we are in how we manage our friendships and relationships, and yet how distinctive and unique the experimental relationships and families we create can be. When greater numbers of straight people come to realise and accept this, I suspect they will have less need to fear gay men and more reason to accept the same extraordinary variety in humans that Alfred Kinsey found and celebrated in his gall wasps. I believe this book's most important contribution to a better understanding of gay men's lives and relationships is in emphasising how their lives have been and are socially constructed in response to varying degrees of social tolerance, and how gay men have shaped their relationships either by conforming to dominant, heterosexual patterns or by shaping them through experimentation to suit their own needs.

Appendixes

Table A.1 International sample, 2009–2011

Code name	Age	City*	Occupation field
Randall	87	Mel	Human services
Herbert	82	Mel	Clerical
Amery	82	Syd	Education
Clancy	81	Mel	Retail
Godfrey	81	Syd	Education
Hector	81	Mel	Small business
Drake	77	Mel	Media
Ambrose	77	Mel	Education
Basil	75	Auc	Retail
Lucas	75	Auc	Transport
Colin	72	NY	Education
Christian	72	Syd	Law
Jeffery	72	Auc	Transport
Arran	70	Mel	Human services
Ashton	70	Syd	Small business
Sean	67	Auc	Small business
Baden	65	Mel	Small business
Alfie	63	Man	Clerical
Fergus	63	Man	Education
Parry	63	NY	Business
Bryce	63	Man	Entertainment
Arthur	62	Lon	Health
Hugh	62	Mel	Education
Alec	62	Syd	Research
Anselm	61	Mel	Education
Ward	59	NY	Education
Marvin	59	LA	Clerical
Bernard	59	HK	Small business
Raymond	58	HK	Business
Austin	57	Auc	Education
Cam	56	LA	Welfare
Logan	56	Auc	Business
Isaac	56	Mel	Health
Ryan	53	Lon	Media
Hilton	53	NY	Human services
Zachary	52	HK	Construction & bldg
Ben	52	Man	Education
Mike	52	Mel	Bureaucracy

(*continued*)

Table A.1 Continued

Code name	Age	City*	Occupation field
Tate	51	Lon	Business
Earl	51	NY	Business
Buck	51	HK	Business
Calvin	51	Mel	Business
Nathan	50	Auc	Small business
Carl	49	Auc	Education
Everett	49	NY	Human services
Ethan	49	Lon	Clerical
Danny	48	HK	Media
Fred	47	Lon	Construction & bldg
Alvin	47	NY	Education
Teddy	47	Mum	Health
Duncan	47	HK	Business
Timothy	46	NY	Human services
Jude	46	LA	Education
Eddie	45	Man	Education
Kendall	44	NY	Finance
Edmund	44	Mum	Agriculture
Jonathon	44	Lon	Business
Callum	43	Mel	Education
Gabriel	43	Auc	Health
Joe	42	HK	Entertainment
Jacob	42	Mel	Research
Noah	42	Auc	Education
Felix	41	HK	Clerical
Connor	41	Lon	Retail
Charlie	40	HK	Entertainment
Kyle	40	Auc	Business
Guy	38	Lon	Business
Liam	37	Syd	Education
Anton	35	Lon	Law
Evan	35	LA	IT
Alexander	34	HK	IT
Findlay	33	NY	Clerical
Aiden	33	Lon	Law
Dylan	32	Syd	Clerical
Jackson	32	NY	Welfare
Leo	31	Syd	Human services
Gavin	31	Auc	Retail
Jem	29	HK	Human services
Curtis	29	HK	Health
Eamon	28	Lon	Construction & bldg
Howard	28	Mum	Health
Denis	27	Mel	Entertainment

(*continued*)

Table A.1 Continued

Code name	Age	City*	Occupation field
William	27	Mum	Business
Bailey	26	Man	Education
Kenny	24	HK	Business
Giiles	23	Mum	Education
Kim	23	Mum	Education
Garth	23	Mel	Education
Jarrad	23	Mel	Education
Zane	22	Mel	Education
Hayden	21	Mel	Education
Jamie	21	Mel	Education
Todd	21	Mel	Education
Dominic	20	HK	Education
Toby	19	Mum	Health
Brody	19	Mel	Education
Dougal	18	Mel	Retail

* City codes: Auc = Auckland, New Zealand; HK = Hong Kong, China; Lon = London, UK; LA = Los Angeles, USA; Man = Manchester, UK; Mel = Melbourne, Australia; Mum = Mumbai, India; NY = New York City, USA; Syd = Sydney, Australia.

Table A.2 Australian sample, 2001–2003

Code name	Age	City*	Occupation field
Reginald	79	Mel	Clerical
Gerald	75	Mel	Construction & bldg
Vernon	75	Ade	Entertainment
Leslie	74	Hbt	Education
Chester	71	Mel	Small business
Harold	71	NSWa	Education
Geoffrey	69	NSWb	Media
Ronald	68	Mel	Education
Charles	67	NSWb	Businessman
Kelvin	66	Mel	Education
Maurice	65	NSWb	Small business
Kenneth	65	Mel	Business
Oscar	65	Mel	Food
John	65	Hbt	Bureaucracy
Brendan	64	Hbt	Bureaucracy
Clive	64	Cbr	Bureaucracy
Terrence	64	Ade	Education
Douglas	63	Mel	Health
Leonard	63	Ade	Retail
Lindsay	62	Ade	Education

(*continued*)

Table A.2 Continued

Code name	Age	City*	Occupation field
Barry	62	NSWb	Agriculture
Edward	60	Cbr	Media
Lionel	59	Mel	Education
Noel	58	Hbt	Education
Roy	58	Hbt	Construction & bldg
Richard	58	Syd	Education
Samuel	56	NSWb	Welfare
Ross	54	Hbt	Bureaucracy
Patrick	53	Hbt	Media
Thomas	52	NSWa	Education
Kevin	52	Mel	Business
Bill	52	Mel	Education
Donald	52	Ade	Health
Michael	52	Mel	Education
Graham	52	Mel	Bureaucracy
Henry	50	NSWa	Human services
Des	50	Syd	Health
Trevor	49	Mel	Food
Stuart	49	Mel	IT
Jerome	49	NSWb	Business
Nigel	49	Cbr	Bureaucracy
Glen	49	NSWa	Transport
Bob	48	NSWb	Media
Alan	47	NSWa	Education
Simon	46	Cbr	Construction & bldg
Neil	46	Mel	Bureaucracy
James	45	Hbt	Education
Scott	45	Mel	Education
Roger	44	Cbr	Education
Mathew	42	NSWa	Law
Ivan	40	NSWa	Health
Ken	40	NSWa	Agriculture
Drew	39	NSWa	Small business
Robert	38	Mel	IT
Travis	38	NSWa	Transport
Neville	37	Mel	Education
Andy	37	Mel	Food
Alex	37	Hbt	Bureaucracy
Jeremy	36	Syd	Finance
Joseph	35	Mel	Human services
Daniel	35	Mel	Human services
Jason	35	Mel	Education
Julius	34	Mel	Education
Paul	33	Mel	Entertainment

(*continued*)

Table A.2   Continued

Code name	Age	City*	Occupation field
Tony	33	Mel	Law
Mick	33	NSWa	Transport
Luke	32	NSWa	Education
Adrian	30	Syd	Finance
Brian	30	NSWa	Transport
Vincent	30	Mel	Education
Harry	28	NSWa	Human services
Ian	28	Hbt	Bureaucracy
David	28	NSWa	Human services
Mark	25	Mel	Education
Myles	24	Syd	Clerical
Lachlan	24	Syd	Clerical
Adam	24	NSWa	Education
Troy	24	Syd	Education
Angus	23	Mel	Education
Jack	22	Syd	Bureaucracy

*City codes: Ade = Adelaide; Cbr = Canberra; Hbt = Hobart; Mel = Melbourne; NSWa = country town in southern New South Wales; NSWb = country town in central New South Wales; Syd = Sydney. Because the two country towns in NSW were relatively small, their names have been disguised so as to protect the interviewees' identity.

Table A.3   Relationship status

Age cohorts	Single	Relationship	Total
70+	8	7	15
50–70	11	17	28
30–50	17	17	34
≤30	6	14	20

Note: Single n = 42 or 43 per cent of the 97 men from the international sample. Of these 42 men, 30 had previously been in relationships, which on average were 6.5 years in length. Relationships n = 55 or 57 per cent of the sample.

Table A.4   Single men

Name	Age	City
Amery	82	Syd
Clancy	81	Mel
Godfrey	81	Syd
Ambrose	77	Mel
Basil	75	Auc

(continued)

Table A.4 Continued

Name	Age	City
Lucas	75	Auc
Jeffery	72	Auc
Colin	72	NY
Fergus	63	Man
Alec	62	Syd
Anselm	61	Mel
Marvin	59	LA
Austin	57	Auc
Cam	56	LA
Ryan	53	Lon
Hilton	53	NY
Mike	52	Mel
Calvin	51	Mel
Earl	51	NY
Carl	49	Auc
Ethan	49	Lon
Everett	49	NY
Teddy	47	Mu
Jude	46	LA
Timothy	46	NY
Kendall	44	NY
Felix	41	HK
Connor	41	Lon
Kyle	40	Auc
Charlie	40	HK
Guy	38	Lon
Evan	35	LA
Anton	35	Lon
Alexander	34	HK
Dylan	32	Syd
Leo	31	Syd
Curtis	29	HK
Eamon	28	Lon
Garth	23	Mel
Jarrad	23	Mel
Giles	23	Mu
Dougal	18	Mel

Table A.5 Fatherhood settings

Code	Age	Married/union &/or children
Bernard	59	Adopted s
Gabriel	43	Civil U + 1s
Neville	37	No + 2d (cousins)
Joseph	35	No + 2s (foster)
Tony	33	1d
Hector	81	55Married* + 1d
John	65	40Married + 2d
Douglas	63	39Married + 4d, 1s
Leslie	74	36Married + 3d, 1s
Randall	87	35Married* + 4ch
Gerald	75	31Married + 2d, 1s
Anselm	61	26Married* + 1d
Drake	77	24Married* + 2d
Henry	50	20Married + 2s, 2d
Terrence	64	20Married + 1s, 1d
Hilton	53	18Married + 2d
Austin	57	15Married* + 3 s
Ross	54	13Married + 1d, 2g/d
Clive	64	11Married + 2s, 1d
Trevor	49	08Married + 1s
Roy	58	08Married + 2s
Scott	45	07Married + 1d

*Length of marriage inferred from material provided in transcripts; years not specified in interview. ch = children; d = daughter; s = son; g/d = granddaughter; g/s = grandson. 55Married = married for 55 years.

Notes

Introduction

1. Royal College of Nursing and UNISON (2004) 'Not just a friend: best practice guidance on health care for lesbian, gay and bisexual service users and their families': http://www.asaging.org/lgbtch-search?title=nursing&body=nursing, accessed 4 December 2012.
2. GLBT is the acronym for gay, lesbian, bisexual, and transgender.
3. D. Altman (1989) 'Aids and the Reconceptualization of Homosexuality' in D. Altman et al. *Homosexuality, Which Homosexuality? Essays from the International Conference on Gay and Lesbian Studies* (London: GMP), p. 35.
4. P. Robinson (2008) *The Changing World of Gay Men* (Basingstoke and New York: Palgrave Macmillan).
5. Having been born in the early 1950s, I belong to the baby-boomer generation. I was in my 50s when I first sent my editor a proposal to write this book, and in my late 50s when I sent her the final manuscript. I was educated at Melbourne University and Oxford University, and was awarded my PhD as a mature-age student in 2007.
6. F. Bongiorno [Review of] Robinson *Changing World* in *Journal of Australian Studies*, 33(3), September 2009. On the myth of the gay male world as a middle-class creation, see, for example, George Chauncey (1994) *Gay New York: Gender, Urban Culture, and the Making of the Gay Male World, 1890–1940* (New York: Basic Books), p. 10.
7. P. Shahani (2008) *Globalization, Love and (Be)longing in Contemporary India* (New Delhi: Sage), p. 50.
8. C. Jenkins (2006) 'Male Sexuality and HIV: The Case of Male-to-Male Sex' (Lucknow and London: Naz Foundation International); copies available at http://www.nfi.net/risks.htm, accessed 8 December 2012.
9. The information sheet I sent potential interviewees said that my research purpose was to interview gay men on the topic of gay age and ageing, and explained that gay men's life stories were one of my chief research interests.
10. D. Altman (2001) *Global Sex* (Sydney: Allen & Unwin), pp. 86–7.
11. S. Seidman (1992) *Embattled Eros: Sexual Politics and Ethics in Contemporary America* (London: Routledge), p. 191.
12. J. Boswell (1980) *Christianity, Social Tolerance, and Homosexuality: Gay People in Western Europe from the Beginning of the Christian Era to the Fourteenth Century* (Chicago: University of Chicago Press), pp. 26–7.
13. N. Elias (2000 [1939]) *The Civilizing Process: Sociogenetic and Psychogenetic Investigations*, trans. E. Jephcott with some notes and corrections by the author. E. Dunning, J. Goudsblom, and S. Mennell (eds), rev. edn (Oxford: Blackwell), pp. 414–21.
14. Robinson *Changing World*, pp. 8–13.
15. D. Altman (1982) *The Homosexualization of America, the Americanization of the Homosexual* (New York: St Martin's Press), p. 22.

16. For more discussion of the idea of gay community, see P. Robinson (2009) 'Gay Men's Experience of Community in Australia', *Journal of Australian Studies*, 33(1), 67–78.

17. On assimilationism, see, for example, P. Moore (2004) *Beyond Shame: Reclaiming the Abandoned History of Radical Gay Sexuality* (Boston, MA: Beacon Press), and R.C. Savin-Williams (2005) *The New Gay Teenager* (Cambridge, MA: Harvard University Press).

18. P. Simpson (2011) 'Differentiating the Self: How Gay Men in Manchester Respond to Ageing and Gay Ageism', Unpublished PhD Thesis: University of Manchester, p. 76.

19. Shahani *Globalization, Love and (Be)longing*.

20. S. Khan (1996) 'Culture, Sexualities, and Identities: Men Who Have Sex with Men in South Asia' (Lucknow and London: Naz Foundation International): http://www.nfi.net/articles_essays.htm, accessed 6 December 2012; J. Seabrook (1995) *Notes from Another India* (London: Pluto Press), and J. Seabrook (1999) *Love in a Different Climate: Men Who Have Sex with Men in India* (London: New Left Books).

21. A. Holleran (1990) *Dancer from the Dance* (London: Penguin Books).

22. For a more thorough discussion of the use of the term 'gay' to describe same-sex-attracted men, see Robinson *Changing World*, pp. xii–xiii.

23. Khan 'Culture, Sexualities, and Identities'.

24. K. Mannheim (1997 [1952]) 'The Problem of Generations' in M.A. Hardy (ed.) *Studying Aging and Social Change: Conceptual and Methodological Issues* (Thousand Oaks: Sage), pp. 22–65.

25. Mannheim 'The Problem', p. 24.

26. Robinson *Changing World*, p. 53.

27. C. Phillipson (2003) 'Intergenerational Conflict and the Welfare State: American and British Perspectives' in A. Walker (ed.) *The New Generational Contract: Intergenerational Relations, Old Age and Welfare* (London: Routledge), p. 212.

28. C. Attias-Donfut and S. Arber 'Equity and Solidarity Across the Generations' in S. Arber and C. Attias-Donfut (eds) *The Myth of Generational Conflict: The Family and State in Aging Societies* (Oxford: Routledge), pp. 7–8.

29. M. Bernard, J. Phillips, C. Phillipson, and J. Ogg (2000) 'Continuity and Change: The Family and Community Life of Older People in the 1990s' in Arber and Attias-Donfut *The Myth of Generational Conflict*, p. 216.

30. Attias-Donfut and Arber 'Equity and Solidarity', p. 3

31. K. Plummer (1995) *Telling Sexual Stories: Power, Change and Social Worlds* (London: Routledge).

32. D. Carr (2001) 'Narrative and the Real World: An Argument for Continuity' in L.P. Hinchman and S.K. Hinchman (eds) *Memory, Identity, Community: The Idea of Narrative in the Human Sciences* (New York: State University of New York Press), pp. 16–17.

33. For more discussion of the self as narratively constituted, see Robinson *Changing World*, pp. 6–8.

34. S. de Beauvoir (1977) *Old Age*, trans. P. O'Brien (Harmondsworth: Penguin Books); N. Elias (1987) *The Loneliness of the Dying*, trans. E. Jephcott (Oxford: Basil Blackwell); P. Laslett (2000) *The World We Have Lost: Further Explored*, 3rd edn (London: Routledge).

35. U. Beck and E. Beck-Gernsheim (2002) *Individualization: Institutionalized Individualism and Its Social and Political Consequences* (London: Sage), p. 133.
36. According to the Australian Bureau of Statistics, in 2011, the median age of death for Aboriginal and Torres Strait Islanders in South Australia was 50.3 years for both males and females; http://www.abs.gov.au/ausstats/abs@.nsf/Latestproducts/3302.0Main%20Features72011?opendocument&tabname=Summary&prodno=3302.0&issue=2011&num=&view=, accessed 6 December 2012.
37. M. Mohanty (ed.) (2004) *Class, Caste, Gender* (New Delhi: Sage), p. 20.
38. G. Pritchard *Pink News*, January 2008: http://www.pinknews.co.uk/2008/01/21/gay-nursing-home-opens-in-germany, accessed 3 December 2012. See also following piece by staff reporter *Pink News*, July 2009: http://www.pinknews.co.uk/2009/07/10/swedish-nursing-home-may-cater-specifically-for-gays, accessed 3 December 2012, and K. Connolly 'LGBT housing project unites generations out in Berlin', *The Guardian*, 28 October 2012. For Australia, see, for example, A. Simmons 'Aged care forcing gays "back into the closet"', *ABC News*, 12 July 2010: http://www.abc.net.au/news/2010-07-12/aged-care-forcing-gays-back-into-the-closet/901768, accessed 20 December 2012; T. Nightingale 'Advocates hail first aged care facilities for gays', *ABC News*, 25 May 2012: http://www.abc.net.au/news/2012-05-25/first-aged-care-facilities-for-gay-seniors/4034230, accessed 20 December 2012.
39. E. White (1986) *States of Desire: Travels in Gay America* (London: Pan Books), p. 62.

1 Collecting 97 Gay Men's Life Stories

1. See Tables A.1 and A.2 of Appendixes.
2. Chapter 4.
3. For details, see Table A.2.
4. For details, see Table A.1.
5. P. Robinson (2008) *The Changing World of Gay Men* (Basingstoke and New York: Palgrave Macmillan), pp. 3–4; R. Sennett and J. Cobb (1973) *The Hidden Injuries of Class* (New York: Alfred Knopf).
6. Robinson *Changing World*, ch. 4.
7. G. Robb (2004) *Strangers: Homosexual Love in the Nineteenth Century* (London: Pan Macmillan), pp. 61–3.
8. A web-cam is a small camera that can be attached to or is built into a computer to allow visual as well as audio communications.
9. Interviews continued via Skype until December 2011.
10. E. White (1986) *States of Desire* (London: Pan Books).
11. I received a positive response to my advertisement posted on the university's G&L website. Four men contacted me from San Francisco, three from Los Angeles, as well as those already mentioned who lived in New York. Because my travel plans were fixed and my budget constrained, I was not able to travel to San Francisco for interviews, which was a pity given the city's long history of gay social and political activism.
12. Interviews held indoors were with Colin (aged 72), Parry (aged 63), Ward (aged 59), Hilton (aged 53), Finlay (aged 33).

13. Colin (aged 72), Parry (aged 63), Ward (aged 59), Hilton (aged 53), Earl (aged 51), Everett (aged 49), Alvin (aged 47), Timothy (aged 46), Kendall (aged 46), Finlay (aged 33), Jackson (aged 32).

14. M. Davis (1992) *City of Quartz: Excavating the Future in Los Angeles* (New York: Random House), pp. 12, 244–50; see pp. 232–6 for discussion of municipal regulations designed to harass homeless people in chic areas of Los Angeles.

15. The four LA men were Marvin (aged 59), Cam (aged 56), Jude (aged 46), Evan (aged 35).

16. The Crown Prince of Gujarat, Prince Manvendra Singh Gohil, is a long-standing advocate of aged-care accommodation for elderly gay men in India generally and specifically in Gujarat.

17. I was in Mumbai 23–28 December 2009.

18. Arthur (aged 62), Teddy (aged 47), Edmund (aged 44), Howard (aged 28), William (aged 27), Giles (aged 23), Kim (aged 23), Toby (aged 19).

19. G. Herhsatter (1999) *Dangerous Pleasures: Prostitution and Modernity in Twentieth-Century Shanghai* (Berkeley: University of California Press).

20. Bernard (aged 59), Zachary (aged 52), Buck (aged 51).

21. T.S.K. Kong (2004) 'Queer at Your Own Risk: Marginality, Community and Hong Kong Gay Male Bodies', *Sexualities*, 7(5), 5–30.

22. Kong 'Queer at Your Own Risk', p. 13.

23. http://tcjm.org, accessed 9 December 2012.

24. Randall (aged 87), Herbert (aged 82), Clancy (aged 81), Hector (aged 81), Ambrose (aged 77), Drake (aged 77), Charlie (aged 70), Baden (aged 65), Hugh (aged 62), Anselm (aged 61), Isaac (aged 56), Mike (aged 52), Howard (aged 51), Callum (aged 43), Jacob (aged 42), Denis (aged 27), Garth (aged 23), Jarrad (aged 23), Zane (aged 22), Hayden (aged 21), Jamie (aged 21), Todd (aged 21), Brody (aged 19), Dougal (aged 18).

25. I included the sole Welsh interviewee in the English part of the sample and did so because his anonymity would have been compromised had I cited only one Welsh interviewee. In doing so, my intention was not to assume British cultural or ethnic homogeneity.

26. For international appeal of the Sydney gay and lesbian Mardi Gras festival, see G. Carbery (1995) *A History of the Sydney Gay and Lesbian Mardi Gras* (Melbourne: Australian Lesbian and Gay Archives), pp. 79, 89, 159, 177, 191–7, 218; for growth and development of Sydney gay scene, see Robinson *Changing World*, chs 5 and 6.

27. Australian Bureau of Statistics Quick Stats, October 2007.

28. According to its web page, Pride history group is a 'not for profit community history group which collects information about Sydney's gay, lesbian, bisexual, transgender and queer past'.

29. Associate Professor Donna Baines of McMasters University put me in touch with Michael Stevens when she was on sabbatical at Auckland University.

30. Auckland (1,303,068), source: 2006 *Census of Population and Dwellings: Report on Initial Results for Auckland Region*, Auckland Regional Council, 2007; Melbourne (3,592,591), Sydney (4,119,190), source: Australian Bureau Quick Stats, October 2007; London (7,172,036), Manchester City (439,500), source: 2001 Census, Office of National Statistics, United Kingdom; Greater Mumbai (16.4 million), source: *UN-Habitat Global Report on Human Settlements 2003, The*

Challenge of Slums (London: Earthscan), Part IV: 'Summary of City Case Studies' pp.195–228; Los Angeles (9,862,049, 2008 estimate), New York (19,280,753, 2005–7 estimates), source: US Census Bureau Quick Facts; Hong Kong (7,067,800, 2010 estimate) website of the Census and Statistics Department, The Government of the Hong Kong Special Administrative Region.

31. For the nature and composition of clandestine gay worlds before gay liberation, see, for example, G. Chauncey (1994) *Gay New York: Gender, Urban Culture, and the Making of the Gay Male World, 1890–1940* (New York: Basic Books); C. Heap (2009) *Slumming: Sexual and Racial Encounters in American Nightlife, 1885–1940* (Chicago: University of Chicago Press); C. Upchurch (2009) *Before Wilde: Sex between Men in Britain's Age of Reform* (Berkeley: University of California Press); G. Wotherspoon (1991) *City of the Plain: History of a Gay Sub-culture* (Sydney: Hale & Iremonger).

32. See R.W. Connell (2010) 'Two Cans of Paint: A Transsexual Story, with Reflections on Gender Change and History', *Sexualities*, 13, 3–19.

33. Chauncey *Gay New York*; J. Seabrook (1995) *Notes from Another India* (London: Pluto Press); J. Seabrook (1999) *Love in a Different Climate: Men Who Have Sex with Men in India* (London: New Left Books).

34. For provenance of 'everyday experiments', see J. Weeks (2000) *Making Sexual History* (Cambridge: Polity Press), pp. 212ff.

2   Single Men

1. U. Beck and E. Beck-Gernsheim (1995) *The Normal Chaos of Love*, trans. M. Ritter and J. Wiebel (Cambridge: Polity Press), p. 145.

2. Beck and Beck-Gernsheim *The Normal Chaos of Love*, p. 145.

3. Beck and Beck-Gernsheim *The Normal Chaos of Love*, p. 145.

4. P. Robinson (2008) *The Changing World of Gay Men* (Basingstoke and New York: Palgrave Macmillan), pp. 160–1, 174.

5. J. D'Emilio and E.B. Freedman (1997) *Intimate Matters: A History of Sexuality in America*, 2nd edn (Chicago: University of Chicago Press), pp. 302–4.

6. D. Altman (1982) *The Homosexualization of America, the Americanization of the Homosexual* (New York: St Martin's Press), p. 88.

7. Robinson *Changing World*, pp. 88–92.

8. For Australian data on one-person households, see, for example, http://www.abs.gov.au/ausstats/abs@.nsf/Lookup/1301.0Main+Features562012#, accessed 7 September 2012. For United Kingdom data on families and households, see http://www.ons.gov.uk/ons/rel/family-demography/families-and-households/2011/stb-families-households.html, accessed 7 September 2012. For data on Germany, see Beck and Beck-Gernsheim *The Normal Chaos of Love*, pp. 14–15, which shows, for example, that, in the late 1980s, 15 per cent of Germans lived alone.

9. Special thanks to Dr Helen Marshall for her observation that increasing numbers of single people might indicate a return to longstanding patterns of delayed marriage.

10. M. Pollak (1986) 'Male Homosexuality – or Happiness in the Ghetto' in P. Ariès and A. Béjin (eds) *Western Sexuality: Practice and Precept in Past and Present Times*, trans. A. Forster (Oxford: Basil Blackwell), p. 57.

11. E. White (1980) *States of Desire: Travels in Gay America* (New York: Dutton), p. 287.
12. A. Giddens (1992) *The Transformation of Intimacy: Sexuality, Love and Eroticism in Modern Societies* (Cambridge: Polity Press), p. 58.
13. Robinson *Changing World*, pp. 115–52.
14. H. Bech (1997) *When Men Meet: Homosexuality and Modernity*, trans. T. Mequit and T. Davies (Cambridge: Polity Press), p. 97.
15. Bech *When Men Meet*, pp. 98–9.
16. Robinson *Changing World*, pp. 137–43.
17. In all, 41 men (or 42 per cent) from the international sample (*n* = 97) were single at the time of interview.
18. See Table A.4.
19. Of the 34 men in the 50–70 age cohort, 17 were single.
20. In Australia, the life expectancy for a male aged 50 in 2008–10 was 81.7 years: http://www.abs.gov.au/ausstats/abs@.nsf/Products/54EE2DFDF75948 B3CA257943000CF07D?opendocument, accessed 9 September 2012. In Hong Kong, the life expectancy for a male child born in 2010 was 80 years: http://www.censtatd.gov.hk/statistical_literacy/educational_materials/statistics_ and_you/index.jsp, accessed 9 September 2012. In India, the life expectancy for males in 2011 was 65.8 years: http://articles.timesofindia.indiatimes. com/2011-05-16/india/29548151_1_life-expectancy-indian-woman-indian-man, accessed 9 September 2012. In New Zealand, the life expectancy of a male child born in 2012 was 78.8 years: http://www.stats.govt.nz/browse_ for_stats/snapshots-of-nz/nz-in-profile-2012/international-comparisons-with-our-top-five-visitor-source-countries.aspx, accessed 9 September 2012. In the United Kingdom, a male child born in 2009 was expected to live until 78.4 years: http://www.bbc.co.uk/news/health-12771594, accessed 9 September 2012. In the USA, the life expectancy for a male aged 50 in 2008 was 79 years: http://www.census.gov/compendia/statab/cats/births_deaths_ marriages_divorces/life_expectancy.html, accessed 9 September 2012.
21. Robinson *Changing World*, pp. 115–33.
22. All the men were asked in the interview if growing older had affected their social life.
23. Mass gay events include circuit parties and leather parties. Cities such as Berlin, Los Angeles, Miami, New York, Rio de Janeiro, and Sydney are known for their mass gay parties. In Melbourne and Sydney in the 1980s, these were often known as 'warehouse' parties because they were held in derelict buildings, often warehouses located at shipping docks when freight transport was undergoing the transformation from cargo to container. Mass leather parties in Berlin are still held in derelict power stations, for example. The term 'circuit' party is a North American expression. See, for example, C. Carrington (2007) 'Circuit Culture: Ethnographic Reflections on Inequality, Sexuality, and Life on the Gay Party Circuit' in N. Teunis and Gilbert Herdt (eds) *Sexual Inequalities and Social Justice*, with a foreword by R. Parker (Berkeley: University of California Press), pp. 123–47. For more on circuit parties today, see this US-based website, which provides monthly information on mass parties in the Americas and Europe: http://www.justcircuit.com/Home.aspx, accessed 9 October 2012.
24. For more on the gay scene, see Robinson *Changing World*, pp. 72–94.

25. Colin (72), New York; Ryan (53), London; Hilton (53), New York; Mike (52), Melbourne; Calvin (51), Melbourne; Carl (49), Auckland; Jude (46), Los Angeles.
26. For more on Greenwich Village as a meeting place for gays and lesbians between the wars, see G. Chauncey (1994) *Gay New York: Gender, Urban Culture, and the Making of the Gay Male World, 1890–1940* (New York: Basic Books), pp. 237–44; on Stonewall Inn and its place in history of gay liberation in US, see D'Emilio and Freedman *Intimate Matters*, pp. 318–25.
27. More information about Body Electric, which was established in 1984, can be found on its webpage: http://www.thebodyelectricschool.com, accessed 10 October 2012.
28. See Robinson *Changing World*, pp. 161–74.
29. P. Robinson (2011) 'The Influence of Ageism on Relations between Old and Young Gay Men' in Y. Smaal and G. Willett (eds) *Out Here: Gay and Lesbian Perspectives VI* (Melbourne: Monash University Publishing), pp. 188–200.
30. Bech *When Men Meet*, p. 12.
31. S.O. Murray (2000) *Homosexualities* (Chicago: University of Chicago Press), p. 440.
32. Regarding specialisation of the commercial gay scene in, for example, Los Angeles and New York in the 1970s and 1980s, see White *States of Desire*, *passim*.
33. G. Robb (2004) *Strangers: Homosexual Love in the C19th Century* (London: Pan Macmillan).
34. A. Stein (1997) *Sex and Sensibility: Stories of a Lesbian Generation* (Berkeley: University of California Press), pp. 152–3.
35. Stein *Sex and Sensibility*, p. 152.
36. Earl (51), New York; Teddy (47), Mumbai; Charlie (40), Hong Kong; Anton (35), London; Leo (31), Sydney; Eamon (28), London.
37. Earl (51), New York; and Charlie (40), Hong Kong.
38. Anton (35), London; Leo (31), Sydney; and Eamon (28), London.
39. Teddy (47), Mumbai.
40. Robinson *Changing World*, pp. 83–92.
41. In this quotation, Anton was not referring to bars or clubs for under-age boys. Referring to '12-year-olds' was ironical and meant to underline the youthfulness of gay venues.
42. Robinson *Changing World*, pp. 137–43.
43. See Chapter 3 for more detailed discussion of works of U. Beck, E. Beck-Gernsheim, A. Giddens, and the individualisation thesis.
44. S. Khan (1996) 'Culture, Sexualities, and Identities', London: Naz Foundation International; http://www.nfi.net/articles_essays.htm, accessed 17 October 2012.
45. S. Nanda (1999) *Neither Man nor Woman: The Hijras of India*, 2nd edn (London: International Thomson), pp. 38, 40.
46. Khan 'Culture, Sexualities, and Identities'.
47. J. Weeks (2000) *Making Sexual History* (Cambridge: Polity Press), pp. 216–20; see also Robinson *Changing World*, pp. 149–50.
48. The men over 60 were Clancy (81), Melbourne; Godfrey (81), Sydney; Ambrose (77), Melbourne; Basil (75), Auckland; Lucas (75), Auckland; Jeffrey (72), Auckland; Alec (62), Sydney; and Anselm (61), Melbourne. The men

under 60 were Cam (56), Los Angeles; Everett (49), New York; Timothy (46), New York; Kendall (44), New York; Kyle (40), Auckland; Guy (38), London.

49. Robinson *Changing World*, p. 140.
50. N. Elias (1987) *The Loneliness of the Dying*, trans. E. Jephcott (Oxford: Basil Blackwell), p. 74.
51. Cam (56), Los Angeles; Everett (49), New York; Timothy (46), New York; Kendall (44), New York; Kyle (40), Auckland; Guy (38), London.
52. For more on extended youthfulness of gay life course, see Robinson *Changing World*, pp. 72–6, 153–4.
53. Godfrey (81), Sydney; Basil (75), Auckland; Jeffrey (72), Auckland; Alec (62), Melbourne; Anselm (61), Melbourne; Connor (41), London; Guy (38), London.
54. Robinson *Changing World*, pp. 164–5.
55. Jake is a social networking group for gay men in London. Its activities include providing information sessions, lobbying, and social events: 'Over the years we have hosted hustings where Jake members grilled politicians on their manifestos and the most glamorous parties in the hottest locations'; see: http://www.jaketm.com, accessed 28 October 2012. Fridae is an equivalent organisation for non-heterosexuals, operating in Bangkok, Hong Kong, Singapore, and other capital cities in SE Asia. Its slogan is 'empowering LGBT Asia'. In May 2012, for example, it hosted a seminar in Bangkok on 'LGBT diversity in the workplace', which focused on improving career prospects for non-heterosexual employees of multinational corporations. Fridae's website is at http://www.fridae.asia/about, accessed 28 October 2012. One of the non-heterosexual networking groups in Melbourne is Globe, which provides 'GLBTI business, professional and like-minded people opportunities to further develop their business interests and network with other professionals and business persons'; one of its better-known groups is Fruits in Suits, which organises social events for gay and lesbian white-collar workers; see: http://www.globemelbourne.com.au, accessed 28 October 2012.
56. For the shadowing quality of homophobia, see Altman *The Homosexualization of America*, p. 22. For the homonormative push of white, gay elites, see, for example, M. Warner (2000) *The Trouble with Normal: Sex, Politics, and the Ethics of Queer Life* (Cambridge, MA: Harvard University Press), pp. 61–80, and M.B. Sycamore (ed.) (2004) *That's Revolting! Queer Strategies for Resisting Assimilation* (Berkeley, CA: Counterpoint LLC), p. 2.
57. On increased workplace insecurity, see, for example, H. McQueen (1998) *Temper Democratic: How Exceptional Is Australia?* (Adelaide: Wakefield Press); R. Sennett (1998) *The Corrosion of Character: The Personal Consequences of Work in the New Capitalism* (New York: W.W. Norton).

3 Long-Lasting Relationships

1. See P. Robinson (2008) *The Changing World of Gay Men* (Basingstoke and New York: Palgrave Macmillan), pp. 125–8.
2. For discussion of changing shape of heterosexual couple relationships, see, for example, Z. Bauman (2003) *Liquid Love: On the Frailty of Human Bonds* (Cambridge: Polity Press); U. Beck and E. Beck-Gernsheim (1995) *The*

Normal Chaos of Love, trans. M. Ritter & J. Wiebel (Cambridge: Polity Press), pp. 5–9; and E. Beck-Gernsheim (2002) *Reinventing the Family: In Search of New Lifestyles*, trans. P. Camiller (Cambridge: Polity Press), *passim*. A useful critique of Beck and Beck-Gernsheim's arguments about the shape and nature of contemporary relationships can be found in C. Smart (2007) *Personal Life: New Directions in Sociological Thinking* (Cambridge: Polity Press), pp. 18–20. For the effects of individualisation on the couple relationship in the 1960s and 1970s, see E. Shorter (1976) *The Making of the Modern Family* (Glasgow: William Collins). For preliminary discussion of companionate marriage as a basis for couple relationships in Australian gay men, see Robinson *Changing World*, pp. 126–8.

3. A.J. Cherlin (2004) 'The Deinstitutionalization of American Marriage', *Journal of Marriage and Family*, 66, 851.
4. L. Stone (1979) *The Family, Sex and Marriage in England 1500–1800*, abridged & rev. edn (London: Penguin Books), pp. 217–24.
5. Smart *Personal Life*, p. 59. For an account of the four types of love, see, for example, Shorter *The Making of the Modern Family*.
6. J. D'Emilio and E.B. Freedman (1997) *Intimate Matters: A History of Sexuality in America*, 2nd edn (Chicago: University of Chicago Press), pp. 265–66.
7. Cherlin 'The Deinstitutionalization of American Marriage', pp. 851–2; J. Murphy (2000) *Imagining the Fifties: Private Sentiment and Political Culture in Menzies' Australia* (Sydney: University of New South Wales Press), p. 56.
8. D'Emilio and Freedman *Intimate Matters*, p. 266.
9. Cherlin 'The Deinstitutionalization of American Marriage', p. 852. For the greater acceptance of cohabitation in the USA and other western countries, see for, example, Cherlin 'The Deinstitutionalization of American Marriage', pp. 849–50; B. Hewitt and J. Baxter (2012) 'Who Gets Married in Australia? The Characteristics Associated with Transition to Marriage 2001–6', *Journal of Sociology*, 48(1), 44–6; and L. Jamieson (1998) *Intimacy: Personal Relationships in Modern Societies* (Cambridge: Polity Press), pp. 32–3.
10. N. Elias (2000 [1939]) *The Civilizing Process: Sociogenetic and Psychogenetic Investigations*, trans. E. Jephcott with some notes and corrections by the author. E. Dunning, J. Goudsblom, and S. Mennell (eds), rev. edn (Oxford: Blackwell); Beck and Beck-Gernsheim *The Normal Chaos of Love*; Beck-Gernsheim *Reinventing the Family*; Bauman *Liquid Love*.
11. E. Illouz (1999) 'The Lost Innocence of Love: Romance As a Postmodern Condition' in M. Featherstone (ed.) *Love and Eroticism* (London: Sage), p. 176; Z. Bauman (2001) *The Individualized Society* (Cambridge: Polity Press), p. 156.
12. A. Giddens (1992) *The Transformation of Intimacy: Sexuality, Love and Eroticism in Modern Societies* (Cambridge: Polity Press), pp. 2, 58, *passim*.
13. Giddens *The Transformation of Intimacy*, p. 58.
14. Beck and Beck-Gernsheim *The Normal Chaos of Love*, p. 172.
15. The following is a small selection from early works on gay and lesbian personal life where the short-term nature of gay men's relationships is discussed: D. Altman (1972) *Homosexual: Oppression and Liberation* (Sydney: Angus & Robertson), pp. 17–18; M. Foucault (2000) 'Sexual Choice, Sexual Act' (1982–3) in *Ethics: Essential Works of Foucault 1954–1984*, vol. 1, trans. R. Hurley and others, ed. P. Rabinow (Harmondsworth: Penguin Books),

p. 150; W.H. Masters and V.E. Johnson (1979) *Homosexuality in Perspective* (Boston: Little, Brown), pp. 229–30; K. Plummer (1981) 'Going Gay: Identities, Lifecycles and Lifestyles in the Male Gay World' in J. Hart and D. Richardson (eds) *The Theory and Practice of Homosexuality* (London: Routledge & Kegan Paul), p. 105; M. Pollak (1986) 'Male Homosexuality – or Happiness in the Ghetto' in P. Ariès and A. Béjin (eds) *Western Sexuality: Practice and Precept in Past and Present Times*, trans. A. Forster (Oxford: Basil Blackwell), pp. 43, 51; R. Robertson (1981) 'Young Gays' in J. Hart and D. Richardson (eds) *The Theory and Practice of Homosexuality* (London: Routledge & Kegan Paul), p. 173; D.J. West (1968) *Homosexuality* (Harmondsworth: Penguin Books), p. 56.

16. See Chapter 5, and Robinson *Changing World*, pp. 115–33.
17. J. Boswell (1980) *Christianity, Social Tolerance, and Homosexuality: Gay People in Western Europe from the Beginning of the Christian Era to the Fourteenth Century* (Chicago: University of Chicago Press), pp. 26–7.
18. For the effect of social hostility on gay men's intimate lives, see Robinson *Changing World*, pp. 21–5, 122–4.
19. The seven men whose relationships were of 30 years' duration and longer included three couples as well as two men who had been formerly married. The age range was 56–87, and comprised a man in his 80s, two men in their 70s, three men in their 60s, and one man in his 50s. Two of the men were from Manchester, four were from Melbourne, and one was from Sydney.
20. The eight men in relationships of between 20 and 30 years included two couples and a man who was formerly married. The age range was 47–81, comprising one man in his 80s, two men in their 70s, one man in his 60s, three men in their 50s, and one man in his 40s. Three men were from Hong Kong, one was from Manchester, two were from Melbourne, one was from New York, and one was from Sydney.
21. The nine men in relationships of between 10 and 20 years' length included a couple, a man who was formerly married, and a man who had a son. The age range was 42–67, and comprised a man in his 60s, four men in their 50s, and four men in their 40s. Two of the men were from Auckland, three were from Hong Kong, one was from Manchester, one was from Melbourne, and one was from New York.
22. Of the 31 men in relationships not classified as 'long-lasting', 10 were in relationships of between eight and five years inclusive, 11 were in relationships of between one and four years inclusive, and 10 were in relationships of less than a year.
23. Christian (72), Sydney; Alfie (63), Manchester; Bryce (63), Manchester.
24. Ashton (70), Sydney; Zachary (52), Hong Kong; Buck (51), Hong Kong; Duncan (47), Hong Kong.
25. Eddie (45), Manchester.
26. Other scholars use a related concept, 'cosiness', as a criterion for companionate marriage. See, for example, J. Finch and P. Summerfield (1999) 'Social Reconstruction and the Emergence of Companionate Marriage, 1945–59' in G. Allan (ed.) *The Sociology of the Family: A Reader*, (Oxford: Blackwell Publishers Ltd.), pp. 23–5.
27. For a more detailed discussion of gay marriage, civil unions and civil partnerships, see Chapters 4 and 5.

28. For more discussion of men's expectation of independence in relationships, see B.D. Adam (2007) 'Relationship Innovation in Male Couples' in M. Kimmel (ed.) *The Sexual Self: The Construction of Sexual Scripts* (Nashville, TN: Vanderbilt University Press), pp. 122–40.

29. R.W. Connell (1987) *Gender and Power: Society, the Person and Sexual Politics* (Stanford, CA: Stanford University Press).

30. P. Bourdieu (2001) *Masculine Domination*, trans. R. Nice (Cambridge: Polity Press), pp. 50–2.

31. The concept living apart together (LAT) was developed by sociologists to describe living arrangements of couples (often gay or lesbian) who continue to live independently in their own flat or house long after the start of the relationship. This is not a recent development. British painter Francis Bacon preferred his boyfriends to live in a flat near him; see J. Hawley 'Dark Night of the Soul', *Saturday Age* 3 November 2012, Good Weekend supplement, p. 24. For more on LAT, see S. Roseneil (2006) 'On Not Living with a Partner: Unpicking Coupledom and Cohabitation', *Sociological Research On-Line*: http://www.socresonline.org.uk/11/3/roseneil.html, accessed 9 December 2012.

32. D'Emilio and Freedman *Intimate Matters*, p. 266; Stone *Family, Sex and Marriage*, pp. 217–24.

33. Stone *Family, Sex and Marriage*, pp. 217–53.

34. Robinson *Changing World*, pp. 119–20.

35. Drake (77), Melbourne; Sean (67), Auckland; Fred (47), London; Jonathon (44), London.

36. The six men comprised a man from the 30-plus group: Drake (77), Melbourne; two men from the 20–30 group: Parry (63), New York, and Ben (52), Manchester; and three men from the 10–20 group: Fred (47), London, Eddie (45), Manchester, and Jonathon (44), London.

37. Fred (47, London); Eddie (45, Manchester); Jonathon (45, London).

38. For distinctions between sexual and companionate relations, see, for example, Smart *Personal Life*, pp. 59ff.

39. Foucault 'Sexual Choice, Sexual Act', p. 150.

40. The equivalent heterosexual term is 'friends with benefits'. The *Age*, 24 March 2011.

41. Adam 'Relationship Innovation in Male Couples', pp. 128, 125. For use of the term 'outlaw sex' and practices it covers, see J. Rechy (1977) *The Sexual Outlaw: A Documentary* (New York: Grove Press Inc.), and for pictoral representations of the same, see D. Hanson (ed.) (2011) *Tom of Finland: The Comics*, vol. 1 (Köln: Taschen GmbH).

42. Adam 'Relationship Innovation in Male Couples', pp. 139, 133.

43. On inequalities in straight relationships, see Smart *Personal Life*, pp. 173–7; Giddens *The Transformation of Intimacy*, p. 2. On equality in gay relationships, see G. Herdt (1997) *Same Sex, Different Cultures: Exploring Gay and Lesbian Lives* (Boulder, CO: Westview Press), p. 154; A. McLaren (1999) *Twentieth Century Sexuality: A History* (Oxford: Blackwell), p. 191; J. Weeks (2007) *The World We Have Won: The Remaking of Erotic and Intimate Life* (Oxford: Routledge), p. 218. Not all historians agree that equality is a distinguishing characteristic of gay relationships, preferring a more nuanced analysis.

4 Fatherhood

1. A shorter, less detailed version of this discussion of gay fatherhood settings and stories appeared in February 2012 in *Australian Policy Online*: http://apo.org.au/research/fatherhood-settings-and-stories-gay-men, accessed 31 January 2013.
2. G. Chauncey (1994) *Gay New York: Gender, Urban Culture, and the Making of the Gay Male World, 1890–1940* (New York: Basic Books), pp. 6–7; A. McLaren (1999) *Twentieth Century Sexuality: A History* (Oxford: Blackwell), pp. 187ff.; J. Weeks, B. Heaphy, and C. Donovan (2001) *Same Sex Intimacies: Families of Choice and Other Life Experiments* (London: Routledge), pp. 159–60.
3. Weeks, Heaphy, and Donovan *Same Sex Intimacies*, pp. 160–3; J. D'Emilio (2002) *The World Turned: Essays on Gay History, Politics, and Culture* (Durham, NC: Duke University Press), pp. 185–90.
4. Randall (87), Melbourne; Hector (81), Melbourne; Drake (77), Melbourne; Clive (64), Canberra; Anslem (61), Melbourne; Bernard (59), Hong Kong; Austin (57), Auckland; Ross (54), Hobart; Henry (50), country Victoria; Gabriel (43), Auckland; Neville (37), Melbourne; Joseph (35), Melbourne; and Tony (33), Melbourne.
5. J. Lindsay and D. Dempsey (2009) *Families, Relationships and Intimate Life* (Melbourne: Oxford University Press), p. 155.
6. Leslie (74), Hobart; John (65), Hobart; Terrence (64), Adelaide; and Scott (45), Melbourne.
7. Gerald (75), Melbourne; Douglas (63), Melbourne; and Hilton (53), New York.
8. Roy (58), Hobart; and Trevor (49), Melbourne.
9. Chapters 2, 3, 5, and 6 are based on the international sample, and Chapter 7 on the all-Australian data set exclusively.
10. Randall (87) was married for 35 years and had a male partner of 37 years; Hector (81) had a male partner of 25 years, and was still married and had been for more than 50 years; Gerald (75) was married for 31 years and had a male partner of nine years; Leslie (74) was married for 36 years and had a male partner of 20 years; John (65) was married for 40 years and had a male partner of 20 years; Douglas (63) had been married for 39 years, had a male lover, and kept a household with his second wife.. While Douglas described himself as gay, his sexual and intimate life more strongly resembled that of a bisexual person.
11. Drake (77) was married for 24 years and had a male partner of 31 years; Terrence (64) was married for 20 years and had a male partner of 24 years; Anselm (61) was married for 26 years and single at the time of interview; Henry (50) was married for 20 years and had a male partner of 10 years.
12. Clive (64) was married for 11 years and had been single for 17 years; Roy (58) was married for eight years and had been single for nine months; Austin (57) was married for 18 years and single at the time of interview; Hilton (53) was married for 18 years and single at the time of interview; Ross (54) was married for 13 years and had a male partner of more than six years; Trevor (49) was married for eight years and had a male partner of 19 years; Scott (45) was married for seven years and had a male partner of eight years.
13. These were a man in his early 80s and one in his early 60s.

14. McLaren *Twentieth Century Sexuality.*
15. N. Elias (2000 [1939]) *The Civilizing Process: Sociogenetic and Psychogenetic investigations*, trans. E. Jephcott with some notes and corrections by the author. E. Dunning, J. Goudsblom, and S. Mennell (eds), rev. edn (Oxford: Blackwell).
16. D. Altman (1972) *Homosexual: Oppression and Liberation* (Sydney: Angus & Robertson).
17. Mark (25), Melbourne.
18. D. Dempsey (2012) 'More Like a Donor or More Like a Father? Gay Men's Concepts of Relatedness to Children', *Sexualities*, 15, 156–74.
19. P. Robinson (2008) *The Changing World of Gay Men* (Basingstoke and New York: Palgrave Macmillan),pp, 145–48. For discussion of gay men's surrogacy experiences, see, for example, Dempsey 'More Like a Donor or More Like a Father?', pp. 156–74.
20. Robinson *Changing World*, pp. 148–9.
21. G. Chauncey (2004) *Why Marriage? The History Shaping Today's Debate Over Gay Equality* (Cambridge, MA: Perseus Books), pp. 110–11; the case, *Bottoms v. Bottoms* was held before the Virginia Supreme Court in 1995, see M.C. Nussbaum (1999) *Sex and Social Justice* (New York: Oxford University Press), pp. 204–5; Weeks, Heaphy, and Donovan *Same Sex Intimacies*, pp. 158–9.
22. Randall (87), Melbourne; Hector (81), Melbourne; Drake (77), Melbourne; Clive (64), Canberra; Anselm (61), Melbourne; Bernard (59), Hong Kong; Austin (57), Auckland; Ross (54), Hobart; Henry (50), country Victoria; Neville (37), Melbourne; Joseph (35), Melbourne; Tony (33), Melbourne.
23. Leslie (74), Hobart; John (65), Hobart; Terrence (64), Adelaide; Scott (45), Melbourne; Gabriel (43), Auckland.
24. Gerald (75), Melbourne; Douglas (63), Melbourne.
25. Roy (58), Hobart; Hilton (53), New York; Trevor (49), Melbourne.
26. Anthony McMahon uses the term 'joys of fatherhood'; see A. McMahon (1999) *Taking Care of Men: Sexual Politics in the Public Mind* (Cambridge: Cambridge University Press), p. 125.
27. J. Weeks (2000) *Making Sexual History* (Cambridge: Polity Press), pp. 216–20.
28. The term belongs to Weeks, Heaphy, and Donovan *Same Sex Intimacies*, pp. 161–3.
29. See, for example, B. Featherstone (2009) *Contemporary Fathering: Theory, Policy and Practice* (Bristol: Policy Press), pp. 24–5.

5 Marriage

1. Same-sex marriage has been an area of research interest since the 1980s, with increased activity in the late 1990s and even more so in the last decade. See, for example, J. Boswell (1995) *The Marriage of Likeness: Same Sex Unions in Pre-modern Europe* (London: Harper Collins); K. Plummer (1981) 'Going Gay: Identities, Lifecycles and Lifestyles in the Male Gay World' in J. Hart and D. Richardson (eds) *The Theory and Practice of Homosexuality* (London: Routledge & Kegan Paul), pp. 93–110; A. Rolfe and E. Peel (2011) '"It's a Double-Edged Thing": The Paradox of Civil Partnership and Why Some

Couples are Choosing Not to Have One', *Feminism and Psychology* 21(3) 317–35; B. Shipman and C. Smart (2007) '"It's Made a Huge Difference": Recognition, Rights and the Personal Significance of Civil Partnerships', *Sociological Research Online* (1). Some scholars have focused on the experiences of lesbians and gay men. While questions of sexual identity and relational equality have seen coalitions form between gay men and lesbians, each has a unique, gendered view on marriage. My perspective in this chapter and more broadly in this book is on the experience of non-representative samples of gay men and gay men only.

2. A. McLaren (1999) *Twentieth Century Sexuality: A History* (Oxford: Blackwell), p. 199; G. Chauncey (2004) *Why Marriage? The History Shaping Today's Debate over Gay Equality* (Cambridge, MA: Perseus Books), p. 3.
3. Isaac (56), Melbourne.
4. G. Hekma (1999) 'Same-Sex Relations among Men in Europe, 1700–1990' in F.X Elder, L.A. Hall, and G. Hekma (eds) *Sexual Cultures in Europe: Themes in Sexuality* (Manchester: Manchester University Press), pp. 99–100.
5. Information on state-by-state legislation in favour same-sex marriage is drawn from N.D. Polikoff (2008) *Beyond (Straight and Gay) Marriage: Valuing All Families under the Law* (Boston, MA: Beacon Press), pp. 110–20.
6. As reported in The *Age*, 5 July 2012; see also J.P. McCormick (2012) 'Same-Sex Marriage Bill to be introduced in France this October', *Pink News* 26 August: http://www.pinknews.co.uk/2012/08/26/same-sex-marriage-bill-to-be-introduced-in-france-this-october, accessed 29 August 2012.
7. McLaren *Twentieth Century Sexuality*, pp. 199–200.
8. G. Herdt (2009) *Moral Panics, Sex Panics: Fear and Fight over Sexual Rights* (New York: New York University Press), pp. 157, 182.
9. Polikoff *Beyond (Straight and Gay) Marriage*, p. 111.
10. Polikoff *Beyond (Straight and Gay) Marriage*, p. 111.
11. C. Frew (2010) 'The Social Construction of Same-Sex Marriage in Australia: Implications for Same-Sex Unions', *Law in Context*, 28(1), 86.
12. M. Kirby (2011) *A Private Life: Fragments, Memories, Friends* (Sydney: Allen & Unwin), p. 91.
13. S. Roberts (2012) 'Australia votes against legalizing equal marriage', *Pink News* 9 September: http://www.pinknews.co.uk/2012/09/19/australia-votes-against-legalising-equal-marriage, accessed 20 September 2012.
14. G. Williams (2012) 'States Leave Canberra Behind in Rush to Same-Sex Marriage', The *Age* 19 September: http://www.theage.com.au/opinion/politics/states-leave-canberra-behind-in-rush-to-samesex-marriage-20120919-266wa.html, accessed 20 September 2012.
15. J. Green (2011) 'French Parliament rejects Gay Marriage Bill', *Pink News*14 June: http://www.pinknews.co.uk/2011/06/14/french-parliament-rejects-gay-marriage-bill, accessed 15 June 2011.
16. S. Gray (2012) 'The Times backs gay marriage', *Pink News* 25 July: http://www.pinknews.co.uk/2012/03/05/the-times-backs-gay-marriage, accessed 7 March 2012.
17. S. Gray (2012) 'Scottish Government will bring forward equal marriage legislation', *Pink News* 25 July: http://www.pinknews.co.uk/2012/07/25/scottish-government-will-bring-forward-equal-marriage-legislation, accessed 26 July 2012.

18. S. Gray (2012) 'Catholic Church in Scotland: Society "should not facilitate gay relationships"', *Pink News* 26 July: http://www.pinknews.co.uk/2012/07/26/catholic-church-in-scotland-society-should-not-facilitate-gay-relationships, accessed 27 July 2012.
19. Alexandra Topping, http://www.guardian.co.uk/society/2013/feb/05/gay-marriage-result-mps-vote?INTCMP=SRCH, accessed 20 February 2013.
20. T.S.K. Kong (2012) *Chinese Male Homosexualities: Memba, Tongzhi and Golden Boy* (London: Routledge), pp. 118–19.
21. M.C. Nussbaum (1999) *Sex and Social Justice* (New York: Oxford University Press), pp. 201–3.
22. G. Simmel (1999 [1895]) 'On the Sociology of the Family', trans. M. Ritter and D. Frisby in M. Featherstone (ed.) *Love and Eroticism* (London: Sage), p. 291.
23. Nussbaum *Sex and Social Justice*, pp. 201–3.
24. M. Warner (2000) *The Trouble with Normal: Sex, Politics, and the Ethics of Queer Life* (Cambridge, MA: Harvard University Press), pp. 61–80. On assimilationism, see, for example, P. Moore (2004) *Beyond Shame: Reclaiming the Abandoned History of Radical Gay Sexuality* (Boston, MA: Beacon Press), and M.B. Sycamore (ed.) (2004) *That's Revolting! Queer Strategies for Resisting Assimilation* (Berkeley, CA: Counterpoint LLC).
25. A.J. Cherlin (2004) 'The Deinstitutionalization of American Marriage', *Journal of Marriage and Family*, 66, 855–6.
26. A condensed, earlier version of this chapter appeared in a refereed paper entitled 'Generational Differences to Gay Marriage' that I presented at The Australian Sociological Association conference at the University of Queensland, November 2012.
27. In the United States, different state jurisdictions use different terminology for formally recognising same-sex civil unions. See D.R. Pinello (2006) *America's Struggle for Same-Sex Marriage* (New York: Cambridge University Press), pp. 160–6.
28. Twenty-three men, or slightly less than a quarter of interviewees, said they opposed gay marriage. And 12 men (or 12 per cent of the sample) said they were unsure.
29. When I first examined the men's answers, I noticed that the proportion of those opposing gay marriage began to increase at the age of 51. My inclination was to divide the group into two subsets but after a seminar with fourth-year students, in which we discussed the week's readings on gay marriage and my analysis in particular, it became clear that a three-way division would be more useful so as to take account of the majority of men aged 31 and under who supported gay marriage. I would like to thank the eight students enrolled in HAF 445 Social Issues at Swinburne University of Technology in semester one 2012 for their help in seeing divisions in my data more clearly.
30. Two of the men from this group were in their 30s; 17 men were in their 20s; and the remaining three men were aged 19, 19, and 18. Ten of the men were from Australia; two were from Britain; four were from Hong Kong; five were from India; and one was from New Zealand.
31. The views of the five men who said that they would support only a civil union or civil partnership but not gay marriage are examined in the next chapter.

32. The longest relationship was six years, and the average length of relationship for men in this group was 14 months.
33. Garth (23), Zane (22), Hayden (21), and Todd (21).
34. P. Robinson (2008) *The Changing World of Gay Men* (Basingstoke and New York: Palgrave Macmillan), pp. 76–83.
35. Curtis (29), Hong Kong; Denis (27), Melbourne; Jarrad (23), Melbourne; Todd (21), Melbourne.
36. L. Jamieson (1998) *Intimacy: Personal Relationships in Modern Societies* (Cambridge: Polity Press), pp. 32–3; and C. Smart (2007) *Personal Life: New Directions in Sociological Thinking* (Cambridge: Polity Press), pp. 13–16.
37. Giles (23), Mumbai; Zane (22), Melbourne.
38. At the time of writing, the Hon. Penny Wong was Minister for Finance in the Gillard Government and Senator Bob Brown was leader of the Greens, a minority party in the 43rd Parliament of the Commonwealth of Australia. Senator Brown resigned as leader of the Greens on 13 April 2012 after 16 years in the Australian Parliament.
39. Reported in The *Age*, 7 July 2012.
40. Jamieson *Intimacy*, p. 157.
41. Two of the men from this group were in their 50s; 23 were in their 40s; and nine were in their 30s. Five of the men were from Australia; eight were from Britain; six were from Hong Kong; two were from India; five were from New Zealand; and eight were from the USA.
42. The views of the eight men who said that they would support only a civil union or civil partnership but not gay marriage are examined in the next chapter.
43. The longest relationship was 21 years, and the average length of relationships for men in this group of men was seven and a half years.
44. The three men who were in civil unions or civil partnerships were Duncan (47), Hong Kong; Eddie (45), Manchester; and Gabriel (43), Auckland. The three men who were in a gay marriage were Danny (48), Hong Kong; Joe (42), Hong Kong; and Everett (49), New York.
45. Ethan (49), London; Felix (41), Hong Kong; Alexander (34), Hong Kong.
46. Danny (48), Hong Kong.
47. Ethan (49), London.
48. Jonathon (44), London; and Dylan (32), Sydney.
49. C. Smart (2008) '"Can I Be Bridesmaid?" Combining the Personal and Political in Same-Sex Weddings', *Sexualities*, 11(6), 770–71.
50. Smart *Personal Life*, pp. 66–79.
51. Cherlin 'The Deinstitutionalization of American Marriage', p. 856.
52. Smart '"Can I Be Bridesmaid?"', p. 767.
53. Six of the men from this group were in their 80s; nine were in their 70s; 10 were in their 60s; and 16 were in their 50s. Seventeen of the men were from Australia; seven were from Britain; four were from Hong Kong; six were from New Zealand; and seven were from the USA. None of the men in this age cohort was from India.
54. The views of the seven men who said that they would support only civil union but not gay marriage are examined in the next chapter.
55. In this age cohort 23 men were in relationships, and 18 were single. The longest relationship was 42 years and the average length of a relationship was 22 years. Of the men in relationships, six men were in civil unions and

one was in a gay marriage. Three of the men in civil unions were in their 60s and three were in their 50s, and came from Hong Kong, Manchester, and New York: Alfie (63), Manchester; Bryce (63), Manchester; Parry (63), New York; Ben (52), Manchester; Buck (51), Hong Kong; Earl (51), New York. The man in a gay marriage was Ward (aged 59) from New York. The men who had previously been in heterosexual relationships comprised six men who were still married or formerly married to a woman and three men who were divorced, a total of nine men in all. From this age cohort there were also seven men who had children, all but one of whom were children from a former marriage or relationship with a woman.
56. Hector (81), Melbourne; Godfrey (81), Sydney; Basil (75), Auckland; Colin (72), New York; Fergus (63), Manchester; Alfie (63), Manchester; Ward (59), New York; Raymond (58), Hong Kong; Austin (57), Auckland; Logan (56), Auckland; Cam (56), Los Angeles; Ben (52), Manchester.
57. Chauncey *Why Marriage?*, p. 96. Others writing on gay marriage or marriage equality have made similar connection. See, for example, Polikoff *Beyond (Straight and Gay) Marriage*, pp. 51–2.
58. Chauncey *Why Marriage?*, pp. 96–104.
59. Robinson *Changing World*, pp. 60–2.

6   Cohabitation

1. For the status of the push for gay marriage in Australia in early 2000s, see P. Robinson (2008) *The Changing World of Gay Men* (Basingstoke and New York: Palgrave Macmillan), pp. 124–5.
2. M.R. Fowlkes (1999) 'Single Worlds and Homosexual Lifestyles: Patterns of Sexuality and Intimacy' in A.S. Rossi (ed.) *Sexuality Across the Lifecourse* (Chicago: University of Chicago Press), p. 175. For useful discussion of same-sex marriage and the public debates it has inspired, especially in the United States, see G. Chauncey (2004) *Why Marriage? The History Shaping Today's Debate over Gay Equality* (Cambridge, MA: Perseus Books); K.E. Hull (2006) *Same-Sex Marriage: The Cultural Politics of Love and Law* (Cambridge: Cambridge University Press); M.C. Nussbaum (2004) *Hiding from Humanity: Disgust, Shame, and the Law* (Princeton, NJ: Princeton University Press), pp. 256–65; and A. Stein (2006) *Shameless: Sexual Dissidence in American Culture* (New York: New York University Press), ch. 8.
3. J. D'Emilio and E.B. Freedman (1997) *Intimate Matters: A History of Sexuality in America*, 2nd edn (Chicago: University of Chicago Press), p. 369.
4. C. Charlotte (2010) 'The Social Construction of Same-Sex Marriage in Australia: Implications for Same-Sex Unions', *Law in Context*, 28(1), 78.
5. Simon Cullen, *ABC News* 19 September 2012: http://www.abc.net.au/news/2012-09-19/controversy-over-cory-bernardi-bestiality-comments/4269604, accessed 20 November 2012. Stephanie Peatling, The *Age* 23 September 2012: http://www.theage.com.au/opinion/political-news/bernardi-keeps-on-losing-20120922-26dof.html, accessed 20 November 2012.
6. J.P. McCormick, *Pink News*, 22 November 2012: http://www.pinknews.co.uk/2012/11/22/new-zealand-committee-told-that-equal-marriage-is-an-abomination-and-could-lead-to-incest, accessed 23 November 2012.

7. Link to 'Freedom to Marry' on Log Cabin Republicans' website: http://www.logcabin.org/site/c.nsKSL7PMLpF/b.8104529/k.9A48/Freedom_to_Marry.htm, accessed 19 November 2012.
8. G. Simmel (1999 [1895]) 'On the Sociology of the Family', trans. M. Ritter and D. Frisby in M. Featherstone (ed.) *Love and Eroticism* (London: Sage), pp. 283–93; C. Donovan (2004) 'Why Reach for the Moon? Because the Stars Aren't Enough', *Feminism and Psychology*, 14(24), 27.
9. Donovan 'Why Reach for the Moon?', pp. 25–8; M.C. Nussbaum (1999) *Sex and Social Justice* (New York: Oxford University Press), p. 202; J. Stacey (2004) 'Marital Suitors Court Social Science Spin-sters: The Unwittingly Conservative Effects of Public Sociology', *Social Problems*, 51(1), 135.
10. G. Herdt (2009) 'Gay Marriage: The Panic and the Right' in G. Herdt (ed.) *Moral Panics, Sex Panics: Fear and the Fight over Sexual Rights* (New York: New York University Press), pp. 191–2.
11. Two of the men from this group were in their 30s; 17 men were in their 20s; and the remaining three men were aged 19, 19, and 18. Ten of the men were from Australia; two were from Britain; four were from Hong Kong; five were from India; and one was from New Zealand.
12. The longest relationship was six years, and the average length of relationship for men in this group was 14months.
13. Curtis (29), Hong Kong; Eamon (28), London; Jarrad (23), Melbourne; Hayden (21), Melbourne; Brody (19), Melbourne.
14. Eamon (28), London; Jarrad (23), Melbourne; Hayden (21), Melbourne.
15. Eamon (28), London; and Hayden (21), Melbourne.
16. Curtis (29), Hong Kong; and Brody (19), Melbourne.
17. For discussion of immigration restrictions, see N.D. Polikoff (2008) *Beyond(Straight and Gay)Marriage: Valuing All Families under the Law* (Boston, MA: Beacon Press), pp. 121–2.
18. Two of the men from this group were in their 50s; 23 were in their 40s; and nine were in their 30s. Five of the men were from Australia; eight were from Britain; six were from Hong Kong; two were from India; five were from New Zealand; and eight were from the USA.
19. Three of the men were in a civil union or civil partnership and three men were in a gay marriage. The men who were in civil unions or civil partnerships were Duncan (47), Hong Kong; Eddie (45), Manchester; and Gabriel (43), Auckland. The men who were in a gay marriage were Danny (48), Hong Kong; Joe (42), Hong Kong; and Everett (49), New York. The longest relationship was 21 years, and the average length of relationships for men in this group of men was seven and a half years. Two of the men were formerly married and one man had an adopted child.
20. Teddy (47), Mumbai; Edmund (44), Mumbai; Callum (43), Melbourne; Liam (37), Sydney; Finlay (33), New York.
21. For more on 'good' gays and homonormativity, see M. Warner (2000) *The Trouble with Normal: Sex, Politics, and the Ethics of Queer Life* (Cambridge, MA: Harvard University Press), pp. 61–80.
22. Decca Aitkenhead, http://www.guardian.co.uk/film/2012/sep/28/rupert-everett-memoir-vanished-years, accessed 3 October 2012.
23. Calvin (51), Melbourne; Charlie (40), Hong Kong; Anton (35), London; Aiden (33), London; Jackson (32), New York.

24. Warner *Trouble with Normal*, p. 85.
25. Nathan (50), Auckland; Alvin (47), New York; Duncan (47), Hong Kong; Fred (47), London; Jude (46), Los Angeles; Eddie (45), Manchester; Jacob (42), Melbourne; Connor (41), London.
26. Six of the men from this group were in their 80s; nine were in their 70s; 10 were in their 60s; and 16 were in their 50s. Seventeen of the men were from Australia; seven were from Britain; four were from Hong Kong; six were from New Zealand; and seven were from the USA. In other words, none of the men in this age cohort was from India.
27. Twenty-three men were in relationships at the time of interview and 18 were single. The longest relationship was 42 years, and the average length of a relationship was 22 years.
28. For more on comparative longevity in gay couple relationships, see Robinson *Changing World*, pp. 122–33.
29. Six of the men were in civil unions or civil partnerships and one was in a gay marriage. Three of the men in civil unions/partnerships were in their 60s and three were in their 50s: Alfie (63), Manchester; Bryce (63), Manchester; Parry (63), New York; Ben (52), Manchester; Buck (51), Hong Kong; Earl (51), New York. The man who was in a gay marriage was in his late 50s and was from New York: Ward (59). The men who had had heterosexual relationships comprised six men who were still married or formerly married to a woman and three men who were divorced. Seven men from this age cohort had children, all but one of whom had children as a result of a former marriage or relationship with a woman. Five of the men were from Melbourne, one was from New York, and two were from Sydney.
30. Randall (87), Melbourne; Ambrose (77), Melbourne; Drake (77), Melbourne; Christian (72), Sydney; Ashton (70), Sydney; Baden (65), Melbourne; Hugh (62), Melbourne; Hilton (53), New York.
31. Sean (67), Auckland; Arthur (62), London; Marvin (59), Los Angeles; Zachary (52), Hong Kong; Mike (52), Melbourne.
32. As mentioned above, I asked the men the following questions in relation to gay marriage: 'Are you married; do you intend to marry? If the circumstances were right, would you marry a man?'
33. See, for example, J.N. Katz (2001) *Love Stories: Sex between Men before Homosexuality* (Chicago: University of Chicago Press) for accounts of intimate and sexual relationships between men from the late 1820s. See also, B.R.S. Fone (1992) *Masculine Landscapes: Walt Whitman and the Homoerotic Text* (Carbondale and Edwardsville, IL: Southern Illinois University Press).
34. ACT UP is the acronym for 'AIDS Coalition to Unleash Power', which was created in New York in 1987. For more information, see P. Moore (2004) *Beyond Shame: Reclaiming the Abandoned History of Radical Gay Sexuality* (Boston, MA: Beacon Press), pp. 83, 93.
35. Amery (82), Sydney; Alec (62), Sydney.
36. Herbert (82), Melbourne.
37. Lucas (75), Auckland.
38. Arran (70), Melbourne; Parry (63), New York; Isaac (56), Melbourne; Tate (51), London; Earl (51), New York.
39. Clancy (81), Melbourne; Jeffrey (72), Auckland; Bryce (63), Manchester; Anselm (61), Melbourne; Bernard (59), Hong Kong; Ryan (53), London; Buck (51), Hong Kong.

7   Living in the Midst of HIV-AIDS

1. In 2011, the UK recorded its highest rate of HIV diagnoses since 1999; see S. Roberts 'UK: HIV infection rate for gay men at record high', *Pink News* 11 November 2012, http://www.pinknews.co.uk/2012/11/29/uk-hiv-infection-rate-for-gay-men-at-record-high, accessed 19 December 2012.
2. See G.W. Dowsett (1996) *Practicing Desire: Homosexual Sex in the Era of AIDS* (Stanford, CA: Stanford University Press), ch. 3.
3. Safe sex and 'safer sex' were terms for sexual practices that some scientists and many gay lobbyists recommended people having casual sex adopt in the early days of the HIV-AIDS epidemic because they were thought likely to prevent transfer of the HIV. Once this was shown to be the case, government medical authorities in many western countries adopted these guidelines and funded safe-sex campaigns among the different groups of men who have sex with men – that is, gay men as well as men who do not identify as gay. The purpose of safe-sex campaigns was to encourage gay men to engage in protected anal sex only, that is, to use a condom whenever they had such sex if they did not know the HIV status of their partner. In its early days, safe sex was recommended for anyone who intended to have casual sex, anal or vaginal. For discussion of changes in sexual practices among gay men as a response to HIV-AIDS, see Dowsett *Practicing Desire*, pp. 77–87.
4. D. Altman (1989) 'Aids and the Reconceptualization of Homosexuality' in D. Altman et al. *Homosexuality, Which Homosexuality? Essays from the International Conference on Gay and Lesbian Studies* (London: GMP), pp. 35, 37.
5. See Dowsett *Practicing Desire*, ch. 3.
6. In the Annual Surveillance Report 2009, the National Centre in HIV Epidemiology and Clinical Research observed the annual number of new HIV diagnoses in Australia has remained steady over the past three years at around 1,000 cases, which represents a return to rates of infection not seen since 1994.
7. The three men are Stuart (49), Jason (35), and Julius (34).
8. See Table A.2 for details of the all-Australian sample, and Chapter 1 for discussion of it and my use of two separate non-representative samples of men for this book.
9. The average age of men in this cohort was 49 and, on average, they came out at 27. Interviewed in 2002, a 49-year-old man would have been born in 1953, would have turned 21 in 1974 and, if he came out at 27, 1980 would have been the year that he did so. Of the 30 men in this cohort, two-thirds were aged 29 or older in November 1982, the year when the first case of AIDS was diagnosed in Australia.
10. Twenty men from the middle cohort (*n* = 30) had been born between 1942 and 1953, and were therefore between 40 and 29 in 1982. For the outbreak of HIV-AIDS in Australia, see Dowsett *Practicing Desire*, p. 61.
11. The average age of these men was 33, and on average they came out at 21. Interviewed in 2002, a 33-year-old man would have been born in 1969 and, if he came out at 21, he would have done so in 1990.
12. Twenty-two men from the young cohort (*n* = 28) were born between 1980 and 1966, and were therefore between 2 and 16 in 1982. Fourteen men, or half the young cohort, were aged 12 or less in 1982.

13. In 1987, an advertising campaign to alert the public to the risks of HIV-AIDS began on Australian television. The television advertisements showed the hooded figure of Death, scythe in hand, stalking people of all ages and types. The highlight of the advertisement showed Death (thereafter in public discourse referred to as the Grim Reaper) bowling a ball in the lane of a bowling alley where the skittles were random human figures, thereby reinforcing the unpredictable nature of the disease's spread. For more information, see P. Sendzuik (2003) *Learning to Trust: Australian Responses to AIDS* (Sydney: University of NSW Press).

14. I would like to thank members of the audience who heard an earlier version of this chapter at the Oral History Conference, Talk About Town in Melbourne, August 2009 for suggesting two of these possible explanations: (a) gay men's desire to refuse any conflation of HIV-AIDS and the gay identity and (b) negative interviewees' desire to distance themselves from the virus.

15. Twenty-one were from the middle cohort and 15 from the young cohort.

16. T.E. Cook and D.C. Colby (1992) 'The mass-mediated epidemic: the politics of AIDS on the nightly network news' in E. Fee and D.M. Fox (eds) 1992 *AIDS: The Making of a Chronic Disease* (Berkely, CA: University of California Press), pp. 84–122; J. Gordon and C. Crossman (1992) '"aids kills fags dead ...": cultural activism in Grand Bend' in J. Miller (ed.) *Fluid Exchanges: Artists and Critics in the AIDS Crisis* (Toronto: University of Toronto Press), pp. 241–54; A. Meredith (1992) 'That last breath: women with AIDS' in Fee and Fox *AIDS: The Making of a Chronic Disease*, pp. 229–44; S. Sontag (1991) *Illness as Metaphor* and *Aids and Its Metaphors* (Harmondsworth: Penguin Books).

17. Twenty-one is 70 per cent of the middle cohort ($n = 30$).

18. The 12 men were: Lionel (59), Roy (58), Noel (58), Kevin (52), Michael (52), Des (50), Jerome (49), Stuart (49), Bob (48), Alan (47), Simon (46), and Matthew (42).

19. For an account of this period of unknowing, see Sendziuk *Learning to Trust*, pp. 11–17.

20. Today, a 'window period' of three months is understood to exist between infection and when the body produces HIV antibodies that can be measured by a blood test. For more details, see H.M. Sapolsky and S.L. Boswell (1992) 'The History of Transfusion AIDS: Practice and Policy Alternatives' in Fee and Fox *AIDS: The Making of a Chronic Disease*, pp. 183–5.

21. The 12 men who spoke of feeling frightened or vulnerable, including three who also spoke of stigma, were: Robert (38), Jeremy (36), Daniel (35), Joseph (35), Jason (35), Julius (34), Mick (33), Ian (28), Mark (25), Adam (24), Troy (24), and Jack (22). The six men who mentioned stigma were: Tony (33), Ian (28), Mark (25), Adam (24), Myles (24), and Angus (23). In other words, the 15 men who referred to fear, vulnerability, and stigma comprised nine who spoke of fear and vulnerability only, three who spoke of fear, vulnerability, and stigma, and three who spoke of only stigma.

22. For more information, see Sendziuk *Learning to Trust*, p. 137.

23. Born in 1974, Ian would have been 13 when the Grim Reaper campaign was shown on television.

24. For the link between homophobia and conservative opposition to discussion of homosexuality in sex education curricula in Australia, see S. Angelides

(2008) '"The Continuing Homosexual Offensive": Sex Education, Gay Rights and Homosexual Recruitment' in S. Robinson (ed.) *Homophobia: An Australian History* (Sydney: Federation Press), pp. 172–92.

25. 'GLBTI' is the acronym for non-heterosexual people, standing for 'gay, lesbian, bisexual, transgender, and intersex'.
26. Fifteen were from the middle cohort and 14 from the young cohort.
27. A. McLaren (1999) *Twentieth Century Sexuality: A History* (Oxford: Blackwell), p. 199.
28. S. Watney (1992) 'The Possibilities of Permutation: Pleasure, Proliferation, and the Politics of Gay Identity in the Age of AIDS' in Miller *Fluid Exchanges*, pp. 329–67.
29. Eleven men (73 per cent) discussed safe sex and four men (27 per cent) monogamy.
30. For more extensive discussion of varying strategies gay men adopted in the face of the disease, see P. Robinson (2008) *The Changing World of Gay Men* (Basingstoke: Palgrave Macmillan), ch. 4; and Watney 'The Possibilities of Permutation', p. 352.
31. The two men who said they withdrew from sexual adventurism were Travis (38) and Mick (33).
32. In the gay world, a relationship such as the one Mick is describing here is known as an 'open' relationship. See Chapter 3 and Robinson *Changing World*, pp. 128–32.
33. For a fuller discussion of 'sero-sorting' and 'strategic positioning', see G. Prestage et al. (2008) *Three or More Study* (Sydney: National Centre in HIV Epidemiology and Clinical Research, University of New South Wales), pp. 2, 42–3, 50–2, 54. My thanks to Mr Daniel Reeders, former campaign co-ordinator for PLWHA Victoria, South Yarra, for his advice about safe-sex policy and health campaigns in Australia.
34. His was the death of a friend.
35. Sixteen were from the middle cohort and eight from the young cohort.
36. For discussion of gay communities' response to HIV-AIDS and their relationship with government health and research strategies in Australia, see Dowsett *Practicing Desire*, ch. 3; for discussion of similar work in the United States, see R.A. Padgug and G.M. Oppenheimer (1992) 'Riding the Tiger: AIDS and The Gay Community' in Fee and Fox *AIDS: The Making of a Chronic Disease*, pp. 245–78.
37. Padgug and Oppenheimer 'Riding the Tiger', p. 258.
38. K. Plummer (1995) *Telling Sexual Stories: Power, Change and Social Worlds* (London: Routledge), p. 96.
39. On growth in homophobia, see A. Stein (2006) *Shameless: Sexual Dissidence in American Culture* (New York: New York University Press), pp. 103–10 and *passim*; D. Eribon (2004) *Insult and the Making of the Gay Self*, trans. M. Lucey (Durham, NC: Duke University Press), pp. xv–xxi.
40. For a summary of the period and published research on the HIV-AIDS epidemic in the West, see Robinson *Changing World*, pp. 54–62.
41. For more on homophobia in secondary schools, see, for example, M. McCormark (2012) *The Declining Significance of Homophobia: How Teenage Boys Are Redefining Masculinity and Heterosexuality* (Oxford: Oxford University Press), and McCormack's interview of 8 April 2012 on the Melbourne gay

and lesbian radio station, JoyFM, as well as some discussion of changes in homophobia in schools over last 15 years: http://badblood.wordpress. com/2012/04/08/mark-mccormack-interviewed-by-dean-beck-lauren-rosewarne, accessed 20 December 2012.

Conclusion

1. D. Altman (1972) *Homosexual: Oppression and Liberation* (Sydney: Angus & Robertson).
2. J. Boswell (1995) *The Marriage of Likeness: Same Sex Unions in Pre-modern Europe* (London: HarperCollins).

Index